EMRAN IQBAL EL-BADAWI

QUEENS AND PROPHETS

HOW ARABIAN NOBLEWOMEN
AND HOLY MEN SHAPED PAGANISM,
CHRISTIANITY AND ISLAM

ONEWORLD
ACADEMIC

Oneworld Academic

An imprint of Oneworld Publications

Published by Oneworld Academic in 2022

ISBN 978-0-86154-445-5
eISBN 978-0-86154-446-2

Maps © Rasha Shammaa

Illustration credits: Sir Edward Poynter, *The Visit of the Queen of Sheba to King
Solomon* courtesy of Wikimedia Commons; Silver drachm of Malichus II with his
wife Shagilath courtesy of Classical Numismatic Group, Inc./Wikimedia Commons;
statue of Julia Domna courtesy of Carole Raddato/Wikimedia Commons; statues of
princesses Dushafri and Simi courtesy of Osama Shukir Muhammed Amin/Wikimedia
Commons; Allat-Minerva courtesy of Dosserman/Wikimedia Commons; Zenobia coin
courtesy of Classical Numismatic Group, Inc./Wikimedia Commons; wall painting of
women with censers at Mary's deathbed courtesy of Karel Innemée; women baking
bread in Syria (*National Geographic Magazine*, March 1908, vol. xix, no. 3) courtesy
of Wikimedia Commons; fresco of holy men with Mavia courtesy of Henri Pidoux/
Wikimedia Commons; illustration from *Siyer-I Nebi* courtesy of Wikimedia Commons;
Elagabalus coin courtesy of Classical Numismatic Group, Inc./Wikimedia Commons.

Typeset by Geethik Technologies
Printed and bound in Great Britain by Clays Ltd, Elcograf S.p.A.

Oneworld Publications
10 Bloomsbury Street
London WC1B 3SR
England

MIX
Paper from
responsible sources
FSC
www.fsc.org
FSC® C018072

For Zacharia, Adam, and Danyal

Chess is a game of life.
The queen is the most powerful piece on the board.
Respect the queen.
Win the game.

Contents

Preface

I DID NOT choose to write this book. This book chose me as its messenger. Lest I be cast as a false prophet for making such a claim, allow me to explain.

While conducting research on holy men in late antique Arabia, I stumbled upon the prominence of regal women instead. Little more than their names are known to many of us. The stories of the region's foremost empress, warrior, and noblewoman are of unprecedented brilliance and enormous consequence. Each woman helped raise an unassuming holy man to the heights of historic notoriety. I began to wonder. Were these women connected at all, how much power did they wield, and were they robbed of this power by men?

Amid this battle of the sexes, I discovered a series of untold stories lurking in the shadows between ancient Near Eastern, biblical, and Islamic traditions. The complex 'narrative history' of these queens and their male prophets shaped the religion, politics, and culture of late antique Arabia, influencing the rise of Arab identity, early Christianity, and the beginnings of Islam. As I dug deeper it became clear to me that the influence of female nobility on male prophecy had a significant impact on the worldview of the eastern churches and the Qur'an, and that their influence was overwritten by generations of religious apologists.

Not everyone has welcomed this project. Some colleagues scoffed at the very idea of excavating "female power" out of the imagined black hole of pre-Islamic Arabia—the *jahiliyyah*. Some of my detractors were concerned that the sheer paucity of documentary evidence made such a venture impossible. Others flatly rejected my vision as an Arabian episode of *The Da Vinci Code*. Of course, I take constructive criticism seriously. But many of my critics simply lacked imagination. They could scarcely concede the patriarchal nature of our evidence, i.e. the Arabic, Syriac, Greek, and Latin sources scholars cherish so dearly. Still, most of my colleagues expressed their enthusiasm for a fresh perspective on the sources, as this project offers. I thank my supporters and detractors alike. Their feedback compelled me to argue my position both rigorously and energetically.

Finally, this book makes bold claims. I know. Some readers may not accept my analysis of female power or concomitant patriarchal traditions due to their own ideological commitments—be they political, religious, or academic. I ask only that you keep an open mind. The evidence, once meticulously laid out, is not so scarce. And the story, when thoughtfully told, is not so far-fetched.

Emran El-Badawi, Houston

Acknowledgements

COMPLETING THIS BOOK would not have been possible without the generous partnership and the careful consultation of esteemed colleagues and dear friends. Essential to my research was a visit to the Centre National de la Recherche Scientifique in Paris, where Laïla Nehmé and Christian Robin kindly offered their wisdom on North and South Arabian epigraphy. I thank a number of colleagues for meeting with me and offering their valuable feedback on the multiple dimensions of this project.

Between my travels to New York and Princeton, Robert Hoyland and Michael Cook helped me explore questions about late antique Arabia and Islamic origins, broadly speaking. My thanks go to Sebastian Brock for his advice in identifying important Syriac literature and Aramaic epigraphy. My heartfelt gratitude goes to Kecia Ali who reviewed an early draft of this project, and whose constructive feedback helped me to situate this project between studies on late antiquity, feminist studies, and Islamic history. Karen Bauer and Gabriel Reynolds generously offered their expertise on the Qur'an. Aziz Al-Azmeh, Fred Donner, Paula Sanders, David Cook, Catharina Rachik, Hani Khafipour, Marie Theresa Hernandez, and Roberta Sabbath shared with me innovative methods for writing history given the sheer lack of documentary evidence we have for late antique Arabia. I am likewise indebted to Kristina Neumann for sharing her wisdom on Roman Syria. And I thank Philip Wood, Azad Sadr, and Marie des Neiges Léonard for their help in improving my introduction.

Thanks go to John Kutsko, Sophia Arjana, and Reza Aslan for their guidance and inspiration over the years. I thank Hildegard Glass,

Michael Fares, Devianee Vasanjee, Rishika Harrylall, and Jessica Ortega for helping to make my research sabbatical a reality despite various challenges, and for their tireless work and friendship always. My gratitude goes to several anonymous reviewers on their constructive feedback on earlier versions of this book. And I offer jubilant praise of the visionaries at Oneworld—especially Novin Doostdar, Jonathan Bentley-Smith, and Rida Vaquas—for transforming dreams into reality. Many colleagues and friends have enriched my research through several discussions and meetings. Nevertheless, the ideas shared in this book, and whatever responsibility accompanies them, are my own.

I am indebted to my students at the University of Houston. Our class discussions in my courses on Women and Gender in Arabic Literature and Early Islamic Society provided fruitful fodder for this project. My appreciation also goes to Majida Hourani and Hazel Thomson for their inspiration and encouragement. Special thanks go to Gale Jenkins, Christine Jenkins, and Brian Eukel for instilling within our family the values of critical thinking, competitiveness, and community through the timeless game of chess.

This book also relied upon the material support of multiple internal grants from the College of Liberal Arts and Social Sciences at the University of Houston. Research towards this book was first presented in 2018 at the Department of Middle Eastern Studies at the University of Texas at Austin, and shared with colleagues in subsequent years at the annual conferences of the International Qur'anic Studies Association, Society of Biblical Literature, and American Academy of Religion.

I am wholeheartedly indebted to Rasha Shammaa. Thank you for designing the maps to this book, for giving me the space to write and travel, and for your tireless support and sacrifice over the years. I thank my children, whose precious youth and energy occasionally conspired against my research, but who compensated for this by helping me transcribe evidence for this project. This feat was undertaken in quarantine during the Covid-19 pandemic of 2020–2021, and it succeeded as a result of their love of reading and storytelling.

Confinement compelled me to complete this book in a state of anguish and isolation. My writing was interrupted by episodes of severe anxiety, and I was haunted by perpetual disruption all around me. Not least among these were the lasting effects and unrest caused by the global pandemic, state-born xenophobia, popular protest, and the encroaching climate crisis. This book was written amid new struggles against age-old injustices. In a world beset by crisis and rife with conflict, writing this book seemed like the right thing to do.

Abbreviations

A	*Arabica*
A2	*Adumatu*
A3	*Aram*
AA	*al-ʿArab*
AAE	*Arabian Archaeology and Epigraphy*
AB	*Al-Bayān: Journal of Qurʾan and Hadith Studies*
AC	*L'Antiquité Classique*
AJSLL	*The American Journal of Semitic Languages and Literatures*
AM	*Al-Manhal*
AOAT	*Alter Orient und Altes Testament*
ATI	*American Theological Inquiry*
AUW	*Al-ʿUsur al-Wusta*
BBVO	*Berliner Beiträge zum Vorderen Orient*
BSOAS	*Bulletin of the American Schools of Oriental Research*
CA	*Current Anthropology*
CIS	*Corpus Inscriptionum Semiticarum*
CM	*The Church and Mary*
CRS	*Comptes rendus des séances de l'Académie des Inscriptions et Belles-Lettres*
DASO	*Dossiers Archéologie et sciences des origines*
DI	*Der Islam*
DT	*Dirasat Tarikhiyyah*
EI²	*Encyclopedia of Islam*, Second Edition
EQ	*Encyclopaedia of the Qurʾān*
GSHA	*GCC Society for History and Archeology*
HJSS	*Hugoye: Journal of Syriac Studies*

HSCP	*Harvard Studies in Classical Philology*
ILS	*Islamic Law and Society*
JA	*Judaïsme ancien/Ancient Judaism*
JAP	*Journal of Applied Psychology*
JECS	*Journal of Early Christian Studies*
JFSR	*Journal of Feminist Studies in Religion*
JIE	*Journal of Islamic Ethics*
JIQSA	*Journal of the International Qur'anic Studies Association*
JJS	*Journal of Jewish Studies*
JNES	*Journal of Near Eastern Studies*
JQS	*Journal of Qur'anic Studies*
JRS	*The Journal of Roman Studies*
JSAI	*Jerusalem Studies in Arabic and Islam*
JSS	*Journal of Semitic Studies*
M	*Man*
MA	*Mediterranean Archaeology*
MAA	*Mediterranean Archaeology and Archaeometry*
MKTA	*Majallat al-Khalij lil-Tarikh wa-l-Athar*
MSLP	*Mémoires de la Société de linguistique de Paris*
MW	*The Muslim World*
O	*Oriens*
O2	*Orientalia*
OC	*Oriens Christianus*
OCIANA	*Online Corpus of the Inscriptions of Ancient North Arabia*
OM	*Orient et Méditerranée*
PEQ	*Palestine Exploration Quarterly*
PO	*Patrologia Orientalis*
PS	*Patrologia Syriaca*
PS2	*Patrimoine Syriaque*
QSA	*Quaderni di Studi Arabi*
R	*Raydan*
S	*Semitica*
SC	*Semitica et Classica*
SI	*Studia Islamica*
SJA	*Southwestern Journal of Anthropology*
SS	*Sociology Study*

SVTQ	*St. Vladimir's Theological Quarterly*
T	*Topoi*
TSASP	*Textile Society of America Symposium Proceedings*
ZDMG	*Zeitschrift der Deutschen Morgenländischen Gesellschaft*

Transliteration and Dates

ARABIC TRANSLITERATION IS based on the system used by the *International Journal of Middle Eastern Studies*. The simplified transliteration system does not mark letters with macrons or dots below. However, the *ta' marbutah* is rendered as *ah* (e.g. Surah, *ummah*). Vowels are limited to *a*, *i*, and *u*. The *'ayn* is rendered as a single open quote ('); the *hamzah* as an apostrophe (').

The transliteration of ancient Arabian dialects, Aramaic, Greek, Latin, and other languages is also based on the simplified system described above, with the additional vowels of *e* and *o*.

The Arabic word *allah* is translated as "God," except when used in contrast to other deities. In such cases it is rendered "Allah."

———

Dates are generally presented according to the Gregorian calendar. Where necessary, pre-Islamic events have been labeled Common Era (CE) or Before the Common Era (BCE).

Events from the Islamic era are dated according to the Hijri then Gregorian calendar (e.g. Marj Rahit, 64/684).

Introduction

QUEENS PLAY A central role in today's popular imagination. Their magnificence has graced numerous television shows around the world, most strikingly in the award-winning series *Game of Thrones*. The show's drama, splendor, and brutality are epitomized in the character of Cersei Lannister. Her power, persona, and predicament as a monarch have parallels in history, although these figures have been caricatured by writers skeptical of female leadership. This demonization of women exercising authority is nothing new. Cersei is portrayed as a cold-hearted, diabolical queen regent who will stop at nothing to secure the crown for her royal bloodline. She is the author and victim of unspeakable cruelty. She develops into a mercilessly ambitious woman, scheming to gain the upper hand in a belligerent world of men and monsters. Her storied bloodline is said to stretch back generations, where it has been locked in a struggle for power with rival houses of nobility. But generations of war between despotic ruling families, external invasions, and military upstarts have left the people in abject misery. The queen's city is ripe for the taking.

One fateful day a strange man appears, planting the seeds of revolution. The high sparrow, as he is known, is the archetype of the pre-modern holy man. His discipline, celibacy, and populism have earned the trust of the broken-hearted multitudes living in poverty. He preaches to them: devotion to a god named "the father"; uncompromising adherence to the laws of a scripture called the *Seven-Pointed Star*; the elimination of wealth, exemplified in the destruction of statues and the seizure of gold; and the shaming of sex and sin. By doing so, he offers the wretched masses a new way of life. But the holy man's mission is military and political as well. By his command an army of newly converted fanatics conquer the city, defeating its incompetent boy king, who is now merely a figurehead. And finally, the holy man presides over a newly formed, all-powerful body of clergy known as the council of septons.

The queen is trapped. She must compromise, or suffer defeat. She speaks words that, while written for modern times, have long echoed in the citadel of ancient imperial history:

The faith and the crown are the two pillars that hold up this world. One collapses; so does the other. We must do everything necessary to protect one another.

The scene is a striking dramatization of reality. From feudal Europe to the ancient Near East, history tells of powerful queens whose subjects and sovereignty were lost to conversion and conquest. In their precarious age, the power once shared by noblewomen and holy men was slowly but surely usurped by the latter. This is what transpired between the queens and prophets of Arabia long ago.

———

This book tells the story of female power in late antique Arabia, its influence over male prophecy there, and the global legacy it left behind. By "female power" I am referring to the agency of female nobility throughout society, notably their capacity to rule independently, undertake warfare, and conduct trade. My research seeks to rebalance decades of scholarship that overstates patriarchal influences within the region's politics, religion, and culture. It also challenges popular assumptions about the marginalized status of Arab women in pre-modern history, or their perceived absence from public life altogether.

Their epic saga is part and parcel of "late antiquity," a period dominated by the conflict between the great empires of Rome and Persia. To understand why female power is central to studying late antique Arabia I pose a central question. What was the religious and political culture of "Arabian society," after the intervention of Rome and before the rise of Islam (*ca.* 106–632 CE)? My answer to this question has been to examine the relationship between female nobility—particularly queens—on the one hand, and holy men—namely bishops, monks, and prophets—on the other. This book examines how the power of female nobility was eventually surpassed by that of holy men. These men became organized within newly independent church hierarchies and subsequent schools of Islamic law.

The foremost heroines of this story are the pagan and pro-Christian queens of Arabia. Their function in society sometimes intersected with that of the priestess or goddess. And their subjects often venerated them through sculpted, saintly, or celestial icons. The legacy these great women left behind was overshadowed by the holy men they employed, a legacy subsequently betrayed, then all but erased by later generations of medieval male authors.

Regal women strategically countered the patriarchal impulse behind Roman imperialism, church councils, and Islamic jurisprudence. Empress Zenobia and queen Mavia deliberately supported the teachings of local bishops—Paul of Samosata and Moses of Sinai—against the will of foreign men, specifically belligerent emperors and their power-hungry clergymen. The Greek-speaking imperial church condemned the teachings of both men as heretical. But those very teachings survived under the auspices of their matron queens, setting in motion seismic debates on the nature of Jesus, Mary, and God which fractured the early churches and laid the groundwork for the rise of Islam. These events paved the way for the foremost noblewoman of Christian extraction and the first Muslim of record, lady Khadijah. She used sheer wealth and political influence to marry a younger man against the will of dissenting Meccan noblemen. She then raised her husband from the deprivation of orphanage to the riches of commerce, helping to transform Muhammad into the greatest prophet to have ever emerged from Arabia.

Method

Our first-hand evidence for late antique Arabia is a patchwork of terse dedications, graffiti, and artwork scribbled onto rockfaces throughout the region. This rich yet fragmented database is supplemented by a wealth of books written by men. They include religious heresiography and political propaganda. This literature often served Near Eastern churches or the Abbasid court in Baghdad. The researcher must, therefore, constantly read between the lines of homilies, saints' lives, and orally transmitted poetry. And so the picture painted of late antique Arabia is often ahistorical, prejudiced, and highly problematic. Serious scholarly debate on female power has only further complicated this picture. But this is where the keen researcher and good storyteller join forces.

The challenges posed by imperfect sources and scholarly debate implore us to "tell a new story." Therefore, I have adopted a hybrid form of "narrative history"—storytelling—in combination with literary analysis, to present the theoretical examination necessary for this project in simple terms. Indeed, *storytelling* is an essential building block of societies constructing *identity*, be it Arabian, Syrian, Roman, Christian, Muslim, or otherwise. This is especially the case for societies convulsed by warfare, scarcity, or migration, as recalled in the exhortations of the Qur'an to its audience (e.g. Q 2:126; 14:37; 24:55; 93).[1]

On the other hand, perhaps these sources are imperfect because the modern researcher seeks an expedient, sequential, and linear path to historical truths. After all, how can we tell truth from fiction through the heaps of poetry in praise of passé chivalry? Or how valuable truly are accounts haplessly extolling saints and demonizing heretics generations after the crafting of an orthodox narrative?

Recent studies have shown that literary sources, especially those based on "oral literature," tell stories *not* to reveal "objective truth" but

1 See Theo de Boer, "Identité narrative et identité éthique," *Paul Ricoeur, L'hermeneutique a l'ecole de la phenomenology*, ed. Jean Greisch, Paris: Beauchesne, 1995, 43–58; Daniel Dennett, *Consciousness Explained*, New York: Little, Brown & Co., 2017, 48. In modern Arab storytelling see Halah Nashif, *Urid huwiyyah: qisas qasirah*, Beirut: al-Mu'assasah al-'Arabiyyah lil-Dirasat wal-Nashr, 1993. In modern social sciences see generally Anna De Fina, *Identity in Narrative: A Study of Immigrant Discourse*, Amsterdam; Philadelphia: John Benjamins Publishing Company, 2003; *Identity and Story: Creating Self in Narrative*, eds. D. P. McAdams et al., Washington: American Psychological Association, 2010; Kurt Röttgers, *Identität als Ereignis: Zur Neufindung eines Begriffs*, Bielefeld: Transcript Verlag, 2016.

rather to create a communal "shared identity."[2] For example, historians of the Byzantine Church or of the Abbasid court did not weave pious, poetic, and panegyric narratives to deliberately lead modern researchers astray. They did so to create a strong Christian or Muslim identity through storytelling.[3]

To this end, every effort has been made in this book to preserve the complexity of our stories, while revealing their parts in chronological order. The normal flow of traditional storytelling from one protagonist to the next, which often privileges men, is supplemented where necessary by literary analysis or cultural storytelling, which I argue better demonstrate the power exercised by women in pre-modern cultures especially.[4] I have endeavored to cite documentary evidence where direct access to data recorded on paper, or carved on rocks, has some bearing on this book's main focus: female power in late antique Arabia. On related matters of secondary focus, modern scholarship is cited freely. In other words, should general arguments made in this book appear more fully explained in prior studies, they are cited without direct reference to primary evidence. Given the sensitive nature of the material covered, the fullest range of scholarly opinions and diversity of researchers has been cited.

Organization

The significance of late antique Arabia's female power and male prophecy introduced here can only be fully appreciated and understood by taking a long historical view. I tell this story in three parts.

PART I, "Divine Queens of Pagan Arabia," covers the rise of female power from the depths of antiquity until the age of Roman–Persian rivalry. Chapter 1 examines the power struggle between women and

2 See Walter Ong, *Orality and Literacy*, New York: Methuen & Co., 1982, 10–16, 137–152; David Bowles and José Meléndez, *Ghosts of the Rio Grande Valley*, Charleston, SC: Haunted America, 2016, 7.

3 Tayeb El-Hibri, *Reinterpreting Islamic Historiography: Harun al-Rashid and the Narrative of the Abbasid Caliphate*, Cambridge: Cambridge University Press, 1999, 13 dubs this "commentary" in place of "facts."

4 Peter Burke, *Varieties of Cultural History*, Ithaca: Cornell University Press, 1997, 66–69, 152–156.

men in late antique Arabia. Chapter 2 integrates numerous queens of this era into the discourse of the pre-Islamic "age of ignorance" or *jahiliyyah*. The cult of the queens shaped Arabia, giving rise to Arabian goddesses whose authority was challenged by the one male god of the Bible and Qur'an, as covered in Chapter 3.

PART II, "Matrons of the Prophets," covers the evolution of Arabian queenship in its Christian context. The power once vested in the female sovereigns, I argue, increasingly passed down to male prophets, *ca.* third–seventh centuries CE. Chapter 4 tells the story of empress Zenobia and Paul of Samosata. Their doomed resistance to Roman incursion, and their assertion of identity occurred during a time when I argue a short-lived, loosely connected "Nativist church" existed (240–337). The story of queen Mavia and Moses of Sinai is the subject of Chapter 5. Their victory over the Romans contributed directly to the blossoming of Arab Christendom (375–500). And the story of lady Khadijah and Muhammad of Mecca is covered in Chapter 6. The final protagonists represent the decisive clash and compromise between Arabia's Christian and pagan communities—Islam.

PART III, "Men of the *Jahiliyyah*," consists of a single chapter. Chapter 7 examines how the patriarchal institutions of empire, church, and war curtailed female power once and for all.

PART I

Divine Queens of Pagan Arabia

I

Origins

Arabian Society in Late Antiquity

Our journey begins squarely within "Arabian society." This phrase refers to empires, kingdoms, and tribes located throughout the Near East, *ca.* second–seventh centuries CE. Most sectors of this society were associated with lucrative trade networks or organized military combat. Their competing cities or tribes connected them, through both alliance and conflict.

Near Eastern trade operated in parallel to the Asian Silk Route and Indian Ocean maritime trade. The main artery of Near Eastern commerce, which lay on the route between South Arabia and Syria, ran through the west Arabian coastal mountain passes known as the Tihamah, stretching from Yemen in the south through the Hijaz in the north.[1] This ancient "highway" evolved into the "Darb al-Bakrah" and gradually connected disparate communities throughout the Arabian Peninsula, Fertile Crescent, and Mediterranean Sea.[2] Crossing the barren Arabian desert were two trade routes running between west and

---

[1] Cf. Hatoon al-Fassi, *"al-Awda' al-siyasiyyah wal-ijtima'iyyah wal-iqtisadiyyah wa-ththaqafiyyah fi jazirat al-'arab," al-Kitab al-marja' fi tarikh al-ummah al-'arabiyyah*, vol. 1, Tunis: al-Munadhamah al-'Arabiyyah li-Ttarbiyah wa-Ththaqafah wal-'Ulum, 2005, 452–485.

[2] Cf. Christian Robin, "'La caravane yéménite et syrienne' dans une inscription de l'Arabie méridionale antique," *L'Orient au cœur: en l'honneur d'André Miquel*, eds. André Miquel et al., Paris: Maisonneuve et Larose, 2001, 206–217 and Q 106. See generally *The Darb al-Bakrah: A Caravan Route in North-West Arabia Discovered by Ali I. al-Ghabban, Catalogue of the Inscriptions*, ed. Laïla Nehmé, Riyadh: Saudi Commission for Tourism and National Heritage, 2018.

east. One of these passed through the northern oasis city of Dumah. The other passed through the southern oasis city of Qaryat al-Faw.

Geography

The Arab peoples of antiquity emerged from the Fertile Crescent and were the "border force" of the ancient and late antique Near East. Ancient Syria was home to several small "Arabias."[3] The Bible suggests "Arabia" encompassed several kingdoms between Syria and North Arabia. These included Qedar, Dedan, and nearby merchant communities (Isaiah 21:13; Ezekiel 27:21). 1 Kings 10 alleges the queen of Sheba left her lavish royal court in the Yemeni highlands to live with the Israelite king Solomon, a tale we shall return to in the following chapter. And "Arabia" lay just outside the Palestinian sphere in which the apostle Paul operated (Galatians 1:17).

We owe our understanding of a single entity known as "Arabia" to Greek and Roman geographers and historians. According to them the land of Arabia referred to communities in the Syrian desert, and their vast network of trade with the Yemen and along the Red Sea.[4] The writings of the geographer Strabo (d. *ca.* 23 CE) and historian Pliny the Elder (d. 79 CE) helped create a discourse linking the South Arabian communities of Minaea, Saba', Qataban, and Hadramaut with North Arabian communities in Nabataea.[5] Ptolemy (d. 170 CE) traversed both land and sea, spreading the imperial designation "Arabia" over three broad climes:

- *Arabia Petraea*, consisting of Petra and former Nabataea
- *Arabia Deserta*, the central lands covered by desert

---

3 Michael Macdonald, "Arabs, Arabias, and Arabic before Late Antiquity," *T* 16.1, 2009, 298.

4 Herodotus, *Histories*, trans. George Rawlinson, Ware, Hertfordshire: Wordsworth, 1996, 227–300; Strabo, *The Geography of Strabo: An English Translation with Introduction and Notes*, trans. Duane Roller, Cambridge: Cambridge University Press, 2014, 646–776; Glenn Bowersock, *Roman Arabia*, Cambridge, MA: Harvard University Press, 1983, 1–11; Robert Hoyland, *Arabia and the Arabs: From the Bronze Age to the Coming of Islam*, London; New York: Routledge, 2010, 2–3; Hatoon al-Fassi, "al-Jazirah al-'arabiyyah bayn istrabu wa blini: qira'ah fi al-masadir al-klasikiyyah," *MKTA* 8, 2013, 57.

5 al-Fassi, "al-Jazirah al-'arabiyyah bayn istrabu wa blini," 81–83.

- *Arabia Felix*, "happy Arabia" in the deep south, where copious rain-fall and flourishing agriculture dominated the green landscape

With time the name "Arabia" stretched to cover the whole peninsula, as evidenced in the writings of Josephus (d. 100 CE), who considered all its inhabitants as far as the southern coast "Arabs." This was during the reign of Roman emperor Trajan (d. 117 CE), whose coins celebrated his expansion into "acquired Arabia."[6]

Communities within the Arabian Peninsula were located in the following regions:

- Hijaz-Nabataea in the northwest
- Najd-Yamamah in the center
- Bahrayn-Gerrha in the northeast
- Yemen-Sheba in the southwest
- Hadramaut in the south and center
- Oman-Mazun in the southeast

Communities were also located throughout "greater Syria," i.e. the widest extent of the Levant or Roman Oriens, including:

- Arabia
- Palestine I–III
- Phoenicia I–II
- Syria I–II
- Euphratensis
- Osrhoene
- Mesopotamia

6 The process of extending the name "Arab" to far-flung communities is described in Fergus Millar, *The Roman Near East, 31 BC–AD 337*, Cambridge, MA: Harvard University Press, 1993, 221, 234; Warwick Ball, *Rome in the East*, London; New York: Routledge, 2002, 60, 110; Macdonald, "Arabs, Arabias, and Arabic before Late Antiquity," 298–301; Greg Fisher, "From Mavia to al-Mundhir: Arab Christians and Arab tribes in the late antique Roman East," *Religious Culture in Late Antique Arabia: Selected Studies on the Late Antique Religious Mind*, eds. Kirill Dmitriev and Isabel Toral-Niehoff, Piscataway: Gorgias Press, 2017, 187.

Across the limits of the Persian realm, communities were located throughout Mesopotamia. These include the northern provinces associated with the Jazirah:

- Adiabene
- Arabistan
- Asoristan (Assyria)

It also included the southern provinces associated with southern Mesopotamia, also known as Iraq:

- Khuzestan
- Meshan

Trade networks and slavery played an integral role as well.[7] An Old South Arabian inscription from Minaea offers evidence of how interconnected Arabian kingdoms were with satellite communities, offering an impressively diverse list of women either married to or enslaved by merchant men. The inscription lists women from Gaza, Awsan, Sidon, Egypt, Qedar, Dadan, Hadramaut, Yathrib, Oman, Qataban, Hegra, Lihyan, Moab, and elsewhere.[8]

Language

Current scholarship argues that the origin of the Arabic language lies between North Arabia and greater Syria, in the environs of the Nabataean sphere, where it was intimately cross-pollinated with the Aramaic language.[9] This region constitutes the ancient homeland of

7 Cf. in relation Kecia Ali, *Marriage and Slavery in Early Islam*, Cambridge, Harvard University Press, 2010.

8 al-Fassi, "*al-Awda' al-siyasiyyah*," 463 cites evidence to this end.

9 Nawaf 'Abd al-Rahman, *Tarikh al-'arab qabl al-islam*, Amman: Dar al-Janadria, 2015, 78; Laïla Nehmé, "Aramaic or Arabic? The Nabataeo-Arabic Script and the Language of the Inscriptions Written in This Script," *Arabic in Context: Celebrating 400 Years of Arabic at Leiden University*, ed. Ahmad Al-Jallad, Leiden: Brill, 2017, 75–79; Ahmad Al-Jallad, "Pre-Islamic Arabic," *Arabic and Contact-Induced Change*, eds. Christopher Lucas and Stefano Manfredi, Berlin: Language Science Press, 2020, 39–42.

Arabia and its surroundings

the Arabic script, and is referred to as "Syro-Arabia." Its peoples, who
shared close cultural, religious, and political bonds, are called "Syro-
Arabian." They shaped and were shaped by direct contact with several
antique nations. According to Hatoon al-Fassi they principally
included the Egyptians, Sabaeans, Aramaeans, Chaldeans
(Babylonians), Persians, and Greeks.[10] Over the course of late antiquity
Syro-Arabians spoke dialects of Arabic, Aramaic, and other Semitic
languages as their native tongue. They also used—to varying degrees—
imperial Greek for public affairs.

---

10 Hatoon al-Fassi, "*al-'Anasir al-sukkaniyyah al-wafidah 'ala shamal gharb al-jazirah
al-'arabiyyah fil-fatrah min muntasaf al-qarn al-sadis q.m. wa hatta al-qarn al-thani lil-
milad*," DT 2.56, 1995, 1–41.

As in any society, Arabian communities were diverse but interconnected. To quote Michael Macdonald, the peoples who identified themselves as "Arab" subsisted within a "complex of language and culture." Over the course of late antiquity these people more or less came to share Arabic as their common language.[11] As early as the first millennium BCE ancient communities appeared in the town of Dumah, located in the deserts west of Babylon and east of Damascus. They formed alliances to resist the powerful Assyrians.[12] These communities were shaped over the coming centuries by generations of Persian, Hellenic, and Roman conquerors.

Communities speaking dialects of Old South Arabian, Old North Arabian, and Aramaic would gradually adopt Arabic as their native tongue in late antiquity. This occurred sometime following the Roman conquests in the second century CE and leading up to the Arab conquests in the seventh century.[13]

Arabs, Saracens, and Ishmaelites

However, the earliest reference to "Arabs" is ancient, and it comes from the north. More specifically, Assyrian records document the great battle of Qarqar (853 BCE), where an alliance of twelve kings finally halted king Shalmaneser III (d. 824 BCE), who had been conquering the cities of Syria one by one.[14] Among the kings were Ben Haddad of Aram, Ahab of Israel, and Gindibu of Arabia. King Gindibu was the first king of Qedar. To him belonged the first recorded Arabic-speaking tribal confederation, located in North Arabia and greater Syria.[15] Arabs could be found throughout much of the ancient Near East. Prior to the second century CE they were attested throughout the northern Arabian

11 Macdonald, "Arabs, Arabias, and Arabic before Late Antiquity," 296, 306, 309.

12 Hatoon al-Fassi, "*Malikat al-'arab fil-alf al-awwal qabl al-fatrah al-mu'asirah*," A2 7, 2012, 32.

13 Macdonald, "Arabs, Arabias, and Arabic before Late Antiquity," 319–320. See further, Jihan Shah Bahay, "*al-Ihtilal al-rumani li-mamlakat al-anbat wal-wilayah al-'arabiyyah 106–305 miladiyah*," PhD diss., King Saud University, 2010.

14 Cf. further al-Fassi, "*Malikat al-'arab*," 23–24.

15 al-Fassi, "*al-Awda' al-siyasiyyah*," 461.

Peninsula, Syria and the Levantine coast, Mesopotamia, Sinai, eastern Egypt, western Iran, and the Kamaran islands off western Yemen.[16]

The identity of late antique "Arabs," while disputed among scholars, was largely influenced by, or asserted in contradistinction to, the great empires surrounding them. Scholars have classified their ranks as:

(1) Settled people—Arabs—dwelling permanently in *Provincia Arabia* from 106 CE onward, or after the annexation of Nabataean lands by Rome

(2) Nomadic Saracens dwelling beyond the Roman *limes*[17]

Others have adopted a more refined distinction, citing the presence of:

(1) Imperial citizens   (*cives*)
(2a) Allies of the imperium   (*foederati*)
(2b) Distant nomads
(2c) Distant city dwellers[18]
(3) Ishmaelites

Ishmaelites became a third classification granted by Palestinian Jews and Syriac Christians to their Arab "cousins." The three groups were imagined, therefore, as sharing common ancestry from the biblical patriarch Abraham.[19]

The taxonomy of these groups—Arabs, Saracens, and Ishmaelites— is coherently presented here, but they have not always been considered one and the same. Pre-modern sources refer to them inconsistently,

16 Macdonald, "Arabs, Arabias, and Arabic before Late Antiquity," 281–283.
17 Ibid., 309.
18 Irfan Shahid, *Byzantium and the Arabs in the Fourth Century*, Washington, D.C.: Dumbarton Oaks, 1984, 17. al-Fassi, "*al-Awda' al-siyasiyyah*," 461 adds the *scenitae* (Arab. *sakiniyyat*) or "tent dwellers."
19 See Robertson Smith, *Religion of the Semites*, London: Adam and Charles Black, 1894, 1, 9, 41; Fergus Millar, "Hagar, Ishmael, Josephus, and the origins of Islam," *JJS* 44, 1993, 23–45, reprinted in *Rome, the Greek World, and the East: Volume 3: The Greek World, the Jews, and the East*, eds. Hannah Cotton and Guy Rogers, Chapel Hill: University of North Carolina Press, 2006, 402.

while modern researchers continually dispute the precise relation between them.

Contemporaneous writings throughout late antiquity, mainly in Greek and Syriac, speak of Arab military leaders (Saracens) and tribal chieftains (phylarchs), numerous kings, and at least one queen— Mavia. These figures presided over barbarian tribes bound to the Romans by treaty and serving them as *foederati*, also known as Qudaʿah-Saracens.[20] Procopius of Caesaria (d. *ca.* 570) identifies a related though seemingly distinct people called Maʿadd, or Maddene-Saracens. These were camel-herding Bedouin used in military action by the Romans as well.[21] About two dozen contemporaneous inscriptions, mainly in Greek, further identify individual "Arabs" in myriad fashions. They were:

- Urban professionals, including tax collectors, merchants and sellers, barbers, gymnasiarchs, and market gardeners
- Rural practitioners, including animal breeders, farmers, and landowners
- Police, guards, and various military functionaries
- Kings and city founders
- City dwellers
- Nomads[22]

In addition to these categories, Arabian communities were composed of:

- Animal herders
- Dairy farmers
- Wine makers
- Ship builders

20 Cf. Fergus Millar, "Ethnic identity in the Roman Near East, A.D. 325–450: Language, religion and culture," *MA* 11, 1998, 159–176, reprinted in *Rome, the Greek World, and the East: Volume 3: The Greek World, the Jews, and the East*, eds. Hannah Cotton and Guy Rogers, Chapel Hill: University of North Carolina Press, 2006, 378–405.

21 Peter Webb, *Imagining the Arabs: Arab Identity and the Rise of Islam*, Edinburgh, Edinburgh University Press, 2017, 74–75 cites Procopius (d. *ca.* 570).

22 Macdonald, "Arabs, Arabias, and Arabic before Late Antiquity," 283–285.

- Seafarers
- Leather and fur makers
- Oasis and terrace agriculturalists

They traded in these very commodities as well. Maritime and river trade were significantly cheaper than overland trade, which was typically limited to expensive, luxury commodities such as spices, gems, and minerals.[23]

Our examination discusses a diversity of Arabs, exploring their often-fragmented society. This fragmentation is frequently attributed to the system of organized socio-political communities linked through kinship, and which the medieval Arab scholars recalled variously as the:

- People   (*sha'b*)
- Tribe   (*qabilah*)
- Settlement   (*'imarah*)

Whatever the most primitive unit may have been, it was self-perpetuating. Meaning, communities based on kinship took the name of an eponymous founder, followed by a continual series of sub-founders. These subsequent generations (*tabaqat*) represented smaller groupings known as the:

- Bloc   (*batn*)
- Clan   (*fakhdh*)
- Smaller units[24]

Politics and Religion

Classical and late antique Arabs are sometimes typecast as bearers of "fabulous wealth, the nomadic lifestyle, and unconquerable

---

23 al-Fassi, "*al-Awda' al-siyasiyyah*," 468–470.
24 Cf. Butrus al-Bustani, *Muhit al-muhit: Qamus mutawwal lillugha al-'arabiyyah*, Beirut: Maktabat Lubnan, 1965, 29.

independence."[25] While this image has been exaggerated in the popular imagination, it did not come from nowhere. Even modern classicists stubbornly clinging to the passé idea that Near Eastern populations existed as little more than quietist Greek-speaking colonies concede the "marginal exception of Arab or Saracen allies under their tribal leaders."[26] It was not diversely fashioned Syrians, Phoenicians, Jews, or Samaritans who did, let alone could, undertake full-scale military rebellion against their Greco-Roman masters, and win. This feat was accomplished with varying degrees of success by populations we identify as Arab. And among their victorious and mighty commanders was a woman—queen Mavia of Tanukh (d. 425 CE)—whose story is told later in this book.

In the pagan times before her, the imperial citizens of Hellenized city states, including Hatra and Palmyra, the city of al-Hirah allied with Persia, the urban center of Kindite trade Qaryat al-Faw, and the various nomads and city dwellers of the Hijaz and Yemen, had in common a surprisingly consistent cadre of chief deities. These included the widespread cults of the goddesses Allat, al-'Uzza, and Manat, *and* divinities styled as daughters of the god Il or El. They also included lesser, regional male gods, notably Hubal in the north and 'Athtar in the south.[27]

It seems Christianity spread in parallel with Arabic. Arabic writing proliferated across the Arabian Peninsula simultaneously with the penetration of the Syrian churches, starting in the third/fourth century CE.[28] Arabic writing came into existence, so to speak, over a century after the Roman conquest of Petra in the north, and seemingly in response to Himyarite expansion from the south. Nabataeo-Arabic inscriptions originating from a sphere of influence around

25 Macdonald, "Arabs, Arabias, and Arabic before Late Antiquity," 319.

26 Millar, "Ethnic identity in the Roman Near East," 381.

27 'Abd al-Rahman al-Ansari (al-Ansary), *Qaryat al-faw: surah lil-hadarah al-'arabiyyah qabl al-islam fi-l-mamlakah al-'arabiyyah al-su'udiyyah/Qaryat al-Fau: A Portrait of Pre-Islamic Civilization in Saudi Arabia*, New York: St. Martin's Press, 1982, 28; Christian Robin, "Les 'Filles de Dieu' de Saba' à La Mecque: réflexions sur l'agencement des panthéons dans l'Arabie ancienne," *S* 50, 2001, 160–161; 'Abd al-Rahman, *Tarikh al-'arab qabl al-islam*, 67.

28 Fisher, "From Mavia to al-Mundhir," 166–167.

Hegra—never fully conquered—coupled with the abandonment of the Zabur-Musnad script, demonstrate the evolution and materialization of the Arabic script.[29]

The evolution of the late Nabataean script into the early Arabic script has been studied widely. Among the diverse spectrum of inscriptions are over a dozen famous texts from along the trade route between Yemen and greater Syria. These include the Raqush Inscription of 267, the Namarah Inscription of 328, the Hima Inscription of 470, the trilingual Zabad Inscription of 512, and a growing collection of largely Christian epigraphic writings from the fifth–sixth centuries. Some have theorized that the abandoning of the Musnad script by late antique Arabic speakers represents an act of defiance against Himyarite dominance.[30] Whatever the precise case may have been, Christianity penetrated Arabia more deeply than its script alone, as the majority of pre-Islamic Arabic-speaking poets were likely Christian or familiar with the growing dominance of Christianity on Arabian soil.[31]

Arabic-speaking communities often competed with one another from within Persian or Roman spheres of influence. By the sixth century, communities in Mesopotamia, Syria, and Yemen were tightly bound to one another through not only trade, but a series of confessional, diplomatic, and military exchanges reverberating from great empire hostilities between Byzantium and Ctesiphon from the north, and Axum from the south. The open channels between seemingly far-flung Arabian communities and their

---

29 Cf. Laïla Nehmé, "A glimpse of the development of the Nabataean script into Arabic based on old and new epigraphic material," *The Development of Arabic as a Written Language,* ed. Michael Macdonald, Oxford: Archaeopress, 2010, 47–80; Beatrice Gruendler, *The Development of the Arabic Scripts: From the Nabataean Era to the First Islamic Century According to Dated Texts,* Atlanta: Scholars Press, 1993. Greg Fisher et al., "Arabs and Christianity," *Arabs and Empires before Islam,* ed. Greg Fisher, Oxford: Oxford University Press, 2015, 314 cites the instrumental role played by the Jafnids (Ghassanids).

30 Christian Robin, "Les Arabes de Himyar, des Romains et des Perses (iiie–vie siècles de l'ère chrétienne)," *SC* 1, 2008, 170.

31 See Louis Cheikho, *Shu'ara' al-nasraniyyah qabl al-islam,* Beirut: Dar al-Mashriq, 1967.

resulting cohesion, whether diplomatic or belligerent, transformed Arabia into a battleground of Christian and Jewish territories on the eve of Islam.[32]

Debating Arabia

Community was, and is, a human construct. Every nation, whether ancient or modern, is an "imagined community."[33] The imagined community under examination here is "Arabian society," a context which is located between the three highly disputed aspects already introduced:

(1) Arabian geography
(2) Arabic language
(3) Arab identity

Scholars debate when a cohesive Arabian ecosystem came into being. The spectrum of opinions varies from origins within the ancient Semites to the centralizing influence of Islam under the medieval Abbasid empire. My goal is neither to reconcile nor to repudiate any particular scholarly position cited throughout this project in passing. Each position possesses the requisite nuance and deliberation deserving of the reader's full attention. Instead, my goal is to enrich the debate by reconsidering the critical role played by the highly organized Abrahamic religions in imagining and reimagining this community. Most significant in this respect are the formation of a national church at the turn of the fourth century CE, and then later a series of caliphates beginning in the seventh century CE.

The very idea that pre-Islamic Arabian peoples enjoyed some measure of cohesion is hotly contested as well. The debate is plagued by

32 Sergius of Rusafa, *The Book of the Himyarites: Fragments of a Hitherto Unknown Syriac Work*, ed. Axel Moberg, London; Oxford; Paris; Leipzig; Lund: C.W.K. Gleerup, 1924, lxxvii.
33 See generally Benedict Anderson, *Imagined Communities: Reflections on the Origin and Spread of Nationalism*, London: Verso, 1983, whose influential work inspired "imagining the Arabs" by Webb, *Imagining the Arabs*, 11.

traditionalist ideology, on the one hand, and infected with hyper-skepticism, on the other.[34] Nationalist-minded scholars have sometimes overstated the antiquity of Arab identity or Semitic culture therein, taking the Arabic sources of medieval Islamic tradition for granted,[35] while Western orientalists, classicists, or missionaries have tended to exaggerate Arabia's fractiousness and stress its indebtedness to Greco-Roman culture.[36] Alternatively, the categorical rejection of sources—whether Arabic or Greco-Roman—has not helped but hindered our understanding. Both the identity and self-awareness of Arabs throughout antiquity is disputed by scholars ad nauseam, with no consensus in sight. Nevertheless, this impasse cannot refute a growing number of studies about ever increasing documentary and literary evidence demonstrating the complex, shared, and long-standing relations between states, tribes, or groups associated with the term *'arab* or their common cultural space.[37]

A critical appraisal of our otherwise imperfect or incomplete sources offers greater promise than outright rejection or blind acceptance. This project will demonstrate the complex, shared, and

---

34 Fred Donner, *Muhammad and the Believers: At the Origins of Islam*, Cambridge, MA: Harvard University Press, 2012, 218–220 and Aziz Al-Azmeh, *The Emergence of Islam in Late Antiquity: Allah and His People*, Cambridge: Cambridge University Press, 2014, 100–154 are centrist assessments of this debate coming from opposing angles. See further Ayad Al-Ani, *Araber als Teil der hellenistisch-römischen und christlichen Welt: Wurzeln orientalistischer Betrachtung und gegenwärtiger Konflikte: von Alexander dem Großen bis zur islamischen Eroberung*, Berlin: Duncker & Humblot, 2014, 13–23.

35 Jirji Zaydan, *Tarikh al-'arab qabl al-islam*, Cairo: Matba'at al-Hilal, 1922; Philip Hitti, *History of the Arabs: From the Earliest Times to the Present*, Basingstoke: Palgrave Macmillan, 2002; Ahmad Dawud, *al-'Arab wa al-samiyyun wa al-'ibraniyyun wa banu isra'il wa al-yahud*, Damascus: Dar al-Mustaqbal, 1991.

36 Millar, "Ethnic identity in the Roman Near East," 378–405, and Webb, *Imagining the Arabs*, 1–3 epitomize this trend. Cf. further Hatoon al-Fassi, "*Nuqtat al-bad' al-tarikhi, min ayn? ru'yah marja'iyyah jadidah*," *GSHA* 9, 2008, 123–140.

37 See G. E. Von Grunebaum, "The nature of Arab unity before Islam," *A* 10.1, 1963, 5–23; Maxime Rodinson, *Les Arabes*, Paris: Presses Universitaires de France, 2002; Hoyland, *Arabia and the Arabs*; Jan Retso, *The Arabs in Antiquity: Their History from the Assyrians to the Umayyads*, London; New York: Routledge, 2014; Ahmad Al-Jallad, "'Arab, 'A'rab, and Arabic in Ancient North Arabia: The first attestation of (')'rb as a group name in Safaitic," *AAE* 31.2, 2020, 1–14; al-Fassi, "*al-Awda' al-siyasiyyah*," 461–468.

long-standing religious and political culture of these peoples *through* examining female power, and its impact on male prophecy.

Debating Female Power

No scholar has yet narrated the impact of Arabian female power on male prophecy. Meanwhile, there is an abundance of modern scholarship on the "history" of ancient Arabia, placing it in the shadow of late antique Byzantium or Rome, or centering it upon pre-Islamic language, rhetoric, tribal customs, or any number of passé discourses.[38] The subject of female power in that scholarship is incidental. Studying women in pre-Islamic Arabia, especially in medieval literary sources, is by and large beholden to male-oriented frameworks of inquiry, notably poetry.[39] Poetry and performed speech were a literary and political vehicle used to convey chivalry, and were typically associated with "masculine virtues" throughout much of late antiquity.[40] Poets were the leaders of their communities, and their utterances were to the

---

38 Cf. Jawad 'Ali, *al-Mufassal fi tarikh al-'arab qabl al-islam*, London: Dar al-Saqi, 2001; Glenn Bowersock, *Roman Arabia*; *The Crucible of Islam*, Cambridge: Harvard University Press, 2017; Irfan Shahid, *Rome and the Arabs: A Prolegomenon to the Study of Byzantium and the Arabs*; *Byzantium and the Arabs in the Fourth Century*; *Byzantium and the Arabs in the Fifth Century*; *Byzantium and the Arabs in the Sixth Century*, 4 vols.; *Byzantium and the Arabs in the Seventh Century*, Washington, D.C.: Dumbarton Oaks, 1984–2010; David Graf, *Rome and the Arabian Frontier: From the Nabataeans to the Saracens*, London: Ashgate, 1997; T. M. Smith, *Arabs: A 3,000-Year History of Peoples, Tribes and Empires*, New Haven: Yale University Press, 2019.

39 Bashir Yamut, *Sha'irat al-'arab fi al-jahiliyyah wa al-islam*, Kuwait: al-Maktabah al-Ahliyyah, 1934; 'Irfan Muhammad Hamur, *al-Mar'ah wa al-jamal wa al-hubb fi lughat al-'arab*, Beirut: Dar al-Kutub al-'Ilmiyyah, 1971; 'Abd Muhanna, *Mu'jam al-nisa' al-sha'irat fi al-jahiliyyah wa al-islam*, Beirut: Dar al-Kutub al-'Ilmiyah, 1990; 'Abd al-Hamid Diwan, *Mawsu'at ashhar al-nisa' fi al-tarikh al-qadim: Mundhu fajr al-tarikh hatta al-'asr al-jahili*, Mansouria, Lebanon: Kitabuna li al-Nashr, 2009; Dalida Akoum, "La représentation de la femme dans la littérature arabe préislamique et dans ses sources," PhD diss., Université Bordeaux Montaigne, 1996.

40 Cf. in relation Shaun Tougher, "In praise of an empress: Julian's speech of thanks to Eusebia," *The Propaganda of Power: The Role of Panegyric in Late Antiquity*, ed. Mary Whitby, Leiden; Boston; Köln: Brill, 1998, 115–116.

Arabs a political weapon and a sacred gospel.[41] Arabic rhymed prose
(*saj'*) was the primary vehicle of prophetic speech and priestly incanta-
tions on the eve of Islam. Most of the prophets and priests recorded
were men. Some were women.[42]

What has seldom been considered is that the deliberate misrepre-
sentation of pre-Islamic religion, politics, and culture—which scholars
widely acknowledge—carries with it the egregious distortion of gender,
broadly speaking, and of female power in particular. Medieval Arabic
scholarship during the Abbasid empire (750–1258) shaped Islam. In
the words of Nadia El Cheikh on the so-called *jahiliyyah* or pre-Islamic
"age of ignorance":

> The texts' formulation of *jahiliyya* was part of a cultural reorienta-
> tion that took place over the course of two centuries with the aim
> of defining ever more sharply what it meant to be an Arab and
> Muslim … Gender-related and sexual imaginings play an impor-
> tant function in self-construction projects, and this is especially
> true in Islamic history.[43]

She emphasizes the importance of characterizing and controlling
women as an instrumental means of constructing a traditional form of
male identity. In doing so "men … used the _heretical woman_ as a vehicle to assert their own orthodox male selfhood."[44] She draws a parallel
between the Abbasid construction of the *jahiliyyah* and the European
practice of colonization:

> Postcolonial historians have, for instance, analyzed the sexualiza-
> tion of cultural difference and the ways in which the gender

41 Mathieu Guidère, "Les poètes et le prophète au debut de l'Islam," *QSA* 5.6, 2010–
2011, 121–122, 136.
42 See generally Ibn Tayfur, *Balaghat al-nisa'*, ed. Ahmad al-Alfi, Cairo: Madrasat
Walidat 'Abbas al-Awwal, 1908.
43 Nadia El Cheikh, *Women, Islam, and Abbasid Identity*, Cambridge: Harvard
University Press, 2015, 2–3.
44 Ibid., 60, emphasis added.

constructs of the dominant imperial culture were used to explain the "uncivilized" nature of the colonized.[45]

El Cheikh adds, finally, that researchers of Islamic history in general, including the pre-Islamic period, have yet to undertake a similar analysis.

In connection with the "gendered imagining of religion," this book argues that male authors of medieval courts portrayed late antique Arabian society in terms that aggrandize pious Christian and Islamic masculinity yet detest impious pagan femininity. This tendency, including patterns of patrilineal kinship, was largely inherited from late antique Greek, Latin, and Syriac church fathers and rabbinic Jews,[46] becoming a staple of classical Islamic ethics.[47]

Beyond the crucial work of El Cheikh, many scholars offer valuable studies on the agency, independence, and major contributions of female nobility in pre- and early Islamic Arabia. In this vein a variety of academic works challenge the narrative of the marginalized Arab woman in late antiquity, including those by religious and secular feminists offering insights about pre-Islamic Arabia.[48] Another handful of studies examine the contribution of queens and nobility during

---

45 Ibid., 8.

46 For biblical precedents of this precise argument see Gail Streete, *The Strange Woman: Power and Sex in the Bible*, Louisville, KY: Westminster John Knox Press, 1997, 101.

47 Ali, *Marriage and Slavery in Early Islam*, 11; Zahra Ayubi, *Gendered Morality: Classical Islamic Ethics of the Self, Family, and Society*, New York City: Columbia University Press, 2019, 127; Cyrus Zargar, "Virtue and manliness in Islamic ethics," *JIE* 1.1–2, 2020, 1–7.

48 Such works include Zaynab Fawwaz, *al-Durr al-manthur fi tabaqat rabbat al-khudur*, Kuwait: Maktabat Ibn Qutaybah, 1891, repr. Cairo: Hindawi, 2014; Nabia Abbot, "Pre-Islamic Arab queens," *AJSLL* 58.1, 1941, 1–22; Layla Sabbagh, *al-Mar'ah fi al-tarikh al-'arabi: fi tarikh al-'arab qabl al-islam*, Damascus: Wizarat al-Thaqafah wa al-Irshad al-Qawmi, 1975; Hind al-Turki, *al-Malikat al-'arabiyyat qabl al-islam: dirasat al-tarikh al-siyasi*, al-Jouf: Mu'assasat 'Abd al-Rahman al-Sudayri al-Khayriyyah, 2008; Hatoon Ajwad al-Fassi, *Women in Pre-Islamic Arabia: Nabataea*, Oxford: Archaeopress, 2007; Nawal El-Saadawi, *al-Untha hi al-asl*, Cairo: Hindawi Foundation, 2017; and Habib al-Zayyat, *al-Mar'ah fi al-jahiliyyah*, Cairo: Wikalat al-Sahafah al-'Arabiyyah, 2018.

medieval and modern Islam, which is an important though altogether different venture.[49]

Sources

What previous studies lack is the connection between female power and male prophecy which this book presents for the first time. In doing so I offer a fresh perspective on cutting-edge studies as well as materials concerning literary, epigraphic, numismatic, and archeological evidence. These sources are mainly in the following languages and dialects:

- Arabic
- Old North Arabian (Thamudic, Safaitic, and Hismaic)
- Old South Arabian (Sabaic and Himyaritic)
- Aramaic (Nabataean, Palmyrene, Hatran, and Syriac)
- Greek
- Latin[50]

Biblical and post-biblical literature which helped shape Arabia is indispensable for the purposes of our examination as well. I make judicious use of the voluminous body of medieval Arabic and Islamic writings on pre-Islamic Arabia (hereafter "Arabic sources" or "Islamic tradition"), while offering a narrative that is historically consistent, and which counter-balances the patriarchy and misogyny made plain in those very sources.

---

49 Fatima Mernissi, *Sultanes oubliées: femmes chefs d'état en Islam*, Paris: Albin Michel; Éditions Le Fennec, 1990, trans. Mary Jo Lakeland, *The Forgotten Queens of Islam*, Minneapolis: University of Minnesota Press, 2003; Shahla Haeri, *The Unforgettable Queens of Islam: Succession, Authority, Gender*, Cambridge: Cambridge University Press, 2020; Leila Ahmed, *Women and Gender in Islam: Historical Roots of a Modern Debate*, New Haven: Yale University Press, 1992.

50 Cf. esp. al-Fassi, *"al-Jazirah al-'arabiyyah bayn istrabu wa blini,"* 55–94; Sulayman al-Dhib [al-Theeb], *al-Kitabat al-qadimah fil-mamlakah al-'arabiyyah al-su'udiyyah*, Riyadh: Kitab al-Majallah al-'Arabiyyah, 2018.

Men Writing about Women

Religious clerics and partisan chroniclers—men—portrayed late antique Arabia as the "dark age" prior to the light of Islam. They were commissioned by powerful Abbasid caliphs and patrons—also men—to document the epic history and mysterious origins of Arabian society once and for all. Only once the caliphate had conquered most of the known world and fully supplanted the Sasanian Empire did the extant works of Arabic literature appear in the Abbasid court *ca.* 750–800 CE. Books reportedly written in the late seventh century at best exist *only* as quoted by later literary works, or they have been lost altogether.[51] The first genres of literature in the second–third/eighth–ninth centuries gave birth to works of:

• Hagiography	(Sirah)
• Conquests	(Maghazi)
• Reports about Muhammad	(Hadith)
• Genealogies of Muhammad	(Nasab)
• Exegesis of the Qur'an	(Tafsir)
• Biographical dictionaries	(Tabaqat)
• Pre-Islamic battle folklore	(Ayyam)
• Poetry	(Shi'r)[52]

51 See Sean Anthony, *Muhammad and the Empires of Faith: The Making of the Prophet of Islam*, Oakland: University of California Press, 2020, 1–23.

52 The most prominent sources include Muhammad b. Ishaq, *al-Sirah al-nabawiyyah*, 2 vols., ed. Ahmad F. al-Mazidi, Beirut: Dar al-Kutub al-'Ilmiyah, 2004, trans. A. Guillaume, *The Life of Muhammad: A Translation of Ibn Ishaq's Sirat Rasul Allah*, Oxford; New York: Oxford University Press, 1955; Ma'mar b. Rashid, *The Expeditions: An Early Biography of Muhammad*, ed. Sean Anthony, New York; London: New York University Press, 2017; Abu Mikhnaf, *Nusus min tarikh abi mikhnaf*, first edition, 2 vols., ed. Kamil S. al-Jabburi, Beirut: Dar al-Mahajjah al-Bayda', 1999; Abu Zayd al-Qurashi, *Jamharat ash'ar al-'arab fi al-jahiliyyah wa al-islam*, ed. Muhammad al-Hashimi, Riyadh: al-Mamlakah al-'Arabiyyah al-Sa'udiyyah, 1981; al-Khalil b. Ahmad, *Kitab al-'ayn: Murataban 'ala huruf al-mu'jam*, ed. 'Abd al-Hamid Hindawi, Beirut: Dar al-Kutub al-'Ilmiyah, 2003; Malik b. Anas, *al-Muwatta: The First Formulation of Islamic Law*, trans. Aisha Bewley, London; New York: Routledge, 2016; Hisham b. al-Kalbi, *Gamharat an-nasab: das genealogische Werk des Hisam Ibn Muḥammad al-Kalbi*, ed. Werner Caskel, Leiden, Brill, 1966; *Jamharat al-nasab*, ed. Naji Hasan, Beirut: Maktabat

These writings weave together Abbasid imperial ideology and rabbinic and ecclesiastical legal piety. They mix history with legend.

This matter is complicated by medieval Persian versus Arab nationalism, and their debate over cultural superiority, or *shuʻubiyyah*, starting in the third/ninth century.[53] Overall, the apologetic impulse and political fabrication behind the otherwise valuable Arabic sources of Classical-Medieval Islam (750–1258) is well documented by modern experts. This is especially the case with respect to crafting the legendary origins of Arabian society centuries before the sources themselves. The extent to which experts debate the utility of medieval sources, however, is a matter beyond the scope of discussion.[54]

Be that as it may, male authors transformed pre-Islamic Arabian society into a caricature. Muslim exegetes going back to reports by Ibn ʻAbbas (d. 68/687) retell stories from ecclesiastical and rabbinic folklore. They ascribe the corrupting temptation of music among the sons of the biblical forefather Cain and the beginnings of adultery to the daughters of Seth.[55] Music was, rather, a staple of Arabia's bustling marketplaces and poetic celebrations where women danced and played the lute.[56] At any rate the fount of exegetical lore—fiction—claims that Satan's

al-Nahdah al-ʻArabiyyah, 1986; Muhammad al-Waqidi, *The Life of Muhammad: al-Waqidi's Kitab al-Maghazi*, trans. Rizwi Faizer, London; New York: Routledge, 2011; Muhammad b. Saʻd, *Kitab al-tabaqat al-kabir*, ed. ʻAli ʻUmar, Cairo: Maktabat al-Khanji, 2001; ʻAli al-Bajawi et al., *Ayyam al-ʻarab fi al-jahiliyyah*, Beirut; Sidon: al-Maktabah al-ʻAsriyyah, 1998.

53 Rina Drory, "The Abbasid construction of the Jahiliyya: Cultural authority in the making," *SI* 83, 1996, 33–50; Fred Donner, *Narratives of Islamic Origin: The Beginnings of Islamic Historical Writing*, Princeton: Darwin Press, 1998, 49, 60–61, 132. See further Rodinson, *Les Arabes*, 90–129.

54 For more on this see Peter Webb, "al-Jahiliyya: Uncertain times of uncertain meanings," *DI* 91.1, 2014, 69–94.

55 Cf. Muhammad b. Jarir al-Tabari, *Tafsir al-tabari: jamiʻ al-bayan ʻan taʼwil ay al-quran*, Cairo: Hajr, 2001, 19:98–100.

56 Hatoon al-Fassi, "*Aswaq al-ʻarab*," *al-Kitab al-marjaʻ fi tarikh al-ummah al-ʻarabiyyah*, vol. 1, Tunis: al-Munadhamah al-ʻArabiyyah li-Ttarbiyah wa-Ththaqafah wal-ʻUlum, 2005, 564; Guidère, "Les poètes et le prophète au debut de l'Islam," 121; Michael Macdonald, "Goddesses, dancing girls or cheerleaders? Perceptions of the divine and the female form in the rock art of pre-Islamic North Arabia," *Dieux et déesses d'Arabie: Images et représentations*, eds. Isabelle Sachet and Christian Robin, Paris: De Boccard, 2012, 278–280.

daughter, Laqis bt. Iblis, corrupted a number of the women among Lot's people, transforming them into the first generation of Lesbians.[57] The association of the "songstress" and demonic temptress with fornication and sorcery was found throughout late antique Babylonian and Syriac writings, including Aphrahat the Persian Sage (d. 345).[58]

Parallel to these traditions was the ancient Sumerian figure of Lilith and what Siegmund Hurwitz calls the "dark aspects of the feminine." She is adopted as the phantom Lamia in Greek writings, and transformed by the Babylonian Talmud and *Alphabet of Ben Sirach* into a ravishing demoness, both seducing men in their sleep and slaying newborn babies.[59] In conversation with the misogyny of their Syriac, Greek, and rabbinic counterparts, the Arabic sources prefer fantastical stories of wayward womenfolk. The authors of these sources explain the tragedy of child mortality like men tormented by their own desires, while twisting the genuine, historical expression of female power.[60] By way of example, this power was often wielded by the priestess. She occupied an institutional office which regulated the agency and social life of women according to older pagan norms, which later sources condemn. Thus, ancient forms of polyandry and open marriage—in which women willingly had sexual relations with multiple, consecutive, or simultaneous male partners—came to represent not female power, but the widespread immorality, rampant lawlessness, and lax marriages of society.[61] In this literature women are portrayed as sexually overactive, yet strangely subjugated. That is to say they are frequently portrayed as unnamed harlots, slaves without recourse, or daughters to be sold if the price is right.

As this book makes eminently clear, political leadership—queenship—was the crown jewel of late antique female power. Since ancient times the role of queen sometimes intersected with that of priestess, and at others with that of warrior. "Priestess-queenship" was attested

---

57 Nihad Ni'mah, *al-Jinn fil-adab al-'arabi*, Beirut: American University in Beirut Press, 1961, 68.

58 Aphrahat, "Demonstrations," *PS* 1, 1894, 1: 265–70 (On Monks).

59 Siegmund Hurwitz, *Lilith: Die erste Eva Eine historische und psychologische Studie über dunkle Aspekte des Weiblichen*, Einsiedeln: Daimon Verlag, 1980, 51–52.

60 Ibid., 47, 114.

61 El Cheikh, *Women, Islam, and Abbasid Identity*, 2.

in ancient North and South Arabia alike, suggesting to some researchers the possibility of a "theocratic society" even before Christianity.[62]
The "warrior-queenship" attested in late antiquity was a phenomenon
native to non-Roman barbarian peoples.[63] But money changes people.
And the "mercantile impulse" of Arabian society soon cultivated a
strong culture of urbanization.[64] With the influx of Abrahamic traditions and Roman laws, the urban centers of Arabia adopted increasingly patriarchal forms of urban political leadership.[65] To secure their
power for future generations, men, I argue, turned to eradicating the
power of their political nemeses—women.

Sources tied to Hisham b. al-Kalbi (d. 204/819) stand out to those
examining female power in late antique Arabia. Ibn al-Kalbi was
himself a prolific author and brilliant medieval researcher. He is
famous for being classical Islam's singular heresiologist of pre-Islamic
Arabian religion. In this discipline he had many predecessors. They
include several Christian and classical authors, not least of whom were
authorities of Semitic background living near or among Syro-Arabian
communities, such as John of Damascus (d. 749), 'Adi b. Zayd (d. *ca.*
600) whom he quotes directly, Epiphanius of Salamis (d. 403), Ephrem
the Syrian (d. 373), Lucian of Samosata (d. *ca.* 180), and others.

Pagan Goddesses

Ibn al-Kalbi's *Book of Idols* is partly built on the *Life of the Prophet* by
Muhammad b. Ishaq (d. 151/768). This hagiography is known in
Arabic as the *Sirah* and serves as our earliest Arabic literary source
after the Qur'an.

But Ibn al-Kalbi is unique. His book is a catalog of the male and
female divinities which populated the late antique Arabian pantheon.
These include gods and goddesses in the vicinity of Mecca's cubic

---

62 Xavier Teixidor, *The Pagan God: Popular Religion in the Greco-Roman Near East*,
Princeton: Princeton University Press, 1977, 86.

63 Shahid, *Byzantium and the Arabs in the Fourth Century*, 192.

64 Marshall Hodgson, *The Venture of Islam*, Chicago: University of Chicago Press,
1977, 1:117, 130.

65 Robert Spencer, "Arabian matriarchate: An old controversy," *SJA* 8.4, 1952, 480–482.

shrine or temple, known as the Kaabah.[66] Among the dozens of deities he records are several known to us through centuries' worth of Arabian inscriptions, including Nasr and Dushara.

The list of Arabian deities also includes eight cited by name in the Qur'an. Among them are the five gods Wadd, Suwa', Yaghuth, Ya'uq, and Nasr, those hypothetically worshipped by Noah's people in Q 71:23. His list also includes the three goddesses known to later Islamic tradition as the "daughters of Allah," namely Allat, al-'Uzza, and Manat, cited in Q 53:19–22. The explicit mention of these deities in seventh-century scripture is unique, because they are last referred to by Old North and South Arabian inscriptions in the fourth century, with the two goddesses Allat and al-'Uzza referenced in the works of fifth–sixth century Christian apologists.[67]

Taken together, the Arabic names of three goddesses—Allat, al-'Uzza, and Manat—communicate the trilogy of life itself: birth, life, and death. The Semitic name *allat* means the "goddess"; it is quite simply the feminine form of *allah*. The name *al-'uzza* conveys the meaning "mightiest, strongest," while *manat* refers to fate, reckoning, or mourning.[68] This trinity of goddesses was worshipped widely by well-established Arabian communities in greater Syria, Mesopotamia, and Yemen, as well as in newly established communities throughout the Arabian Peninsula—including Mecca in the Hijaz—and trading communities on the Mediterranean.[69]

66 Hisham b. al-Kalbi, *Kitab al-asnam*, ed. Ahmad Zaki Basha, Cairo: Dar al-Kutub al-Misriyyah, 1924; *The Book of Idols: Being a Translation from the Arabic of the Kitab al-Asnam*, trans. Nabih Faris, Princeton: Princeton University Press, 1952. See Ibn Ishaq, *Sirah*, 60–65.

67 See further Valentina Grasso, "The gods of the Qur'an: The rise of Hijazi henotheism during late antiquity," *The Study of Islamic Origins: New Perspectives and Contexts*, eds. Mette Mortensen et al., Berlin: De Gruyter, 2021, 297–324.

68 Cf. in relation Hashim al-Mallah, *al-Wasit fi tarikh al-'arab qabl al-islam*, Beirut: Dar al-Kutub al-'Ilmiyyah, 1971, 134; Firas al-Sawwah, *Lughz 'ishtar: al-uluhah al-mu'annathah wa asl al-din wal-usturah*, Damascus: Dar 'Ala' al-Din, 1996, 292–299, 92–100, 207–233.

69 See Christian Robin, "L'attribution d'un bassin à une divinité en Arabie du Sud antique," *R* 1, 1978, 39–64; "Les 'Filles de Dieu' de Saba' à La Mecque," 113–192; "À propos des 'filles de dieu,'" *S* 52–53, 2002–2007, 113–192; al-Mallah, *al-Wasit fi tarikh al-'arab qabl al-islam*, 321.

The goddesses figure importantly in the famous Islamic catalog of pre-Islamic deities, the *Book of Idols* by Ibn al-Kalbi. In that work, the entry on al-ʿUzza is the longest of any deity, suggesting her supremacy in the Arabian pantheon of late antique Hijaz. She is described as "the greatest idol among the Quraysh."[70] Meanwhile the male god Hubal, claimed to be the major deity of the Meccan Kaabah in the *Sirah* of Ibn Ishaq, has a meagre entry immediately appended to that of al-ʿUzza. These idiosyncrasies require careful examination and they demand a critical reading of his text, supplemented with documentary evidence where possible.

As is the case with other pagan pantheons, the functions of these three deities in the mythology or cultic practice of late antique Arabia were occasionally interchangeable, notably the role of Allat at first and later al-ʿUzza as "queen of heaven." This was a divine title originally carried by the ancient Mesopotamian goddess Inanna, but inherited by several succeeding goddesses and devotional figures for millennia. Their ranks include the Canaanite Asherah, the Arabian al-ʿUzza, the Christian figure of Mary as mother goddess and god bearer, and the Muslim figure of Fatimah, daughter of Muhammad.[71]

Ibn al-Kalbi assigns these deities to the cities where Muhammad sought sanctuary. Thus, he claimed Hijazi urban trading centers took three female deities as matron:

(1) Allat in Taʾif
(2) al-ʿUzza in Mecca
(3) Manat in Yathrib

How much truth this claim holds is not entirely certain. However, the three cities seem to have developed as a tightly knit commercial and cultic consortium. Ibn al-Kalbi's claim that Manat and Allat are ancient

70 Cf. Ibn Ishaq, *Sirah*, 63 vs. Ibn al-Kalbi, *Kitab al-asnam*, 13–27. See also al-Mallah, *al-Wasit fi tarikh al-ʿarab qabl al-islam*, 239, 403; Gerald Hawting, *The Idea of Idolatry and the Emergence of Islam: From Polemic to History*, Cambridge: Cambridge University Press, 1999, 139.
71 Cf. generally Diane Wolkstein and Samuel Kramer, *Inanna: Queen of Heaven and Earth: Her Stories and Hymns from Sumer*, New York: Harper & Row, 1983; Sayyid al-Qimani, *al-Usturah wal-turath*, Cairo: Maktabat Ibn Sina, 1999, repr. Cairo: Hindawi, 2017. My forthcoming book researches the divinity of Fatimah.

adoptions while al-'Uzza is more recent, though entirely possible, contradicts his suggestion elsewhere that the former are al-'Uzza's two daughters. Furthermore, an exception to our list of previously known Arabian deities are the divine couple Isaf and Na'ilah, whose names were introduced to us through the work of Ibn al-Kalbi. He claims the divine couple desecrated the Kaabah of Mecca by engaging in sexual intercourse during the formative period of the sanctuary's history.[72]

Ibn al-Kalbi echoes the cultural memory preserved by his peers and predecessors, that ancient Mecca was a monotheistic city founded by none other than the biblical patriarch Abraham, and that some centuries later the Arab chieftain 'Amr b. Luhayy, of the Azd tribe and founder of the Khuza'ah tribe, introduced pagan gods from Syria and the north.[73] The stories woven around the contrived accounts of Abraham or 'Amr are telling nonetheless. Ibn al-Kalbi's account of the origins of monotheism *and* idolatry may be an embellished cultural memory. But it recalls, at the very least, the northern origins of Arabic-speaking tribes, including their queens and goddesses, a subject of further examination in the coming chapters. Like Mecca's imagined patriarchs, its goddesses, he claims, also came from the north. His suggestion that Allat and Manat were ancient deities, while al-'Uzza was a recent arrival, suggests a seismic shift in Meccan society on the eve of Islam. This was the result of large-scale war, persecution, and conversion.

Ibn al-Kalbi is also remembered as the greatest genealogist of Arabia's tribes. The medieval study of genealogy is connected to the neighboring encyclopedic ventures of Tabaqat and Hadith. These became hallmarks of classical Islamic scholarship and medieval Arab culture. His *Comprehensive Genealogy* alongside his other genealogical works, and the *Great Book of Generations* by his successor Muhammad b. Sa'd (d. 230/845), are essential resources for excavating the memory of Arabian queens among later generations. Invaluable in this regard is Ibn Sa'd's final volume, which is dedicated to biographies of the earliest Muslim women.

72 Ibn al-Kalbi, *Kitab al-asnam*, 22, 27, 39. See also Ibn Ishaq, *Sirah*, 163–164; al-Fassi, "al-Awda' al-siyasiyyah," 458.
73 Ibn al-Kalbi, *Kitab al-asnam*, 8.

Recent memories of "believer queens," reverberate throughout these rich sources. Among them Zenobia, Mavia, and Khadijah were the stars of Arabian queenship in its Christian phase (third–seventh centuries). However, the more distant memories of late antique Arabia's "pagan queens" were largely lost. These women were the less-known predecessors who laid the foundations for Arabian queenship in its pagan phase (first–third centuries).

Pagan Queens, First–Third Centuries CE

The medieval Arabic sources have virtually nothing historical to say about the pagan queens of Arabia. Our knowledge of them as heads of state and landed noblewomen come from inscriptions, monuments, and coins left behind by the Aramaic- and Arabic-speaking kingdoms located in the desert steppes between North Arabia, Syria, and Mesopotamia. Our examination begins with the Nabataean kingdom (*ca.* 312 BCE – 106 CE). This realm is popularly known for establishing permanent trade networks throughout Arabia, especially between Syria and Yemen, and connecting the global markets of the Indian Ocean with those of the Mediterranean Basin. The kingdom's geographical limits included:

- Petra, its capital located in Transjordan
- Hegra, its second largest city located in the Hijaz
- Sinai[74]

The authors of the Hebrew Bible acknowledge the Nabataeans as descendants of ancient Ishmaelites (Genesis 25:13). It is little known, however, that Nabataean women were bearers of great economic, political, and religious authority. They were merchants, landlords, and priestesses.[75] I argue that the power of Nabataean female nobility

---

74 al-Fassi, "*al-Awda' al-siyasiyyah*," 454. See further Mehdy Shaddel, "Studio onomastica coranica: *al-Raqim, caput nabataeae*," *JSS* 62.2, 2017, 303–318.

75 Cf. Hatoon al-Fassi, "Kamkam the Nabataean priestess: Priesthood and society in ancient Arabia," *From Ugarit to Nabataea: Studies in Honor of John F. Healey*, eds. George Kiraz and Zeyad al-Salameen, Piscataway: Gorgias Press, 2012, 1–14.

peaked around the first century CE, when queens ruled at times independently and helped bring the cities of Petra and Hegra to their apex
(*ca.* 9 BCE – 106 CE). They include:

- Huldu (d. *ca.* 16 CE)
- Shagilath I (d. *ca.* 40 CE)
- Gamilath (d. 106 CE)

Following the golden age of queens, the Nabataean realm was
conquered by the Romans. Nabataea lost its Hijazi lands and shrank to
the smaller province of "Arabia." The power and prestige of pagan
queenship declined dramatically. Or it shifted to newly independent
Arabian realms in Syria and Mesopotamia. Notable among them were
the city states which Rome would dominate in the coming centuries.
They include:

(1) Emesa
(2) Hatra
(3) Palmyra—granted the title *Civitas Libera ca.* 129 CE by emperor
    Hadrian (d. 138 CE)[76]

By way of comparison, other conquered peoples also suffered a decline
in the status of their women as a direct consequence of Roman
conquest. They include the Etruscans, whose women enjoyed a level of
power and freedom which shocked their Greek and Roman counterparts.[77] This is not to say that Etruscan and Arabian women enjoyed
identical status before Roman conquest, only that this conquest nega-
tively impacted the status enjoyed by each.

By the second and third centuries, Roman political influence and
Abrahamic religions had begun the gradual but inevitable process of
restricting the autonomy of women throughout Arabian society, and
empowering men at their expense. This patriarchal evolution is
demonstrated in the short-lived kingdoms of Emesa, Adiabene, and

---

76 al-Mallah, *al-Wasit fi tarikh al-'arab qabl al-islam*, 163.
77 Larissa Warren, "The women of Etruria," *Women in the Ancient World: The Arethusa
Papers*, eds. John Peradotto and John Sullivan, Albany: SUNY Press, 1984, 229–233.

Osrhoene. The ruling class of these metropolises became increasingly dominated by non-Arabian men. Their chief deities, furthermore, became the male gods El-Gabal, Yahweh, or Christ. Thus, the "Semitic high god" was crafted by the hegemonic power of Roman culture. This god was also shaped by select emperors, and a multitude of holy men who quite simply detested female power. Just consider the misogyny of the apostle Paul of Tarsus (d. *ca.* 67 CE).[78]

Believer Queens, *ca.* 249–619 CE

The memory of pro-Christian Arabian queens is preserved in the poetic verse and battle folklore recorded in the medieval Arabic sources. Zenobia (d. 274), the empress of the Roman East, and Mavia (d. 425), the queen of Tanukh, are celebrated as heroes who fended off the Roman scourge. These historical figures were much more than symbols of what we may consider pre-modern Arab nationalism, as the medieval authors would have us believe. They also supported local Christian communities.

Late antique Greek and Latin histories give us a somewhat more historical glance at Zenobia and Mavia, beyond the largely whimsical stories in the Arabic sources.[79] The former protected and promoted the bishop of Antioch named Paul of Samosata (d. 275). This was notably the case once the early church condemned him for the so-called "heresies" of Monarchianism and Adoptionism.[80]

Mavia established the first pan-Arabian *foederatus* serving Rome. She spearheaded the conversion of the Arabs to what would later become West Syrian (Monophysite) and East Syrian (Nestorian) churches. This feat she undertook with the help of a mysterious monk from Sinai called Moses (d. late fourth century).[81] Conversion may

---

78 Cynthia Westfall, *Paul and Gender: Reclaiming the Apostle's Vision for Men and Women in Christ*, Ada, MI: Baker Publishing, 2016 seeks to rectify this problem for believers.

79 David Powers, "Demonizing Zenobia: The Legend of al-Zabba' in Islamic Sources," *Histories of the Middle East*, eds. M. E. Roxani et al., Leiden: Brill, 2010, 147.

80 Gustave Bardy, *Paul de Samosate: étude historique*, Louvain; Paris: Spicilegium Sacrum Lovaniense; Champion, 1923, 115.

81 See Shahid, *Byzantium and the Arabs in the Fourth Century*, 411.

have begun among the tribes of Tanukh and Kalb, but Christianity inevitably became a signature of subsequent *foederati*, namely the tribes of Salih and Ghassan.

Both Zenobia and Mavia supported the theologies of Paul and Moses as a means to counter-balance the growing power of an imperial, foreign church doctrine and hierarchy. These theological trajectories were sanctioned by queens and contributed to the doctrine of God's single nature. The popularity of this doctrine competed with that of the powerful emperor sitting in Byzantium, and in contradistinction to what would become the Chalcedonian (Melkite) Church established by his holy men.[82]

The Monophysite flock of Syria, Egypt, Ethiopia, and Arabia would, to varying degrees, resist Greek Byzantium. In the Arabian province of Hijaz, the theology of God's single nature may have contributed to the rise of Islam, sanctioned by late antique Arabia's final queen, deprived of a proper regnal title.

The twilight of Arabian queenship came in the person of Khadijah bt. Khuwaylid (d. 619), Muhammad's first wife.[83] Although she did not carry a regnal title, she is remembered as the preeminent exemplar of Arabian female nobility at the advent of Islam. The sources esteem her as the "princess of Quraysh," "Khadijah the great," and as the original "mother of the believers." She was the very first Muslim and, moreover, recognized as the wealthiest woman, and one of the most powerful leaders, among the Quraysh tribe and the city of Mecca. She is identified as a widow and the inheritor of a prosperous commercial enterprise between Syria and Yemen. The sources claim she was much older than Muhammad and the facilitator of his career as a merchant and prophet. These features, while acknowledged generally, are deliberately downplayed by the very same sources. The likelihood that Khadijah came from a Christian family has received meagre scholarly attention.[84]

82 Averil Cameron, "The Cult of the Virgin in Late Antiquity: Religious Development and Myth-Making," *CM* 39, 2004, 13 cites the "competition model."

83 al-Fassi, "*Malikat al-'arab*," 13.

84 Cf. generally Abu Musa al-Hariri, *Qiss wa nabi: bahth fi nash'at al-islam*, Beirut: s.n., 1979, trans. Joseph Azzi, *Le prêtre et le prophète: aux sources du coran*, Paris: Maisonneuve

I argue in this book that Khadijah is the last in a long line of late antique Arabian queens. Her royal bloodline was in decline. Like her predecessors she delegated her power to a holy man. The seeds for this model for gendered delegation of power were planted in antiquity, especially in the petitioning of female nobility of their "more powerful" male counterparts, principally kings.[85] The nobility of Khadijah's bloodline and the holiness of Muhammad's mission were passed down to their daughter Fatimah (d. 10/632), and later her husband 'Ali (d. 40/661), who were transformed through medieval Islamic tradition into the holiest objects of devotion after God and Muhammad. The Islamic "holy family" or *ahl al-bayt* would shape Shii and Sunni piety and politics for centuries to come.[86]

The lives of "believer queens" transformed Arabia as much as they did the Abrahamic traditions. Indeed, their memory is no less important than those of the biblical matriarchs examined by others. By way of comparison these include Hagar the "mother of Islam," Esther the "Jewish heroine," and Mary the "Christian matriarch."[87]

Female power flourished in both pagan as well as Christian communities. What follows is a survey of pre-Islamic Arabia's preeminent queens. Their illustrious ranks include women of historical as well as mythical reputation.

---

et Larose, 2001; Khalil 'Abd al-Karim, *Fatrat al-takwin fi hayat al-sadiq al-amin*, Cairo: Mirit li al-Nashr wa al-Ma'lumat, 2001.

85 Tikva Frymer-Kensky, *In the Wake of the Goddesses: Women, Culture, and the Biblical Transformation of Pagan Myth*, New York: Ballantine Books, 1992, 130.

86 See Ali Shariati, *Fatemeh fatemeh ast*, Tehran: Nashr-i-Ayat, 1978, trans. Laleh Bakhtiar, *Ali Shariati's Fatima is Fatima*, Tehran: Shariati Foundation, 1981, 35. My thanks go to Hani Khafipour and David Cook for their insights.

87 Cf. generally Debbie Blue, *Consider the Women: A Provocative Guide to Three Matriarchs of the Bible*, Grand Rapids: Eerdmans, 2019.

2

Queenship

In the Beginning

In the beginning was the queen. And the queen ruled as a goddess. And the queen was a goddess.

This is the story of female power in Arabia in a nutshell, from its rise in the first millennium BCE through to its slow and gradual fall in late antiquity. However, the prevalence of queens was not attested evenly throughout the Arabian Peninsula, nor in its Syrian or Mesopotamian environs. Before enumerating the many queens of pre-Islamic Arabia whose names have come down to us, and their various achievements, we must separate fact from fiction.

Queens figured importantly in the north, but not in the south. Their sovereignty was felt throughout the cities of greater Syria and northern Arabia. The north's distinct social, religious and political culture made it the abode of great queens. So is there any historical truth to the stories about the queen of Sheba?

The Queen of Sheba—Myth or Reality?

The legendary queen of Sheba is often taken as the archetype of Arabian queenship in antiquity. According to the stories of scripture and exegesis alike, she was the queen of ancient Saba' (thirteenth century BCE–third century CE) in South Arabia.[1]

---

1 al-Fassi, "*Malikat al-'arab*," 16–20.

Renouncing Wealth in 1 Kings 10

The Bible narrates a regal visit by the Sabaean queen to Solomon, king of Israel. The story goes that

> [the queen] heard of the fame of Solomon ... due to the name of the Lord. She came to Jerusalem with a very great retinue, with camels bearing spices, and very much gold, and precious stones; and when she came to Solomon, she told him all that was on her mind. Solomon answered all her questions; there was nothing hidden from the king that he could not explain to her. When the queen of Sheba had observed all the wisdom of Solomon, the house that he had built, the food of his table, the seating of his officials, and the attendance of his servants, their clothing, his valets, and his burnt offerings that he offered at the house of the Lord, there was no more spirit in her. So she said to the king, "The report was true that I heard in my own land of your accomplishments and of your wisdom, but I did not believe the reports until I came and my own eyes had seen it. Not even half had been told me; your wisdom and prosperity far surpass the report that I had heard. Happy are your wives! Happy are these your servants, who continually attend you and hear your wisdom! Blessed be the Lord your God, who has delighted in you and set you on the throne of Israel! Because the Lord loved Israel forever, he has made you king to execute justice and righteousness." Then she gave the king one hundred twenty talents of gold, a great quantity of spices, and precious stones; never again did spices come in such quantity as that which the queen of Sheba gave to King Solomon. (1 Kings 10; cf. 2 Chronicles 9)

The point of the biblical story is expressed in the conclusion of the episode. God made Solomon the wealthiest and wisest king on earth (1 Kings 10:23–24). Gail Streete adds about biblical queens:

> The one wise, independent and foreign queen who does no harm is the queen of Sheba ... This sexually independent and clever

queen, "mastered by Solomon," cannot control him and therefore poses no further threat.[2]

Renouncing Power and Pagan Faith in Q 27

The Qur'an elaborates on the biblical story. It adds that God gave Solomon control over the winds, demons, and beasts of the land. After his love of earthly wealth caused him to forget the Lord, he repented and his dominion over the earth was restored (Q 38:30–40).

In Q 27 we learn that among his formidable army of demons, men, and birds was the hoopoe, dispatched to far-off lands. Upon returning from Saba' (Sheba) the bird reports back to Solomon. There he found a people living in great abundance, with woman ruling over them with a mighty throne. Satan tempted them into worshipping the sun instead of the one God. Solomon is livid at hearing this news. The king immediately begins plotting the downfall of the queen, sparking a series of correspondences and pitting his royal court against hers. The queen receives his letter and reads it before her noble advisers, stating:

> "Oh you nobles, a truly distinguished letter has been conveyed unto me. Behold, it is from Solomon, and it says, 'In the name of God, The Most Gracious, The Dispenser of Grace: Exalt not yourselves against Me, but come unto Me in willing surrender!' Oh you nobles, give me your opinion on the problem with which I am now faced. I would never make a decision unless you are present with me." They answered, "We are endowed with power and with mighty prowess in war, but the command is thine. Consider, then, what thou wouldst command." Said she, "Verily, whenever kings enter a country they corrupt it, and turn the noblest of its people into the most abject. And this is the way they behave. Hence, behold, I am going to send a gift to those, and await whatever the envoys bring back."

2 Streete, *The Strange Woman*, 104, 105.

Solomon furiously rejects the queen's gifts, claiming his God's gifts are greater.

> Now when it arrived unto Solomon, he said, "Do you people mean to add to my wealth? But that which God has given me is better than all that He has given you. Nay, it is you that would rejoice in this gift of yours. Go thou back unto them. For we shall most certainly come upon them with forces which they will never be able to withstand, and shall most certainly cause them to be driven out, despicable and humbled!"

The queen judges a visit to the belligerent king's court is necessary to prevent the massacre of her people. When Solomon learns of her imminent visit, he dispatches one of his demons to steal her throne and bring it to his court. This magical gesture symbolizes the conquest of her realm and the loss of her dominion before she ever sets foot into Solomon's court. At any rate when the queen arrives, the story goes that she was mesmerized by the opulent court and many servants of the king, whereupon she has a change of heart.

> She has arrived at the truth without any help from us, although it is we who have been given knowledge before her, and have surrendered ourselves unto God. Although that which she has been wont to worship instead of God had kept her away. For, behold, she is descended of people who deny the truth.

The queen finally surrenders to the one God of Solomon:

> "Oh my Sustainer, I have been sinning against myself. But I have now surrendered myself, with Solomon, unto the Sustainer of all the worlds!" (See Q 27:15-44—trans. Muhammad Asad, edited)

The passage integrates the well-known biblical story with a condemnation of ancient Sabaean sun worship. The worship of the sun, moon, and stars was indeed practiced in South Arabia, and among other

segments of late antique Arabia (Q 41:43).[3] Q 34, entitled "Saba,"
compares the splendor of this ancient kingdom to the gardens of
paradise. The Sabaean people "turned away" and God punished them
with a great flood, expulsion, and migration (cf. Q 34:12–19; 56:46–
78). Islamic tradition teaches that this episode refers to the breaching
of the Ma'rib dam, and the dispersal of South Arabian communities
throughout the peninsula in the fifth–sixth centuries CE.[4]

Evidence for South Arabian Queens?

In this context we find the legendary epic of Sayf b. Dhi Yazan (d. 578),
which tells of how Sasanian Persia brought about the end of Himyarite
power. It is celebrated in an Arabic literary masterpiece dated to the
fifteenth century CE. Its story takes place between the world of military
struggles undertaken by humankind, and the world of magical spells
cast by demonkind. King Sayf's mother, Qamariyyah, is described in
ahistorical terms, as the evil temptress of his father and jealous usurper
of her son's rightful power. Far from being history, the story is a master-
ful retelling of ancient Near Eastern themes and *topoi*.[5] Nevertheless,
Qamariyyah was not our queen of Sheba.

South Arabia certainly had kings, whose exploits were as famous or
infamous as their names. Their wives were, therefore, queens through
royal marriage. Could one of these be the long sought-after queen of
Sheba? It is unlikely. Sabaic inscriptions preserve the memory of a
queen, namely Malak Halak bt. 'Alhan Nahfan, queen of Hadramaut
(second century BCE). Her father, brother, and husband all served as
king at some point in their lives.[6] The same records cite the names of
other noblewomen, including Dhat Hadar, Dhat Yafra', and Dhat Bani
'Irq.[7] However, there is no evidence that these highborn women led

3 Al-Azmeh, *The Emergence of Islam in Late Antiquity*, 73, 183–186.
4 Tabari, *Tafsir*, 16:254.
5 See further Lena Jayyusi, *The Adventures of Sayf Ben Dhi Yazan: An Arab Folk Epic*,
Bloomington: Indiana University Press, 1996.
6 Cf. further al-Fassi, "*Malikat al-'arab*," 17, 20; Balqis al-Hadrani, *al-Malikah balqis:
al-tarikh wal-usturah wa-rramz*, Cairo: Matba'at Wahdan, 1994, 114 cites evidence in this
regard.
7 Ibid., 115.

armies, undertook missions to foreign lands, or conducted public life as independent queens or regents. There is evidence, nevertheless, of matriarchal or matrilineal relationships in South Arabia, which is beyond our focus here and taken up elsewhere.[8]

One final detail in this matter is that there are numerous Old South Arabian inscriptions mentioning women. However, the overall message this evidence provides about female power is mixed. The epigraphic evidence suggests women owned property and built temples. The women are mentioned for their frequent cultic activity, because they appear heavily burdened with sins—more than men that is.[9] Overall, South Arabia simply did not have the formidable tradition of queenship ascribed to it by legend.[10]

Trophy Wife or Triumphant Queen?

Medieval Arabic sources build upon the Qur'an and Bible, telling tall tales of a romance between the Israelite king and Sabaean queen. In qur'anic exegesis she is given the name Bilqis, which is an Arabic rendering of Greek *pallakis* meaning "concubine." In other sources she is reported to have been married off to king Solomon, or another king. The Ethiopian national epic known as "The Glory of Kings" was translated from Arabic in 1322. It tells the story of how Ethiopian civilization abandoned the worship of constellations and embraced the one God of Israel. The link between Israel and Ethiopia is the marriage between king Solomon and the re-envisioned queen of Ethiopia named Makeda. Their purported son Menyelik I (tenth century BCE) is believed to be the ancient forefather of Christian Ethiopia, the center of which was Axum. Makeda is portrayed as the perfect bride, who after falling under the spell of Solomon says to him:

8 Joseph Chelhod, "Du nouveau à propos du 'matriarcat'," *A* 28.1, 1981, 76–106.

9 al-Fassi, "*al-Awda' al-siyasiyyah*," 467.

10 Aram Shahin, "Struggling for communitas: Arabian political thought in the great century of change (*ca.* 560–*ca.* 660 AD)," PhD diss., University of Chicago, 2009, 688–689.

Blessed art thou, my lord, in that such wisdom and understanding have been given unto thee. For myself I only wish that I could be as one of the least of thine handmaidens, so that I could wash thy feet, and harken to thy wisdom, and apprehend thy understanding, and serve thy majesty, and enjoy thy wisdom. O how greatly have pleased me thy answering, and the sweetness of thy voice, and the beauty of thy going, and the graciousness of thy words, and the readiness thereof. The sweetness of thy voice maketh the heart to rejoice, and maketh the bones fat, and giveth courage to hearts, and goodwill and grace to the lips, and strength to the gait. I look upon thee and I see that thy wisdom is immeasurable and thine understanding inexhaustible, and that it is like unto a lamp in the darkness, and like unto a pomegranate in the garden, and like unto a pearl in the sea, and like unto the Morning Star among the stars, and like unto the light of the moon in the mist, and like unto a glorious dawn and sunrise in the heavens. And I give thanks unto Him that brought me hither and showed thee to me, and made me to tread upon the threshold of thy gate, and made me to hear thy voice.[11]

A separate body of medieval traditions holds that the queen of Sheba was the daughter of a human father and a demoness mother, making her part Jinn. This made the exchange between her and Solomon the subject of truly fantastic stories within medieval Islamic tradition. These stories were forged in conversation with Jewish and Christian lore, where the character of the queen of Sheba exerts immense power.[12] If there were any historicity to a powerful queen of Sheba, it would come not from the Bible or Qur'an. But it could have been inspired by royal matrilineal succession in the neighboring state of Nubia.[13]

---

11 *The Kebra Nagast: The Glory of Kings*, ed. E. A. W. Budge, Rockville, MD: Silk Pagoda, 2007, 26.

12 See Jamal Elias, "Prophecy, power and propriety: The encounter of Solomon and the queen of Sheba," *JQS* 11.1, 2009, 57–74.

13 Giovanni Ruffini, *Medieval Nubia: A Social and Economic History*, Oxford: Oxford University Press, 2012, 242–245.

The queen of Sheba visits king Solomon

As this brief literary survey illustrates, the queen of Sheba is not depicted in historical let alone realistic terms. She is portrayed in some traditions, rather, as king Solomon's most prized conquest and convert. This image is developed further in medieval literature where she is depicted as Solomon's "concubine" or the "least of his handmaidens." In contrast to this image, however, she is portrayed by other traditions as a powerful Jinn-queen.

Echoes of Zenobia and Aurelian in Q 27

The reader cannot mistake, however, the strong protest against the destructive behavior of kings within the queen's voice in the Qur'an. There is a tension between the predatory masculine power celebrated in Q 27:22–44 and the simultaneous resentment of that very power.[14]

---

14 al-Fassi, *"Malikat al-'arab,"* 17–18. See further Zishan Ghaffar, *Der Koran in seinem religions- und weltgeschichtlichen Kontext: Eschatologie und Apokalyptik in den mittelmekkanischen Suren,* Leiden: Brill, 2017, 75–110, with thanks to Catharina Rachik for her insights.

This tension arises from the clash between fiction and history, which demands some investigation.

While Q 27:22–44 clearly retells the biblical myth of the queen of Sheba, and her submission to king Solomon and his God, the qur'anic narrative recalls the details of an encounter between an historic "queen and king" who loomed large in the memory of late antique Arabian society. They are, namely, the empress Zenobia of Palmyra (d. 274) and the Roman emperor Aurelian (d. 275).

The connection between the queen of Sheba in Q 27 and the historical Zenobia is only speculated on by some Arabic sources. The renowned exegete Muhammad b. Jarir al-Tabari (d. 310/923) describes the only queen in the Qur'an as a sun-worshipping demon, whose legs were hairy and hooved like a donkey![15] His guesswork is often buried in centuries of Jewish and Islamic folk traditions demonizing the autonomy, power, and femininity of the queen of Sheba.[16] Like other works of Tafsir, exegetical storytelling is pregnant with fantasy but lacking in historicity. These stories conflate the historical queens of Sheba, Qedar, and Palmyra, discussed later, with the semi-legendary kings of Tanukh and Lakhm.[17] Bluntly, Tabari taps into ancient stories of real queens for whom we have reliable evidence—demonizing them—in order to craft new stories about glorious kings, for whom we have virtually no evidence. The queens are portrayed, furthermore, as unruly agents of rebellion and paganism. The kings are paragons of monotheism and social order.[18] The perennial conflict between the representations of late antique Arabian women and men in the sources is developed throughout this book.

Let us return to the narrative details of Q 27:22–44. In the passage following the hoopoe's mission, king Solomon sends a stern letter

---

15 Tabari, *Tafsir*, 18:45–47. Cf. also al-Fassi, "*Malikat al-'arab*," 14; Al-Azmeh, *The Emergence of Islam in Late Antiquity*, 111.

16 Jacob Lassner, *Demonizing the Queen of Sheba: Boundaries of Gender and Culture in Postbiblical Judaism and Medieval Islam*, Chicago: University of Chicago Press, 1993; Fabrizio Pennacchietti, *Three Mirrors for Two Biblical Ladies: Susanna and the Queen of Sheba in the Eyes of Jews, Christians, and Muslims*, Piscataway: Gorgias Press, 2006.

17 Cf. Isabel Toral-Niehoff, *al-Hira: Eine arabische Kulturmetropole im spätantiken Kontext*, Leiden; Boston: Brill, 2013, 43–58.

18 Cf. in relation Frymer-Kensky, *In the Wake of the Goddesses*, 204.

demanding the queen's unconditional surrender (vv. 28–31). Upon receiving the harshly worded epistle the queen, like all true leaders, soberly consults with her advisers without whom she makes no decision (v. 32). They deliberate yet nevertheless defer to her, whereupon she utters words of eternal wisdom:

> When kings enter a city, they devastate it, and subjugate its dignified people. Thus they always do. (vv. 33–34)

The temperate queen then sends the bellicose king lavish gifts, to which he responds with scorn and savagery, calling for war and the humiliation of her people (vv. 35–37)—precisely as the queen's words prophesied. Prior to making war, the king conjures a ruse to "convert" the magnificent queen by snatching her throne using one of his demons (vv. 38–40). These narrative details may be summarized as follows:

(1) The king's threat
(2) The queen's consultation
(3) Her rejected gifts
(4) His bringing war and humiliation
(5) His snatching her throne

These details are a homiletic retelling of the diplomacy and warfare between Roman emperor Aurelian and Palmyrene empress Zenobia during the third century.

First, according to the *Historia Augusta*, the contending monarchs initially exchanged letters in a frantic diplomatic effort, ultimately doomed to fail. Aurelian demanded Zenobia's complete surrender. She defiantly rejected submission in hopes of valiantly dying in battle like her predecessor and hero Cleopatra, while consulting her most trusted advisers. Her trusted inner circle was said to be composed of four men of the highest repute: the generals Zabbai and Zabdas, the philosopher Longinus, and the bishop Paul of Samosata, revisited at length in Chapter 4. They were instrumental to Palmyra's survival, and its defense against Rome's coming onslaught. Longinus' boldness helped shape Zenobia's defiant policy against Aurelian, for which he ultimately paid with his life.[19]

It is possible Zenobia then offered Aurelian gifts to stave off further escalation and possible war, and that he subsequently felt insulted by the overture. This is unlikely however. Far more likely is that vv. 33–34 evoke this very exchange with Zenobia's husband, Odenathus (d. 267). The latter's gifts to the Persian king of kings Shahpur I (d. 270) years earlier were indeed met with great fury and thrown into the Euphrates river.[20] In any case, Aurelian would ultimately amass two great armies to assail Palmyra through the mountains of Anatolia from the north, and through Egypt from the south. The breaking of the Palmyrene army by Roman forces, notably at Emesa, and Zenobia's humiliating defeat before Aurelian, became the stuff of legend. The emperor celebrated his conquest of Palmyra by promoting the cult of the male god Elagabal, whom we will explore further in Chapter 7. Be that as it may, Zenobia's disgrace is enshrined in the apocryphal legends of her suicide, notably preserved in the medieval Arabic sources, building on the Greek historian Zosimus (d. *ca.* 520).[21]

There remains the matter of the throne, which I argue refers to the spurious legend of an ornate war chariot within which Zenobia was allegedly imprisoned by Aurelian after her defeat. She was said to have been shackled by golden chains and paraded through Rome itself.[22] This spectacle, though entirely fabricated, served as a chilling message for posterity.

Given the preceding explanation, Q 27:22–44 "qur'anizes" the historical and legendary qualities of stories about emperor Aurelian and empress Zenobia. In other words, it transforms them into king Solomon and the queen of Sheba. This transformation took place, furthermore, in conversation with rabbinic Jewish interlocutors around the seventh century, which is when the *Targum Sheni Esther*

---

19 Nathaniel Andrade, *Zenobia: Shooting Star of Palmyra*, Oxford; New York: Oxford University Press, 2018, 205–207.

20 Andrade, *Zenobia*, 147.

21 Cf. further Yasmine Zahran, *Zenobia: Between Reality and Legend*, Oxford: Archaeopress, 2008, 15–16.

22 Ibid., 12, 16.

may be dated.[23] However the story came to be, it glorifies victory of male power over female power. It imposes the one God of Solomon as justification for the conquest and humiliation of the queen and her people. Any further discussion of the mythical origins and patriarchal objectives behind the queen of Sheba story is beyond the scope of this chapter and has been debated extensively elsewhere.[24]

Beyond the pages of scripture and exegesis there is no hard evidence for the historical existence of the queen of Sheba. The biblical authors crafted her legendary persona, among other things, to exaggerate ancient Israel's political influence over international trade routes originating in South Arabia. Israel's short-lived kingdom (1050–931 BCE) likely did not enjoy such power, nor is it likely that the queen of Sheba existed as she is portrayed. Alas, she is a myth.

A History of Arabian Queenship, *ca.* 738 BCE – 636 CE

If the queen of Sheba is mythical, she is a myth extrapolated from fragments of reality. We have no documentary evidence for independent queens in South Arabia at all.[25] However, there is a plethora of documentary and literary evidence for queens in North Arabia and greater Syria. A number of scholars, having agonized over trying to square the literary figure of the queen of Sheba with the history of Arabia, have identified her with the queens of Qedar in the north, the first great Arabic-speaking kingdom (ninth–fifth century BCE; more on which shortly). If the meeting of Israelite kings and Arabian queens has any historical merit, then the queens could have only come from the north, not the south.[26]

Ancient Arabian queenship and female power thrived in the north, as this chapter demonstrates. More specifically, I am referring

23 Jillian Stinchcomb, "The Queen of Sheba in the Qur'an and late antique Midrash," *The Study of Islamic Origins: New Perspectives and Contexts*, eds. Mette Mortensen et al., Berlin: De Gruyter, 2021, 88.

24 For the mythical nature and literary evolution of the queen of Sheba and other "biblical queens," namely Esther, see generally Deborah Coulter-Harris, *The Queen of Sheba: Legend, Literature and Lore*, Jefferson, NC: McFarland and Co., 2013.

25 Cf. Abbot, "Pre-Islamic Arab queens," 2.

26 This is the view of Abott and al-Fassi, "*Malikat al-'arab*," 14–17.

here to the great kingdoms of ancient and late antique North Arabia and greater Syria, reaching Mesopotamia. Power swung wildly from one corner of Arabian society to another, due to Roman and Persian intervention, especially with the rise and fall of state structures standing among the ancient, Hellenic, and semi-nomadic kingdoms. These were namely: Nabataea, Palmyra, and Quraysh. Thus, the centers of power within Arabian society shifted from one region to the next, and with them sprouted new generations of ruling female nobility.

<u>Ancient Kingdoms</u>

(1)	Qedarites of Dumah	(ninth–fifth centuries BCE)
(2)	Lihyanites of Dedan	(sixth–first centuries BCE)
(3)	Nabataean Kingdom of Petra and Hegra	(*ca.* 312 BCE – 106 CE)

<u>Hellenized City States</u>

(4)	Sampsiceramids of Emesa	(64 BCE – 235 CE)
(5)	Kingdom of Hatra	(*ca.* 150–241 CE)
(6)	Empire of Palmyra	(260–274 CE)

<u>Settled Nomadic States</u>

(7)	Tanukhids of northern Syria	(*ca.* 275–425 CE)
(8)	Kindite Kingdom of Qaryat al-Faw and Dumah	(*ca.* 200 BCE – 540 CE)
(9)	Lakhmid Kingdom of al-Hirah	(266–633 CE)
(10)	Ghassanid Kingdom of Bosra	(220–638 CE)
(11)	Taghlibids of the Jazirah and Najd	(fourth–seventh century CE)
(12)	Tamimids of Najd and Bahrayn	(sixth–seventh century CE)
(13)	Qurayshids of Mecca	(sixth–seventh century CE)

Qedar

There is ample evidence of female power within these ancient communities. By way of cursory mention, one of the earliest recorded Arabian oases is that of Tayma. It was located in Hijaz between the

Ancient kingdoms of Arabia

ancient empires of Egypt and Mesopotamia. Its lucrative resources and strategic location were much coveted, and it was ultimately settled in the first millennium BCE by the Qedarites. This city is believed by some to be named after the Mesopotamian goddess of the sea—Tiamat.[27] It is thanks to the Mesopotamian influence of the Assyrians and Babylonians that we know about the antiquity of Arabian queenship at all. Their influence culminated in the conquest of all Hijaz, including the oases of Tayma, Fadak, Dadiʿu, and Yathrib, by the last Neo-Babylonian king, Nabonidus (d. 539 BCE), who made

27 Retso, *The Arabs in Antiquity*, 601–603 makes the connection to various Assyrian and Babylonian goddesses. See further ʿAbd al-Rahman al-Ansari, *Tayma' multaqa al-hadarat*, Riyadh: Dar al-Qawafil, 2002.

it his empire's second capital, and about whom there are several inscriptions.[28]

Documentary evidence from these ancient Arabian communities demonstrates that women readily owned property and traded it freely.[29] At the highest level, an impressive list of independent Arabian queens has come down to us through Assyrian records. To say this differently, our earliest evidence of Arabian sovereignty in the north coincides with our earliest evidence for Arabian queenship. The records include the names of queens conquered and then entrusted to rule by the powerful Neo-Assyrian Empire in the seventh–eighth centuries BCE.

Among the Qedarites they are: the military generals Zabibi (738– 733 BCE)—whom some identify with the queen of Sheba[30]—Samsi, and Yatie; as well as the priestesses Telkhunu and Tabua. What is more, while Hazael "king of the Arabs" (d. *ca.* 676 BCE) submitted to Assyrian king Esarhaddon (d. 668 BCE), Telkhunu formed an alliance with Babylon to resist Assyrian incursion. She was the priestess-queen, known in Assyrian as *apkallatu* or in Arabic as *afkal*. Both Telkhunu and Hazael were captured and taken to Nineveh. However, the prowess of Arabia's queens impressed the Assyrian king, who appointed not Hazael, but Telkhunu's daughter Tabua as priestess and vassal queen at Dumah. Others suggest that Telkhunu's exile to Assyrian lands was the result of conflict with Hazael and her Arab community in Dumah. Likewise, Tabua is said to have become high priestess, rather than taking the title of queen, and returned her people's idols from Assyrian custody to their Arabian home.[31] These acts of protest from the community, on the one hand, and bearing the community's trust, on the other, underscore the power of Qedarite queens and priestesses, and the independence with which they conducted their public life.

---

28 al-Fassi, "*al-Awda' al-siyasiyyah*," 454.
29 Husayn Abu al-Hasan, *Qira'ah li-kitabat lihyaniyyah min jabal 'akmah bi mintaqat al-'ula*. Riyadh: Maktabat al-Malik fahd al-wataniyyah, 1997, inscription 100; Mahdi Alzoubi et al., "Woman in the Nabataean society," *MAA* 13.1, 2013, 154–157.
30 Cf. al-Fassi, "*Malikat al-'arab*," 16.
31 al-Fassi, "*Malikat al-'arab*," 24, 28–30; Abbot, "Pre-Islamic Arab queens," 4–7.

There are, finally, several biblical references to the Ishmaelite lands of Tema and Dumah (e.g. 1 Chronicles 1:30; Isaiah 21:11–14).

Lihyan

Lihyanite inscriptions make one explicit attestation to a queen by name. She may have been called Asif. Still there were others. Lihyanite queens were independent, and controlled property including fields and tombs. They also built temple idols and served the gods. Dozens of inscriptions cite the work of Lihyanite queens, including the function of collecting taxes for the temple at Dhu Ghaybah. Also, epigraphic evidence from Dedan and Tayma demonstrates the prominence of female landowners and their gravesites among the Lihyanites. Still, we know basically nothing about the biographies of Lihyanite or early Nabataean queens. We do know, however, that their polities clashed with one another over one major foreign policy. The Lihyanites were close allies of Ptolemaic Egypt, while the Nabataeans were its bitter enemies.[32]

Nabataea

As the Assyrian conquests moved west, they would meet fierce resistance from the queens of Nabataean tribes who, despite their courage and capability, were no match for the Assyrian colossus. They would go on to subjugate Arabian queens in Nabataean territory, namely: Baslu of Ikhilu, Yapa'a of Dhikrani, and Adia.[33] Although the names of their queens disappear for centuries, the Nabataeans would thrive and prove resilient for a long time to come.

The kingdom was in truth more of a commercial network. At its peak it ruled over southern Syria, northern Arabia, and Sinai. The centrality of trade made society immensely wealthy and it became a haven for cosmopolitanism and urbanization. From its splendid rock-hewn cities in Petra and Hegra (cf. Q 26:149), Nabataean queens and kings controlled trade throughout the Arabian Peninsula, Syria,

32 al-Fassi, "*al-Awda' al-siyasiyyah*," 34, 462–465, 471.
33 al-Fassi, "*Malikat al-'arab*," 33.

Mesopotamia, and parts of Egypt and Ethiopia. Maritime routes between the Mediterranean and the Red Sea connected the ports of Gaza, Aqaba, and Leuce Kome. Caravan routes passed through the region's grandest metropolises, including Damascus, Jerusalem, Babylon, Memphis, Alexandria, Aden, and Axum, as well as through dozens of smaller towns and marketplaces.

Notable in this regard was the southern trading outpost known as Dhat Kahl (Qaryat al-Faw), taken from the Lihyanites by the Nabataeans, a site which would only truly flourish later under Kindah. Nabataea's coffers were filled through the trade of luxury goods, including bitumen, incense, myrrh, and other spices. The medieval Arabic sources claim that Muhammad defeated the last of Banu Lihyan near Petra.[34]

The Nabataeans were Arabs ruling over Arabs and non-Arabs alike.[35] That is to say, they were Arabic speakers ruling over speakers of different languages, using Aramaic for public life. Mercantile skills made literacy essential, but Arabic was a regional vernacular tongue whose global importance had not yet emerged. The closely related language of Aramaic on the other hand was already the Middle Eastern language of trade, or lingua franca. The Nabataeans adopted it for all purposes of public life, including commerce, politics, and religion.

The multitude of cultural influences on society is accentuated in the architecture of its major cities—Petra and Hegra—where Arabian, Hellenic, Mesopotamian, and Egyptian forms come together seamlessly. Even the kingdom's name, "Nabataea," refers not to trade, but rather to "flowing water." This is a testament to their unprecedented water engineering, construction management, and urban planning. In the hot and dry deserts of antiquity the Nabataeans monopolized both the water supply and international trade.[36]

---

34 al-Fassi, "*al-Awda' al-siyasiyyah*," 454; Ibn Ishaq, *Sirah*, 435.

35 See Jerome Norris, "Peuples et groupes sociaux en Arabie du nord-ouest aux époques nabatéenne et romaine," PhD diss., Université de Lorraine, 2014; John Healey, "Were the Nabataeans Arabs?" *A3* 1, 1989, 38–44.

36 John Eadie and John Oleson, "The Water-Supply Systems of Nabataean and Roman Humayma," *BSOAS* 262, 1986, 49–76.

The neighboring cultures of antiquity found Nabataean wealth and ingenuity impressive. The Greek historian Diodorus Siculus (d. *ca.* 30 BCE) shares insights which seem to define the prototypical under-standing of Arabs for posterity. He says of the Nabataeans:

For the sake of those who do not know, it will be useful to state in some detail the customs of these Arabs, by following which, it is believed, they preserve their liberty. They live in the open air, claiming as native land a wilderness that has neither rivers nor abundant springs from which it is possible for a hostile army to obtain water. It is their custom neither to plant grain, set out any fruit-bearing tree, use wine, nor construct any house; and if anyone is found acting contrary to this, death is his penalty. They follow this custom because they believe that those who possess these things are, in order to retain the use of them, easily compelled by the powerful to do their bidding. Some of them raise camels, others sheep, pasturing them in the desert. While there are many Arabian tribes who use the desert as pasture, the Nabataeans far surpass the others in wealth although they are not much more than ten thousand in number; for not a few of them are accus-tomed to bring down to the sea frankincense and myrrh and the most valuable kinds of spices, which they procure from those who convey them from what is called Arabia Eudaemon. They are exceptionally fond of freedom; and, whenever a strong force of enemies comes near, they take refuge in the desert, using this as a fortress; for it lacks water and cannot be crossed by others, but to them alone, since they have prepared subterranean reservoirs lined with stucco, it furnishes safety. As the earth in some places is clayey and in others is of soft stone, they make great excavations in it, the mouths of which they make very small, but by constantly increasing the width as they dig deeper, they finally make them of such size that each side has a length of one plethrum. After filling these reservoirs with rain water, they close the openings, making them even with the rest of the ground, and they leave signs that are known to themselves but are unrecognizable by others. They water their cattle every other day, so that, if they flee through waterless places, they may not need a continuous supply of water. They themselves use as food flesh and milk and those of the plants that grow from the ground which are suitable for this purpose; for among them there grow the pepper and plenty of the so-called wild honey from trees, which they drink mixed with water. There are also other tribes of Arabs, some of whom even till the soil, mingling with the tribute-paying peoples, and have the same customs as the Syrians, except that they do not dwell in houses. It appears that such are the customs of the Arabs. But when the time draws near for the national gathering at which those who dwell round about are accustomed to meet, some to sell goods and others to purchase things that are needful to them, they travel to this meeting, leaving on a certain rock their possessions and their old men, also their women and their children. This place is exceedingly strong but unwalled, and it is distant two days' journey from the settled country.[37]

Given the kingdom's wealth and power, it resisted Judea and reaped the benefits of bitter rivalry between Ptolemaic Egypt and Seleucid Syria (*ca.* 305–65/30 BCE). The Nabataeans also formed marriage alliances with the Jewish-Arabian kingdom of Edom, where the daughter of Aretas IV (Arab. *al-harith*; d. 40 CE), Phasaelis, was married to Herod Antipas (d. 39 CE), before he left her for Herodias (d. 39 CE). This episode of palace intrigue is recorded by Josephus, Mark 3, 8 and Matthew 2, 14.

The names of Nabataean queens reappear in the final and most prosperous century of the kingdom's independence, *ca.* 30 BCE – 106 CE, by which time the kingdom was under centuries of Egyptian, Hellenic, and Roman cultural influence. During this time Nabataean coins bearing the names and busts of kings and queens jointly appear, beginning with king Obodas III (r. 30–9 BCE). The coins were minted in the Roman style, and the queens depicted were often the mother or sister of the king. This attestation demonstrates that the practice of sibling marriages between brother and sister was practiced by Nabataean royalty and probably inherited from the pharaohs of

---

37 See Diodorus Siculus, *Library of History*, vol. 19, trans. C. H. Oldfather, Cambridge: Harvard University Press, 1933, 94–95.

Malichus II and Shagilath II

Egypt.[38] The titles appear as "queen, king's sister, his wife or king's mother."[39]

At any rate the names of at least four queens come down to us. Two are the wives of Aretas IV: Huldu (d. *ca.* 16 CE) and Shagilath I (d. *ca.* 40 CE). Shagilath II (d. *ca.* 71 CE) was sister-wife of Malichus II (d. 71 CE) and then served as queen regent of her son Rabel II (d. 106), who later married the very last ruling Nabataean queen, Gamilath (d. 106 CE).[40] Further queens represented on first-century CE coins include Phasal, Hagru, Sa'dat, and others.[41] al-Fassi draws parallels between them and Cleopatra VII (d. 30 BCE). who styled herself as high priestess, and divine mother of the people.[42]

All this is to say that, despite our scanty data, the prominence of Nabataean queens as late as the Roman period demonstrates a long-standing, unbroken tradition of female power and queenship in the Arabian sphere. Historians affirm that the Nabataean kingdom reached its apex during the first century CE, especially with respect to the status

38 Ibid., 8. This is debated by Alzoubi et al., "Woman in the Nabataean society," 155.
39 al-Fassi, "*Malikat al-anbat*," 27.
40 Hatoon al-Fassi, "*Malikat al-anbat: dirasah tahliliyyah muqaranah*," A2 16, 2007, 27.
41 Alzoubi et al., "Woman in the Nabataean society," 155. For a comprehensive list of later Nabataean queens and their titles see al-Fassi, "*Malikat al-'arab*," 35.
42 al-Fassi, "*Malikat al-anbat*," 31–33. See further Ditlef Nielsen, "Die altsemitische Muttergöttin," *ZDMG* 92.17, 1938, 514.

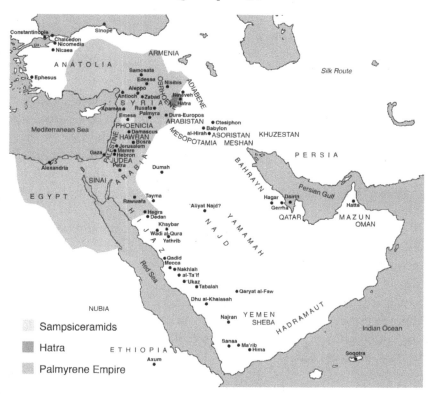

Hellenized city states of Arabia

of women. Scholars have attributed this relative golden age to the following factors: increased agricultural and other production, population growth, division of labor, increased commercial taxation, slave trade, new credit-based economic instruments, and relative peace in the Mediterranean Basin. Roman economic pressure compelled the Nabataeans to surge economically, partaking in mining, embroidery, agriculture, and other crafts before their overthrow. At any rate, if Nabataean kings are celebrated by historians as the stewards of political power and economic success, as they are,[43] then so too should their queens.

---

43 See al-Fassi, "*al-Awda' al-siyasiyyah*," 465, 472–474; Alzoubi et al., "Woman in the Nabataean society," 155.

Roman Emesa and Hawran

To what extent did Arabian queens exercise power within the Roman Empire? The answer to this question is found in the Semitic ruling families of Syro-Arabia. They include the royal house of Emesa (Homs), otherwise known as the Sampsiceramids. This name may have originally been *shams jiram*, a tribal totem which in Arabic may approximate "celestial sun." This royal house was indeed famously known for worshipping the sun as their high god and patron. His name was Elagabal. This name in Arabic is *ilah al-jabal* or "god of the mountain."

The mighty queens of this royal family rose to the rank of Roman empress. Their ascent through the Roman hierarchy was achieved through the fateful marriage of emperor Septimius Severus (d. 211), himself of Punic ancestry, to his Emesan bride Martha. She is known to posterity as empress Julia Domna (d. 217). She and her descendants clung to power by installing male heirs under their tutelage as emperors, which, though brilliantly executed, ultimately led to their doom. In this respect history tells of three episodes of splendor and tragedy.[44]

Julia Domna may have enjoyed a senatorial appointment for some time. Otherwise, she busied herself with Rome's finest philosophers, artists, and men of letters. Before Septimius Severus passed, he made both his jealous sons, Geta (d. 212) and his older brother, Caracalla (d. 217), co-emperors. As widow, Domna's impossible task was to prevent the rupture of the empire between her squabbling sons. She was no match for the malevolent Caracalla, who murdered Geta before her eyes, and then violently usurped the throne. Gibbon states of Domna, "She was doomed to weep over the death of one of her sons, and over the life of the other."[45] Some years later she tasted the bitterness of losing her other son. Caracalla's cruel reign came to an end when one

---

44 Julie Langford, *Maternal Megalomania: Julia Domna and the Imperial Politics of Motherhood*, Baltimore: Johns Hopkins University Press, 2013, 87.

45 Edward Gibbon, *The Decline and Fall of the Roman Empire* (Edited and Abridged), New York: Random House, 2009, 90.

Julia Domna

of his own soldiers murdered him. Unable to bear much more agony, Julia Domna took her own life soon thereafter.[46]

The next two episodes of Arabian queenship in the Roman Empire come through Julia Domna's younger sister, Julia Maesa (d. 224), who enjoyed immense power and fortune from behind the throne. As Augusta from 218 to 224, she served as the Roman Empire's matriarch, regent, and kingmaker. It was she who meticulously orchestrated the return of the Severan dynasty from their sojourn in Emesa to the

46 Langford, *Maternal Megalomania*, 22.

Roman throne. Her army overthrew emperor Macrinus (d. 218), and she installed two of her grandsons as emperor, namely Elagabalus (d. 222) and Severus Alexander (d. 235). The former was the son of Julia Soaemias (d. 222), and the latter the son of Julia Mamaea (d. 235). As regents of the young emperors they ruled jointly with their sons.

The authority so well exercised by these women, however, made the male emperors appear both weak and cowardly before their men. Mamaea is even said to have joined Alexander in his military campaign against Germania, which infuriated the Roman army. The supremacy of the Emesan queen regents made Rome restless. When the hand of fate moved to eliminate the last of the Severan line, it slew both mother and son. Julia Soaemias and her son Elagabalus were assassinated in 222, followed by her sister Julia Mamaea and her son Alexander in 235, plunging the empire into the "crisis of the third century" lasting some fifty years.[47] This appears the more plausible scenario, with alternate theories suggesting the involvement of Julia Maesa and Julia Mamaea in the murder of Julia Soaemias and Elagabalus. At any rate, before his death Alexander founded the religious calendar the *Feriale Duranum* in Dura Europos, Syria. In it Julia Maesa is one of several Roman female empresses raised to the status of "divine mortals."

Back in Rome, chaos ensued. By the mid third century, a series of short-lived emperors had arisen from all corners of the empire. Among them was another Syro-Arabian pretender to the throne. He was known as Philip the Arab (d. 249) of Trachonitis or Jabal Hawran, and he is believed by some to have been the first Roman emperor to practice Christianity.[48] Constantine (d. 337) may not have been, as the popular imagination would have it, the first emperor to convert to the new faith. In any case, Chapter 7 returns to the profound legacy of Rome's Semitic emperors upon the religious and political culture of Arabian society itself.[49]

---

47 Abbot, "Pre-Islamic Arab queens," 11.
48 Shahid, *Rome and the Arabs*, 36–37.
49 Ayad Al-Ani, *Araber als Teil der hellenistisch-römischen und christlichen Welt*, 83–91.

Hatra and the Persian Gulf

Several Arabian communities thrived within the trading hubs of Seleucid Mesopotamia and port cities in the Persian Gulf, dominating international trade there and growing wealthy in the process. They included Hatra, Meshan/Charax, Gerrha, and Maka (later Mazun). The Kingdom of Hatra (*ca.* 150 BCE – 241 CE) belonged to the Parthian sphere, where its Arabian kings ruled under the influence of Persian, Mesopotamian, and Hellenic cultures. The city's thriving trade funded uniquely opulent temples. Its female royalty enjoyed significant power, though maybe not at the level of their counterparts elsewhere. The presence of at least a dozen exquisite life-size statues of them have immortalized their names and majestic appearance for posterity. Among them are statues of the noblewomen Bat Malki and Maritu bt. Shariku, the priestess Martibu, and temple musicians.[50]

Among Hatra's magnificent statues are priestly kings and queens, in service of deities including the god Baalshamin and goddess Atargatis. They include princess Dushfari, daughter of king Sanatruq II (d. 241) and queen Batsimia, who are otherwise better known for raising the crown prince, Abdsimia.[51] Hatra's queens enjoyed significant authority, as evidenced by the wealth of material culture the city produced for the study of the religious and political culture of Arabian society.

Palmyra

Rome was in turmoil during much of the third century. The empire was beset on two fronts by powerful foes: the Germanic Goths in the west and the Persians in the east. Rome could only muster the resources to fend off one foe at a time. And it was compelled to defend its western borders. The east was ripe for the taking by the large Sasanian Empire (224–651 CE). However, the small, independent Syro-Arabian settlement of Palmyra in Syria stood between it and its Roman

---

50 See al-Fassi, "*al-Awda' al-siyasiyyah*," 455–458, 466–467.

51 Klaas Dijkstra, *Life and Loyalty: A Study in the Socio-Religious Culture of Syria and Mesopotamia in the Graeco-Roman Period Based on Epigraphic Evidence*, Leiden; New York; Köln: Brill, 1995, 234.

Princess Dushfari and her daughter Simi

nemesis. Its king, Septimius Odenathus (d. 267), became a Roman citizen and later governor of Syria Phoenice for the empire during the Severan dynasty, which as discussed earlier saw a number of Semitic pretenders to the imperial throne.

Odenathus took up the task of defending Rome against the Persian king of kings, Shahpur I (d. 270), and succeeded brilliantly. Given the titles Augustus and Imperator, he became emperor of the Roman East, and later adopted the Persian title "king of kings of the East."[52] Odenathus' dazzling victories came to an end with his assassination in 267.

The mantle of leadership immediately passed to his wife, the famed Zenobia (d. 274), who served as regent of their son Vaballathus (d. 274) in typical Roman fashion. Zenobia was a noblewoman who

52 See plate 3946, *CIS* 2.3, 1953, 12.

belonged to the upper echelons of Palmyrene life. Her rise to power was facilitated no doubt through the power enjoyed by Palmyrene noblewomen, who owned property and traded it freely.[53] These qualities made her a suitable wife to the city's ruler, Odenathus. Once her husband had conquered parts of the East and made himself king, Zenobia's fortunes rose once again as she became queen. After the king's passing, she expanded upon his territorial and political ambitions.

Zenobia immediately pursued the expansion of the Palmyrene realm after the passing of her husband. Once she had conquered Mesopotamia, Asia Minor, and Egypt by 271, she assumed the title of empress of the East and began minting coins in Antioch and Alexandria. She removed the portrait of emperor Aurelian (d. 275) and replaced it with portraits of herself and her son Vaballathus, whom she now dubbed Augustus. Aurelian was already marching on Palmyra by this time; and in 272 the two met in a great battle at Emesa.

Zenobia was defeated, stood trial, and was either hauled off to Rome, or sentenced to some form of imprisonment or house arrest in which she died under obscure circumstances.[54] The fact that the Roman sources—authored by men—tell contradictory tales of her humiliation and bravery are a testament to just how stunning Zenobia's military victories were, and how close a woman came to dominating the Roman Oriens.[55]

Uncertain rumors of her Jewish or Christian sensibilities only accentuate the shock and confusion felt by Roman authors, and the unlikely triumph of her many conquests.[56] Built upon ancient roots, the Palmyrene Empire (260–274) was short-lived but shone brightly. Zenobia captured the imagination of Latin- and Arabic-speaking authors for centuries to come.

---

53 Andrade, *Zenobia*, 60.

54 Pat Southern, *Empress Zenobia: Palmyra's Rebel Queen*, London: Bloomsbury, 2008, 159.

55 Cf. Andrade, *Zenobia*, 207; Al-Ani, *Araber als Teil der hellenistisch-römischen und christlichen Welt*, 93–95.

56 Bowersock, *Roman Arabia*, 134; Andrade, *Zenobia*, 187.

Settled-nomadic states of Arabia

Tanukh and the Roman Foederati

The growing rivalry between Rome and Byzantium, on the one hand, and Sasanian Persia, on the other, demanded the enlisting of Arabian allies bound by treaty or *foederati*. They policed the frontier between both realms, acting as military buffer states.[57] The Roman Empire had learned a hard-fought lesson during the crisis of the third century. Emperor Constantine became explicitly pro-Christian in 313 and constructed Constantinople as an eastern capital soon after. The empire thereafter had recourse to 'Christian *foederati*' during the

---

57 Retso, *The Arabs in Antiquity*, 624; Shahid, *Byzantium and the Arabs in the Fourth Century*, 15.

fourth century.[58] Christianity increasingly became the currency of both religious and political capital. That is to say, political pragmatism was as much an incentive for conversion to the new faith as was the religious conviction of Arabian tribes defending the Roman Oriens. Chief among these tribes were the Tanukhids of the fourth century, the Salihids of the fifth century, and Ghassanids of the sixth century.

Not unlike their Palmyrene predecessors, the Tanukhid king al-Hawari (d. 375) and his queen, Mavia (d. 425), governed their realm during its final glory days. Similar to Zenobia and second only to her, Mavia looms large as a heroic warrior-queen in Classical and Arab history.[59] Greek and Latin sources give us a glimpse of her life and activity. Following the untimely death of her husband in 375, queen Mavia initiated her own conquest of Palestine and Egypt, defeating every Roman garrison and army that stood in her way.

The reason for this woman-led Arabian insurrection was not an attempt to vanquish the new Christian empire, by now an impossible venture in any case, but rather to establish a legitimate Christian Arab realm. Mavia fought for Roman approval of an Arabian bishop—her choice—which she courageously won. This singular act by a truly remarkable woman would have a profound impact upon the religious and political culture of Arabian society, to which we will return in Chapter 5.

Kindah

The tribe of Kindah (*ca.* 200 BCE – 540 CE) was distinctive in Arabia. Its powerful pan-Arabian partnership with Himyar, including strategic marriages and new kinship ties, captivates students and scholars alike. While its queens did not rule independently, a number of its female nobility served as queens in the northern Kindite capital of Dumah and nearby 'Aliyat Najd, the Lakhmid capital of al-Hirah, and the Ghassanid capital of Bosra.[60]

---

58 Shahid, *Byzantium and the Arabs in the Fourth Century,* 331.
59 Al-Ani, *The Arabs from Alexander the Great until the Islamic Conquests,* 96–97.
60 al-Fassi, "*al-Awda' al-siyasiyyah,*" 452–453.

Hind bt. Zalim was second wife to the founder of the Kindite realm in the north, Hujr b. 'Amr (fourth–fifth century), as identified by the Arabic sources.[61] Her impressive character is attested to by how often her name appears in these sources, wherein she receives the nickname "the Hind of all Hinds."[62] Her husband, the king, was famously known as the "eater of bitter herbs," a peculiar name likely referring to the herbs of Passover, and ultimately signifying his Jewish origins.[63] Segments of Kindite nobility converted to Judaism, following the path of their Himyaritic kindred and their first Jewish forefather, As'ad Abu Karib (d. 430). Among the inscriptions of neighboring Hijaz and Transjordan are several invocations by or about Jews.[64] This includes a Safaitic prayer to Allat for the protection of Jews,[65] raising the tantalizing possibility of pagan-Jewish syncretism. A century earlier, a Nabataeo-Arabic inscription dating to the year 303 demonstrates that communities in the Hijaz celebrated the Jewish "feast of unleavened bread."[66] In short, like their Christian rivals, Jewish Arabs became a staple of Arabia throughout the fourth century.

Back to Hujr: he was a man with a voracious appetite for power. Hind was a pugnacious woman who did not care much for her power-hungry husband. It is alleged she had an affair with a member of the Shaybanids, a tribe who were enemies of the Kindites. She is reported to have protested to her lover Ziyad about her husband Hujr: "By Allah, I do not hate any living soul as I hate him; but I have never seen

61 See Gunnar Olinder, *The Kings of Kinda of the Family of Akil al-Murar*, Lund: C. W. K. Gleerup, 1927, 39–40.

62 al-Bajawi, *Ayyam al-'arab fi al-jahiliyyah*, 42.

63 See in relation Christian Robin, "Les religions pratiquées par les membres de la tribu de Kinda (Arabie) à la veille de l'Islam," *JA* 1, 2013, 215.

64 Robert Hoyland, "The Jews of the Hijaz in the Qur'an," *New Perspectives on the Qur'an: The Qur'an in Its Historical Context 2*, ed. Gabriel Reynolds, London; New York: Routledge, 2011, 92–115; Christian Robin, "Les rois de Kinda," *Arabia, Greece and Byzantium. Cultural Contacts in Ancient and Medieval Times*, eds. Abdulaziz al-Helabi et al., Riyadh: King Saud University, 2012, 94.

65 Cf. KRS 37; ASWS 217 in OCIANA, http://krc.orient.ox.ac.uk/ociana/corpus/pages/OCIANA_0031773.html; http://krc.orient.ox.ac.uk/ociana/corpus/pages/OCIANA_0020665.html.

66 *The Darb al-Bakrah*, 2018, 185–186 discusses the UjadhNab 538 inscription.

a stronger man than he is, whether he is asleep or awake."[67] The jealous husband ultimately had Hind killed.

A second Hind was daughter or sister of Imru' al-Qays b. Hujr (d. 544), the last Kindite king. He was also arguably the greatest poet of all pre-Islamic Arabia. Beyond finding her name in his poetry, nothing is known of her.

Kindah produced another noblewoman with the same name. This time Hind bt. al-Harith b. 'Amr b. Hujr was queen of al-Hirah, and wife of the pagan persecutor of Christians, al-Mundhir III b. Nu'man (d. 554). Hind was the object of an inter-tribal marriage which kept the peace between Kindah and its rival Lakhm. The two parties were not merely competitors. The former became partly Jewish, while the latter became largely Christian.[68] The importance of Hind's role, therefore, no matter how servile in appearance, makes her another important heroine in the story of Arabian queenship. After the passing of her husband, al-Mundhir, Hind served as regent to their son 'Amr, and founded a convent in her name, "Hind's convent."

Tribal alliances between Kindah and Lakhm produced yet a fourth Hind recorded in the Arabic sources. As Arabia's most ravishing poet and princess, Hind bt. al-Nu'man attracted the attention of both men and women. She became wife to 'Adi b. Zayd (d. *ca.* 600), the famous Christian poet and secretary of king Nu'man III b. al-Mundhir (d. 602). Once the king had tired of his secretary, he had 'Adi imprisoned and then killed. After a wild and adventurous life, Hind is said to have followed the example of her Kindite predecessor and retired to a convent she built carrying her name, the "convent of Hind the younger."[69]

Ghassan and Lakhm

Another Kindite noblewoman by the name of Mariya bt. Zalim, sister of the more prominent Hind al-Hunud, became the wife and queen of the

67 Abbot, "Pre-Islamic Arab queens," 16.
68 This point disagrees with Abbot, "Pre-Islamic Arab queens," 18.
69 Abbot, "Pre-Islamic Arab queens," 20.

Ghassanid king in Bosra, al-Harith b. Jabalah (d. 569).[70] Other than her impressive assortment of pearl jewelry, virtually nothing is known of her.

Their daughter was princess Halimah bt. al-Harith (d. late sixth century), after whom the famous battle of Halimah was named. The battle took place in 554 in Qinnasrin (Chalcis), Syria. Halima's story in pre-Islamic battle folklore is reminiscent of Helen of Troy, whose intense beauty attracted the ablest generals across the land. The Christian king is said to have given his daughter a fragrant perfume to spread among the brave soldiers of the Ghassanid army. He offers his daughter's hand in marriage to he who would slay his pagan Lakhmid arch nemesis al-Mundhir III, along with his Tamimid allies. A brave Ghassanid knight by the name of Labid b. 'Amr stepped forward, accepting the challenge, slaying the Lakhmid king and bringing his head back to al-Harith. He is offered Halimah's hand in marriage as reward. The selfless soldier declines, preferring to return to battle instead.[71]

Back in al-Hirah, the Lakhmids also developed a rivalry with Taghlib, a powerful tribe with communities stretching from Najd in central Arabia, through the northern reaches of the Jazirah in Mesopotamia. Rivalry spilled over into conflict during the reign of king 'Amr III b. al-Mundhir (d. 570). He is known to posterity as 'Amr b. Hind, i.e. after his mother.

One day, the Lakhmid king sought to humiliate the Taghlibid chieftain and famous warrior-poet, 'Amr b. Kulthum (d. 589), and his mother, Layla bt. al-Muhalhil, one of Arabia's most esteemed noblewomen. When Hind sought to disgrace Layla at a royal banquet by commanding her to carry a tray of food like a menial slave, the latter exclaimed, "Arise oh Taghlib!" Her son heeded his mother's cry. He sprang up, unsheathed his sword, and slew the king.[72] The precise details of the story, no matter how fantastic, attest to the continued power exercised by Arabian queens and regents well into the sixth century.

70 Ibn al-Kalbi, *Nasab ma'add wal-yaman al-kabir*, ed. Naji Hasan, Beirut: Maktabat al-Nahdah al-'Arabiyyah, 1988, 433.
71 Ibrahim, *Ayyam al-'arab fi al-jahiliyyah*, 54.
72 Abbot, "Pre-Islamic Arab queens," 19.

Tamim and Hanifah

In this volatile social context, a number of Arabian holy men, and one woman, emerged to liberate the masses from the hold of foreign political hegemony and competing church hierarchies. They united the masses under a more ecumenical Arabian ministry. While these movements may have appeared provincial from the perspective of Byzantium or Ctesiphon, they were indigenous if not deliberately nativist. Their memory is preserved in the medieval Arabic sources, which describe the Arabian prophets as military leaders not unlike the Judges of the Hebrew Bible.

Among them are Christian "counter-prophets" who challenged Muhammad's religious and political authority, including the prophetess Sajjah bt. al-Harith of Taghlib and Tamim (d. late seventh century). The narrative details of the story were embellished to conform to medieval Islamic orthodoxy. However, the scandal of so many highborn prophets and a prophetess from powerful Christian tribes challenging Muhammad is ample proof of their historicity. One narrative claims Sajjah married a fellow prophet, the notorious Maslamah b. Habib of the Hanifah (d. 12/634). The latter was disparaged by the sources as "petty Maslamah the liar."[73] Sajjah and her male hosts in Bahrayn and Mesopotamia likely belonged to the East Syrian Church.

At any rate, after the death of Muhammad in 10/632, the first caliph, Abu Bakr (d. 12/634), fought the powerful Christian tribes of eastern Arabia in the "wars of apostasy," as the medieval Arab authors called them. Maslamah is said to have been killed in battle. Sajjah is said to have submitted to Islam, which may or may not be true. After this she is mentioned no more.

Quraysh

In the Hijaz the noblewoman and wealthy merchant by the name of Khadijah bt. Khuwaylid of the Quraysh (d. 619), lived on the crossroads of the West Syrian Church before becoming history's first Muslim. Her royal lineage and indispensable role as the conduit to Muhammad's prophetic ministry will be explored fully in Chapter 6.

73 Ibn Ishaq, *Sirah*, 666.

Suffice it for now to say that the Arabic sources claim she was the granddaughter of Asad b. 'Abd al-'Uzza (fifth century), whose ancestors clearly served the goddess al-'Uzza, and whose name was bequeathed to one of the clans of the Quraysh tribe. She was also the ninth granddaughter of Fihr b. Malik (third century), the semi-legendary founder of Quraysh itself.[74]

The Quraysh are believed to have settled in Mecca later than other tribes, with the city being significantly older.[75] The origins of the famed city are disputed. Some claim a connection between the name "Mecca" and Greek *macoraba* citing Ptolemy (d. 170 CE). Others claim a connection between "Quraysh" and Latin *Dabanegoris* citing Pliny the Elder (d. 79 CE).[76]

Regardless, Khadijah was believed to be an exceptionally wealthy member of the Qurashi nobility. Her daughter through Muhammad, Fatimah (d. 10/632), would carry forward the remnants of Arabian regnal deification, and become the saintly matron of the Shia and the mother of their Imam-based lineage. Khadijah's great-nephew 'Abd Allah b. al-Zubayr (d. 73/692) was proclaimed commander of the faithful in Mecca for some years, before the Umayyad Empire crushed the "counter-caliphate" in 692. Essentially, Khadijah's role as matriarch and prophet maker belonged to the tradition of her Emesan and Nabataean predecessors.

A near contemporary of Khadijah was Hind bt. 'Utbah (d. 13/636), governess of Mecca and wife to its ruler and chief merchant, Abu Sufyan b. Harb (d. 31/653). She was a frightening warrior and formidable leader. Their son Mu'awiyah (d. 60/680) would go on to become the first caliph of the Umayyad dynasty (660–750) and one of the most powerful men in the late antique world. The Arabic sources claim she was a bitter enemy of Muhammad, slaying his uncle Hamzah at the battle of Uhud (3/625) and tearing into his blood-soaked liver with her

74 Ibn al-Kalbi, *Jamharat al-nasab*, 21.
75 al-Fassi, "*al-Awda' al-siyasiyyah*," 458.
76 Harri Holma, "Que signifie, chez Diodore de Sicile, le nom propre arabe Βανίζομεν(εῖς)?" O2 13, 1944, 356–360; Carl Rathjens, "Die alten Welthandelsstrassen und die Offenbarungsreligionen," O 15, 1962, 115–129. Cf. further discussion by Ian Morris, "Mecca and Macoraba," *AUW* 26, 2018, 1–60.

bare teeth. Hind's fury would later serve Muhammad after her conversion, whereupon her brave combat and powerful battle cries are much celebrated.[77] Her fearlessness during the battle of Yarmuk in 636 is reminiscent of the warrior queen of Tanukh and the empress of Palmyra, upon whose path she valiantly trod.

The extent of Qurashi female warriors and noblewomen cited is beyond our focus here. Of course, the phenomenon of such dynamic and commanding women was not limited to Arabia. For instance, Near Eastern antiquity preserves the illustrious name of the Ptolemaic Cleopatra (d. 30 BCE), the obscure memory of the Jewish-Persian Helena of Adiabene (d. 56 CE), and Pharantzem of Christian Armenia (d. 370 CE). However, this survey makes it abundantly clear that ancient and late antique Arabian society enjoyed a long-standing, unbroken tradition of female power and queenship.

Final Remarks

Our survey does not cite the name of a single, independent Arabian queen from the south. We have none. The distinction between South and North Arabia goes deeper than the gender of their respective monarchs. But that is beyond our scope.

Queenship had a powerful effect upon religious imagination. Arabian paganism, therefore, abounding with female divinities, was tied to queenship. Queens were represented in the guise of goddesses, which in turn exerted considerable influence upon Arabian paganism, Christianity, and Islam.

77 El Cheikh, *Women, Islam, and Abbasid Identity*, 18.

3

Divinity

Queen, Priestess, and Goddess

Having demonstrated the antiquity of Arabian queenship, our attention now turns to the impact its legacy had on the religious and political culture of late antique Arabian society. In the words of Hatoon al-Fassi:

> Arab men gave women respect and consideration, worshipping her as *goddess*, obeying her as *queen* and submitting to her as *priestess*.[1]

Much like commemorating heads of state on national holidays or on monetary currency today, ancient Near Eastern queens and kings were often depicted within temples or as statues, mandated by the gods or worshipped among their ranks.[2] The promotion of pre-modern queens, kings, and nobility to the status of deities was especially pervasive in the most ancient Near Eastern civilizations in the Nile valley and Mesopotamia.

The ancient Sumerians buried their male and female leaders side by side, suggesting both were deified among the people.[3] Still, they may have emulated their Egyptian rivals, whose queen Khamerernebty II was first to be represented as the goddess Hathor, as early as the third

---

1 al-Fassi, "*Malikat al-'arab*," 35, translated by the author.
2 Frymer-Kensky, *In the Wake of the Goddesses*, 61.
3 al-Fassi, "*Malikat al-'arab*," 15.

millennium BCE.[4] Subsequently, the Sumerian goddess Inanna, after whom Arabian goddesses were modeled, was simultaneously the queen, priestess, and goddess of heaven.[5] These functionaries would be unequivocally condemned in the Bible and Qur'an. That being said, modern scholarship offers new perspectives on the biblical matriarch Sarah. Among these is the figure of "Sarah as priestess."[6]

Among the perennial enemies of biblical tradition are the notorious figures of Pharaoh and Nimrod. Likewise, the Qur'an denounces them due to their contempt for the one God, and for asserting themselves as gods instead (cf. Q 2:258; 79:24). The Arabian pantheon of deities was shaped as much by local monarchs as it was by neighboring cultural influences. It was shaped by hybridization with Syrian and Mesopotamian deities. To this end, the visual representations and artforms found within North Arabian epigraphy demonstrate conventions adopted from Babylonian and Assyrian cultures.[7]

We will see how female power and queenship in Arabia contributed to this pantheon, and how it gave rise to the worship of the so-called "daughters of Allah" as understood by Q 53:19–22. I argue that in Arabia and neighboring societies, the institution of priesthood transformed humans into gods, and was hence an instrumental source of power.[8] Our examination begins with a careful investigation of ancient Egyptian and Mesopotamian influences, followed by consideration of Arabian society in the form of Nabataean, Hatran, Palmyrene, Roman, and biblical communities, culminating in the "daughters of Allah." The effacement of Arabian female power by Abrahamic monotheisms will be uncovered and dissected.

---

4 Oskar Kaelin, *"Modell Ägypten" Adoption von Innovationen im Mesopotamien des 3. Jahrtausends v. Chr.*, Fribourg: Academic Press Fribourg, 2006, 26.

5 Wolkstein and Kramer, *Inanna*, 153–158, 182.

6 See generally Savina Teubal, *Sarah the Priestess: The First Matriarch of Genesis*, Columbus, OH: Swallow Press, 1984.

7 Michael Macdonald, "Three dimensions in two: Convention and experiment in the rock art of Ancient North Arabia," *The Archeology of North Arabia: Oases and Landscapes*, ed. Marta Luciani, Vienna: Austrian Academy of Sciences, 2016, 317–336.

8 See in relation Guy Stroumsa, *Self and Self-Transformation in the History of Religions*, Oxford: Oxford University Press, 2002, 102.

Ancient Egyptian and Mesopotamian Influences

The deification of queens and the development of female power in Arabian society had ancient origins. As the earliest recorded civilizations on earth, ancient Egypt and Mesopotamia exerted considerable influence upon the religious and political culture of Arabia, including its ecosystem of queens, priestesses, and goddesses. We cannot make a full survey of their pantheons and monarchs here, but we can easily demonstrate the parallel relationship between kings and queens, on the one hand, and gods and goddesses, on the other. Such mythical or theological features as "sacred marriage"— the sexual union of woman and man known in Greek as *hieros gamos*—and the resulting dualities or trinities are ubiquitous. Furthermore, the mythology surrounding the most famous pairs of divinities convey twin narratives about the death of the male god who then rules over the earth/underworld, and his resurrection by the winged female goddess of the sky.[9] They include primarily:

- Inanna and Dumuzi (Ishtar and Tammuz) in Mesopotamia
- Isis and Osiris in Egypt

Their stories would contribute to the doctrines of death, resurrection, and rebirth in the Abrahamic religions.

al-Fassi asserts that ancient Arabian communities, including those on the Persian Gulf coast, adopted the worship of the queen of heaven or mother goddess, emerging from ancient Sumeria. The goddess Inanna was manifested as:

- Isis in Egypt
- Ishtar in Babylonia
- Atargatis in Syria
- Astarte in Phoenicia
- Gaia, Rhea, or Sibyl in Greece

9 Cf. Wolkstein and Kramer, *Inanna*, 125; Frymer-Kensky, *In the Wake of the Goddesses*, 51–57; al-Sawwah, *Lughz ʿishtar*, 320–323.

Their vitality may have been partly owed to patterns of matriarchy or matrilineality in those societies. Those societies, al-Fassi adds, re-enacted sacred marriage between Inanna and Dumuzi, typically through the high priestess and king. The cult of the Arabian goddess was as deep as it was broad. In this respect, al-Fassi cites an inscription from Thaj (possibly the site of Gerrha), mentioning the name of a woman Amat Han Allat bt. Hawn bt. Taym Manat of the Jibsid clan of the Hudan tribe.[10] Theophoric names in conjunction with high goddesses Allat and Manat were extremely common, and in this case interwoven over generations.

Bread Offering vs. Blood Offering

The Sumerian deities Inanna and Dumuzi represent the meeting and merger of ancient communities throughout the ancient Near East. The former represented agriculture and fertility, and was readily associated with the procreative power of the mother goddess. The latter represented pastoralism and animal sacrifice, and was associated with the father god. Their sacred marriage retells the timeless story of nomadic tribes settling in rural communities throughout the Mesopotamian plains and the Nile Delta.

Cultic offerings to the mother goddess included temple- or shrine-based prostitution and bread cakes in the shape of a moon or human figurine, often fed to the poor. Cultic offerings to the father god typically required blood sacrifice, which scholars debate originated with the sacrifice of human victims, a barbaric custom which may have evolved into the sacrifice of animal victims, often a lamb.[11] This partly explains the female and male qualities of God manifested throughout the Hebrew Bible, New Testament, and early Islamic tradition, as well as their cultic offerings.[12] These include, for example, the "unleavened bread" offered by the ancient Israelites before fleeing Egypt (Exodus 12:18), sacrificing Jesus as the "lamb of God" (John 1:29), and the

---

10 Hatoon al-Fassi, "al-Nizam al-umumi bayn al-nuqush al-hasa'iyyah (al-thajiyyah) wal-nuqush al-nabatiyyah," A2 28, 2013, 43, 47.

11 al-Qimani, al-Usturah wal-turath, 107–111, 144.

12 Cf. Barker, The Mother of the Lord, 107–128.

martyrdom of al-Husayn at Karbala 61/680, who is mourned and commemorated as a sacrifice. Cultic offerings to the divine mother and divine father are symbolized by the "body and blood of Christ" during the Eucharist (cf. Mark 14:22–25; John 6:53–57).[13] The different symbols of an Abrahamic covenant came much later than their ancient Egyptian and Mesopotamian archetypes.

The Egyptian Wife of Amun

Pharaonic rulers loomed large in the cultural consciousness of the Lihyanite and Nabataean kingdoms during the first millennium BCE. But there is reason to believe that Egyptian influence began much earlier, owing to the sheer supremacy of its priestly institutions.

As early as the second millennium BCE, monumental evidence from Thebes demonstrates the important role played by the office of the "wives of Amun." The chief Egyptian deity, Amun, was the primordial father and god of creation. The divine masculine was responsible for creation in Egyptian mythology. Amun's simultaneously terrible and life-giving power unleashed the annual flooding of the Nile river. The deluge was considered the release of Amun's semen upon the earth, releasing the divine couple of Air (male) and Moisture (female). His wife was known as the "hand of Amun."[14] And among her duties was to bring him to sexual climax, controlling the flow of his semen, both preserving Egypt from devastation and granting it the gift of a plentiful harvest.[15] In human terms, Amun's wife was high priestess. After performing ritual purification only she, apart from Pharaoh himself, could enter Amun's forbidden sanctuary. The wife of Amun wielded immense power within society. And in time she emerged exclusively from the royal class.

To this end Hatshepsut (d. 1458 BCE) was regent of her son and future pharaoh, Thutmose III (d. 1425 BCE). But she also served as wife of Amun. Her ambition was limitless. She soon declared herself pharaoh.

13 al-Qimani, *al-Usturah wal-turath*, 92.
14 Mariam Ayad, *God's Wife, God's Servant: The God's Wife of Amun (ca. 740–525 BC)*, London; New York: Routledge, 2009, 3–4.
15 Ayad, *God's Wife, God's Servant*, 148–149.

Her political success as a ruler would not have been possible without her religious authority as the wife of Egypt's chief deity. Among her priestly duties was promoting the "feast of drunkenness," a festival dedicated to the goddess of love, Hathor. There, male and female participants—including the wife of Amun—celebrated life and creation by becoming intoxicated, partaking in sexual rites, and then praying to the goddess.[16] The feast demonstrates both the sexual agency of women and the parity of men and women in the eye of the goddess, at least among certain communities of ancient Egyptian society. Hatshepsut's religious office as high priestess—the wife of Amun—imputed the qualities of divinity to her and her successors as Egyptian queens. Two centuries later, the metamorphosis of queen to goddess would be complete.

Queen Nefertari (d. 1255 BCE) was not merely the wife of the great pharaoh Ramses II (d. 1213 BCE). She was, more importantly, Egypt's second in command, owing to both her political achievements and religious authority. She not only enacted peace accords with Egypt's arch-rival, the Hittites, ending years of bloodshed, but established herself as the wife of Amun. It is only natural, given her vast political and religious authority, that Nefertari was elevated in monumental reliefs to the status of goddess, standing with Horus and Isis.[17]

It bears reminder, in our case, that the promotion of Egyptian queens to goddesses was *only* possible through the transformative power vested in the office of high priestess. That is to say, the role of priestess was the intermediary or gatekeeper between queenship and divinity. One had to first serve the gods before becoming one. Moreover, sexual intercourse represented a celebration of female power, fertility, and creation. In all this the priestess performed both acts of purity as well as sexuality, neither seen as contradictory.

That being said, as in many societies, men of power resisted the rise of female power in ancient Egypt. Preempting their wrath, pharaoh Hatshepsut had herself depicted on the walls of her temple as a man with a beard. After her untimely passing, her resentful stepson, Thutmose III, rose to power. Before becoming a great pharaoh himself he had many of his stepmother's monuments defaced. He eliminated the office of the

16 Ibid., 45.
17 Cf. in relation Ayad, *God's Wife, God's Servant*, 6–8.

wives of Amun, which was not reinstated until the queen Nefertari some two centuries later.[18] The supplanting of Egyptian queenly influence by a rising crown prince is echoed in the purported rise of male power in neighboring Ethiopia during the tenth century BCE, where the legacy of Menyelik I overpowered that of legendary mother the queen of Sheba.[19] Similarly, while the temple of Nefertari features large statues of both her and Ramses II, the male pharaoh built an even greater temple of Ramses featuring four colossal statues of himself.

The ebb and flow of female power in Egypt, and elsewhere in the Near East, would continue for centuries. Its deathblow was delivered during the reign of the Ptolemaic queen Cleopatra VII (d. 30 BCE), who was little more than a puppet pharaoh before the growing might of the male emperors of Rome, to whom we will return shortly.

The Babylonian Priestess of Ishtar

Sumerian and subsequent Mesopotamian civilizations worshipped Ki, the goddess of the earth. Her male consort An was god of the sky.[20] Among their divine offspring was the goddess of love and fertility Inanna, known as Ishtar among the Babylonians. The goddess was considered the queen of Babylon, Nineveh, and nearby cities. She was the inspiration behind the legendary Jewish figure of Esther (d. *ca.* 465 BCE), queen of ancient Persia and savior of the Jewish people after the Babylonian exile (Esther 2). Her rescue of the Jewish people is commemorated in the spring festival of Purim.

Returning to Ishtar, as the heavenly queen ruling over earthly kings she was vilified by later authors as the "whore of Babylon" (Revelation 17). Ishtar's influence upon the biblical canon is palpable in both the condemnation as well as appropriation of her female power. Her power is, therefore, adopted in the Bible as a "wanton wife," "Zion as woman," or both "whore" and "virgin" simultaneously.[21]

18 Ibid., 45, 65–67.
19 al-Fassi, "*Malikat al-'arab*," 19.
20 al-Qimani, *al-Usturah wal-turath*, 93 cites the symbols of the father in the sky and mother in the earth.
21 Frymer-Kensky, *In the Wake of the Goddesses*, 169.

Ishtar-Inanna ruled the cities of Mesopotamia and its environs from the heavens. Her authority as queen of the city was delegated to her high priestess. One of her most important duties included re-enacting the mating of Inanna and Dumuzi at the spring festival. The ritual saw males and females engage in sexual union. They were joined by the high priestess who engaged in intercourse with the high priest or king, promising the people agricultural prosperity for another year.[22]

The cult of Ishtar-Inanna and her temple priestesses and prostitutes spread throughout the ancient Near East, reaching Aphrodite among the Greeks and Venus among the Romans. Ishtar's Arabian counterparts are many. They include:

- Belti of Palmyra
- 'Athirat of Tayma
- Allat of Hawran
- al-'Uzza as *al-zuhrah* (Venus)[23]

It was the goddess Allat, however, who was most often the consort of the male god of Petra, Dushara, or perhaps Allah owing to the fact that Arabic *allat* is simply the feminine form of *allah*, before her demotion and condemnation as one of his three daughters in Q 53:19–22. Onomastic evidence in Old North Arabian, especially Safaitic and Lihyanite, Old South Arabian, and Syriac, attest to ambiguous graphemes which could refer to either *allat* or *allah*. Some examples include *WHBLH*, *M'DLD*, or *'BDLH*.[24]

The worship of Inanna and her counterparts by so many premodern societies makes her the most recognized, commanding, and celebrated goddess of Near Eastern antiquity, including Arabia. In the words of renowned Sumerian historian Samuel Kramer:

---

22 Ibid., 62–63.
23 See Christian Robin, "'Athtar au féminin en Arabie méridionale," *New Research in Archaeology and Epigraphy of South Arabia and its Neighbors*, ed. A. V. Sedov, Moscow: State Museum of Oriental Art and Institute of Oriental Studies, 2012, 333–366.
24 Sergius, *The Book of the Himyarites*, lxxvi.

Female deities were worshipped and adored all through Sumerian history ... but the goddess who outweighed, overshadowed, and outlasted them all was a deity known to the Sumerians by the name of Inanna, "Queen of Heaven," and to the Semites who lived in Sumer by the name of Ishtar. Inanna played a greater role in myth, epic, and hymn than any other deity, male or female.[25]

It is worth remembering that the mythological power of Inanna was preserved as both "queen of heaven and earth." Her epithets also included the "first daughter of the moon" and the "morning and evening star" (i.e. the planet Venus). She is queen of the night and queen of the city, as mandated through her high priestess.[26] Inanna or her Arabian counterparts were associated with closely related primeval celestial bodies, namely:

- The eight-pointed star (Ishtar)
- Venus (Allat, al-'Uzza)
- The moon (Manat)[27]

Her connection to the human world, and the power she exerted among the people, was manifested through sacred marriage. By participating in this spring ritual the king or high priest was copulating with the goddess herself. The spring festival demonstrates the divine status of ancient Mesopotamian royalty. It teaches that women enjoyed a great measure of agency, and that both women and men enjoyed some degree of social equality.

The Primacy of Nabataea

The Nabataean kingdom was the longest lasting and arguably wealthiest Arabian kingdom of antiquity. The empire bequeathed its language, global network of trade, and a host of patron and matron deities to its successor states. The kingdom's sheer affluence and unprecedented

25 Wolkstein and Kramer, *Inanna*, xv quotes him.
26 Ibid., 41, 93, 160, 166, 174.
27 al-Mallah, *al-Wasit fi tarikh al-'arab qabl al-islam*, 239.

central authority granted women a level of power and independence unique among their Arabian peers. The strength of Nabataean govern-ance allowed women to rely on the security of law and order, rather than the whims of strong men.[28] To this end noblewomen were active in political and economic life, recorded in deeds of property and depicted wearing fine garments and jewelry. These features of Nabataean life suggest that pre-Islamic women were not sowing the seeds of widespread immorality as Islamic tradition suggests, but rather that they enjoyed great autonomy and affluence.

Nabataean queens played no small part in passing on these valued Arabian customs. Like their Mesopotamian, Egyptian, and South Arabian neighbors, the Nabataean priestly class came from the ruling, royal house (cf. 1 Peter 2:9). A priestess or *kahinah* was typically a queen, consort, or princess who served as guardian of a particular goddess's temple, gifts, or fertility cult. Priestly houses or tribes were typically rooted within a local sanctuary for countless generations, visited and worshipped by more recent tribal clients.[29] Priestesses, female attendants, and female worshippers typically frequented the temple of a goddess, given the fact that Arabian cults were sometimes gender specific.[30] This was not always the case. The temple was tended to by a company of servants, slaves, and prostitutes, and it functioned as the central institution of the city. Beyond its religious role, the temple facilitated childbirth, healing, life ceremonies, tax collection, lending, and banking. Within the hierarchy, however, the task of oracle, or "fortune teller," almost always fell upon the priestess.[31]

Priestess of Manat

A handful of Nabataean inscriptions confirm that both priests and priestesses served female deities throughout the realm. They included:

- Allat in Hawran

---

28 al-Fassi, "*al-Awda' al-siyasiyyah*," 465 cites evidence in this regard.
29 Smith, *Religion of the Semites*, 79–80, 145.
30 Robin, "À propos des 'filles de dieu,'" 144.
31 al-Fassi, "Kamkam the Nabataean priestess," 1–10.

- al-ʿUzza in Sinai
- Manat in Hegra

The functions and the status of a late antique Arabian priestess are typified in the tomb inscription of Kamkam bt. Waʾilah bt. Haram, dated 1 BCE. She was a third-generation priestess, serving the major deities of Hegra, including Dushara, Hubal, and Manat. The fact that her name is matrilineal in form suggests her priestly duties may be tied to polyandry. Finally, Kamkam's tomb inscription ordains a fine not to the king but to the high priest, known in Nabataean Aramaic as *apkala* or in Arabic as *afkal*. The distribution of power in Nabataea was complex—and the priesthood wielded instrumental authority.[32]

Goddess-Queen in Petra and Hegra

There is evidence for the "blending of the queen and the goddess," most likely Ishtar-Atargatis, during the reign of Shagilath I or Shagilath II (*ca.* 30–71 CE).[33] The queen and the goddess were adorned with the same features, including the crown of leaves and other symbols of fertility.[34]

At the "temple of winged lions" in Petra, consecrated 26 CE, the statue of al-ʿUzza is that of a queen in appearance, donning a crown, veil, and earrings. Evidence suggests the cult of al-ʿUzza spread to the Sulaymids of Hegra. This was a clan reportedly belonging to the tribe of Shayban in the later Arabic sources, and whose priests may have witnessed the final days of her cult under Muhammad centuries later. There is, furthermore, evidence from Hegra and Petra that queen Huldu was high priestess and protector of Allat and Manat, and that she "adopted the crown of Isis, the Egyptian equivalent to goddess

32 Ibid. See further Mohammed Maraqten, "Der Afkal/Apkallu im arabischen Bereich: eine epigraphische Untersuchung," *AOAT* 252, 2000, 263–284; al-Fassi, "*al-Nizam al-umumi*," 43.
33 Yaʾakov Meshorer, *Nabataean Coins*, Jerusalem: Hebrew University of Jerusalem, 1975, 34.
34 Alzoubi et al., "Woman in the Nabataean society," 157.

Allat." Ptolemaic queens were readily identified with the goddess Isis-Tyche. al-Fassi adds of Huldu, "It seems that she represented the qualities of Isis synchronized probably in one of the major Nabataean goddesses."[35]

In the Nabataean borderlands, where so-called Thamudic inscriptions are found, the deities Dushara, Allat, and others are mentioned along with basileophoric names. These include "servant of Shagilath" or *'abd shaqilat*, "servant of Aretas" or *'abd harithat*, and the like. These are identical in form to better known theophoric names such as *'abd allat* and *'abd allah*.[36]

The rock-hewn chapel at Petra contains within it an inscription commemorating Obodas I (d. 85 BCE), whom it calls "Obodas the god." The inscription also honors the artisan, the artisan's god, Aretas king of the Nabataeans, his unnamed "sister" queen of the Nabataeans, and the remaining male and female members of the royal, divine house.[37]

The representations of Nabataean kings and queens generally evoke the imagery of the "divine couple" found in prayer niches. The divine couple were gods associated with the king and his family; they consisted of Dushara and his consort, Allat *or* Manat *or* al-'Uzza.[38] All this is to say this nomenclature and these practices only corroborate the phenomenon of regnal deification, as monarchs ascended to divine status, becoming objects of worship in specific cases.

Queenship had a profound impact upon the religious and political culture of Arabian society. By the late Nabataean era (first century BCE–first century CE) queens were elevated to the status of goddess, both in practice and representation. This transformation was often mediated by the office of priestess, and had its parallel among kings,

35 al-Fassi, *Women in pre-Islamic Arabia*, 19, 28, 41.

36 Ibid., 26. Allat is the only goddess in the list of "patron" deities by Teixidor, *The Pagan God*, 178.

37 Francisco Sánchez, *Nabatu: The Nabataeans through their Inscriptions*, Barcelona: University of Barcelona, 2015, 69–71.

38 John Healey, *The Religion of the Nabataeans: A Conspectus*, Leiden: Brill, 2001, 81; Blair Fowlkes-Childs, Michael Seymour, *The World between Empires: A Picture Album*, New York: Metropolitan Museum of Art, 2019, 4, 37–38; Retso, *The Arabs in Antiquity*, 606.

priests, and gods. Throughout Arabia one could find the high goddess in the guise of priestess.[39] Furthermore, the monumental and iconic traditions of Nabataea, Hatra, and Palmyra demonstrate that historical queens, e.g. Huldu or Zenobia, were depicted as goddesses, especially Inanna or her many counterparts: Allat, Atargatis, or Athena. What is more, there is evidence that the role of the goddess-queen remained active in the fourth century or later, when Christianity emerged as a major religion.

Pagan-Christian Petra

There is reason to believe the divine status of Nabataean queens and kings endured through Christian times. Back at the temple of winged lions in Petra, evidence suggests the building was used during both pagan and Christian periods, even after the infamous earthquake of 363 CE which struck the Levant causing widespread damage. Scholars have debated, given the absence of a statue of a goddess on site, if a queen or priestess stood in place of the ancient cultic icon.[40] That is to say, the queen or priestess was the equal of the goddess. Despite the paucity of evidence in this case, the intersection of divinity and queen-ship is entirely expected given the interwoven relationship between the Arabian queen, priestess, and goddess introduced earlier.

What is intriguing, however, is that this otherwise pagan custom would survive even after the realm was Christianized. The persistence of pagan practices in late Roman Arabia is also in line with evidence that the descendants of storied Nabataean nobility considered them-selves "Nabataean" long after Roman conquest and Christian conver-sion.[41] It may have also contributed to the Qur'an's criticism that many Christian Arabs strayed from the Gospel, and that they lapsed into pagan customs during the *jahiliyyah*.

39 Robin, "Les 'Filles de Dieu' de Saba' à La Mecque," 144, 146.
40 Healey, *The Religion of the Nabataeans*, 43.
41 *The Petra Papyri*, vols. 1–5, eds. Antti Arjava et al., Amman: American Center of Oriental Research, 2002–2018, 1:59; Macdonald, "Arabs, Arabias, and Arabic before Late Antiquity," 302.

Whatever the case, the conquest of Nabataea moved the centers of Arabian trade and economic prosperity further north to the newer metropolises of Hatra and Palmyra. They were located in greater Syria and Mesopotamia and flourished in the second and third centuries CE. The city states inherited the Arabian pantheon of the once great Nabataean kingdom and adapted it to their highly syncretic form of religious and political culture. The opulence and wealth of those city states provide us with a great deal of material culture on queens, priest-esses, and goddesses. The images, icons, and statues of their goddesses were fashioned, quite simply, as female monarchs.[42]

Allat in Hatra, Palmyra, and Beyond

In Hatra, where the city's ancient Arabian and Mesopotamian cultural roots were enriched by Hellenic and Parthian cultural influences, stat-ues of goddesses were depicted seated on thrones as queen, or stand-ing in the temple as priestess. Chief among the goddesses was Allat, often depicted as the Greek goddess Athena at the temple of Allat.[43] Certain shared features of Allat in the realms of both Palmyra and Hatra are significant, namely: her royal dress (especially veil, necklace, and diadem), and her association with temple musicians, as well as other female and male deities.[44]

Allat was depicted as Athena in Palmyra too. She stood beside the sun god Shamash and a third deity at a temple northwest of the city, as though they were queen, king, and princely companion.[45] At the temple of Baalshamin she is depicted in the manner of ancient Inanna, seated on a throne over a male lion. Another bas-relief depicts Zenobia herself as Allat-Inanna, seated on a throne, presiding over a dog and

---

42 Signe Krag, *Funerary Representations of Palmyrene Women: From the First Century BC to the Third Century AD*, Turnhout: Brepols, 2018, 129–132 discusses the importance of the funerary context.

43 Javier Teixidor, *The Pantheon of Palmyra*, Leiden; Boston: Brill, 1979, 61.

44 Cf. al-Fassi, "*al-Awda' al-siyasiyyah*," 467, 476–477. See further Cynthia Finlayson, "The women of Palmyra: Textile workshops and the influence of the silk trade in Roman Syria," *TSASP* 385, 2002, 9.

45 See Teixidor, *The Pantheon of Palmyra*, 52–64.

Allat-Minerva

below the eagle god Nasr, while tended to by a female servant.[46] The scene is striking as it vividly brings to life the deification of queens as goddess.

In the second century or later, Allat was depicted in Damascus as Minerva, standing tall and wielding her lance. During this time, she was also depicted in a bas-relief in distant Tai'f, Hijaz, seated on a camel. Was this scene also an allusion to a Hijazi Arabian queen? We may never know. However, in all cases, there is no mistaking the power epitomized by the goddess Allat *as* queen, whose iconographic representations demonstrate her dominion over both human civilization and beasts of the wild.[47]

Goddess of Roman Slave Rebellion

Long before the tyranny of Julius Caesar, Rome's conquest of the Mediterranean created an influx of slaves from across Asia, Africa, and Europe. This led to numerous slave rebellions, including three full-scale insurrections. For a while they threatened Rome's grasp over its

46 Cf. in relation Krag, *Funerary Representations of Palmyrene Women*, 111–114.
47 al-Sawwah, *Lughz 'ishtar*, 145–150.

Italian and Sicilian holdings in the second–first centuries BCE. Roman slaves organized rebellions against their Italian overlords in three "Servile Wars," during 135–132, 104–100, and 73–71 BCE. The historical details of these wars are documented fully by others.[48]

What is of startling significance for us here is the banner under which the first wave of subjugated rebels battled. To the slaves of Rome, the rejection of its cruel masters and its repressive aristocracy came in the person of Eunus (d. 132 BCE), an enslaved Syrian from Apamea turned prophet. It also came in the form of the Syro-Arabian goddess Atargatis (Allat-Inanna) whom he served. He claimed to receive divine revelation from his matron goddess. Eunus cleverly reinforced the power of his Arabian matron with that of the Greek goddess Demeter, thereby appealing to the broadest spectrum of the ancient imperium's suffering servants. Among his thousands of loyal, marching faithful, he crowned himself king Antiochus in Henna, Sicily. By doing so, Eunus came to personify the role of a Seleucid slave-king in defiance of Rome. His reign was supposedly foretold by the goddess Atargatis, as she is said to have foreseen the future back in their Syro-Arabian homeland.[49] Eunus' brilliant rebellion was short-lived but it cast a long shadow upon Rome's predatory aristocrats. And it left a powerful legacy among their malcontented Hellenic and Syro-Arabian subjects.

Eunus planted the seeds of two further Servile Wars, under the leadership of Hellenized slaves. These included the little-known Salvius (d. 100 BCE) who was directly inspired by Eunus and also fancied himself a Seleucid slave-king by the name of Tryphon (d. 100 BCE). Finally, it inspired the famous Spartacus of Thrace (d. 71 BCE), who captured the imagination of playwrights and politicians for centuries to come.

Most importantly, the Syro-Arabian duo—i.e. the prophet Eunus and goddess Atargatis—served as an early prelude to the exercise of female power through male prophecy for late antique Arabian society. Unlike the martial culture through which Rome dominated its colonies, Hellenic aristocrats—both Seleucid and Ptolemaic—generally adopted the cultures of the Near East and Egypt, including the role of

48 Theresa Urbainczyk, *Slave Revolts in Antiquity*, London: Routledge, 2016, 42–56.
49 H. J. W. Drijvers, *Cults and Beliefs at Edessa*, Leiden: Brill, 1980, 100.

high priestess and mother goddess.[50] Thus, during the twilight of the Seleucid dynasty and the gradual ascendency of Semitic dynasties the people chose their representatives to resist the scourge of Rome. The throngs, known in Greek as the *demos* or in Arabic as the *ummah*, went for the Arabian goddess par excellence and her prophet.[51]

Qaryat al-Faw—Northern Goddesses in the South

Arabian goddesses ruled over the lowly and lavish alike. As introduced in the preceding chapter, the tribe of Kindah is unique among regional powers on account of its "central Arabian" characteristics. The centrality of this cosmopolitan identity is manifested in the exceptionally rich material culture of its ancient capital in the south, Qaryat al-Faw (*ca.* 200 BCE – 400 CE). It sat along one of the two peninsular east–west trading highways, as introduced in Chapter 1. The oasis city grew wealthy off trading goods across Najd and Yamamah, in the very heart of the inhospitable Arabian desert. Seventeen water wells served its populace; organized farming and hunting nourished them. It fostered a literate public, and was empowered by strong transnational relations with its neighbors. Its aspirations were realized in its sophisticated marketplace, temple, palace, and tombs. The city's architecture demonstrates a "unique Arab style" found in Petra, Hatra, Palmyra, Palestine, and other Near Eastern and North African enclaves.[52]

Commerce transformed this remote outpost in south-central Arabia into a magnificent trading center, housing the goddesses of Kindah's northern neighbors, namely Allat, al-'Uzza, and Manat. Of course, their cult existed alongside the tribe's ancestral male idol, Kahl, as well as several other female idols. They include Shams or the sun. This deity's gender was female, unlike Shamash to the north. And the Kindites shared her cult with their southern kindred and rivals,

---

50 al-Fassi, "*Malikat al-anbat*," 31.

51 Cf. in relation H. J. W. Drijvers, "Die Dea Syria und andere Syriche Gottheiten im Imperium Romanum," *Die Orientalischen Religionen Im Römerreich*, ed. Maarten Vermaseren, Leiden: Brill, 1981, 245.

52 al-Ansari, *Qaryat al-faw*, 16–20, 28.

Himyar and Saba', in addition to the Egyptian goddess Isis and the Roman goddess Minerva.[53]

Qaryat al-Faw harbored a cornucopia of both licentious art and pious-regal iconography. The rich cultural confluence demonstrates an understudied if bewildering role played by female power in a truly fascinating city. Its more indulgent nature is displayed in several artifacts, extending to a female statue holding the "horn of plenty," and a clay figurine of an "ugly woman" with a "male organ." Its pious-regal iconography includes a dark bronze statue of a goddess with small arms stretched out, a white limestone bust of a crowned "goddess or princess," and an exquisite wall mural painted in the Christian-Byzantine style. The mural presents a mother and child, fish, and male figure crowned by women or angels with grape clusters (cf. John 15:5).[54]

Sooner or later Arabia became part of the larger religious fabric known as Christendom. With it queenship evolved to suit a world increasingly dominated by imperial bishops, desert monks, and urbanized prophets. We turn to them next.

---

53 Ibid., 20, 24, 28; Nielsen, "Die altsemitische Muttergöttin," 512–515, 524.
54 al-Ansari, Qaryat al-faw, 25–26, 108, 120, 134–139.

PART II

Matrons of the Prophets

4

Zenobia, Paul, and the Nativist Church (240–337 CE)

Palmyra, Rome, and al-Hirah

Septimia Zenobia Augusta (*ca.* 240–274), as she is commemorated on the coins struck in her name, was Empress of the East. Her late husband was Septimius Odenathus (*ca.* 220–267), Roman governor of Syria Phoenice and "king of kings" once he vanquished Persia in battle. After his murder, she ruled as regent of their short-lived son, Lucius Julius Aurelius Septimius Vaballathus Athenodorus (*ca.* 259–274). She first ruled as "mother of the king of kings" and then later as "Augusta." Egypt, Syria, Arabia, and most of Anatolia were hers to rule until the Romans sacked Palmyra in 272, some say taking its queen back to Rome into captivity. She is said to have lived out the remainder of her days under house arrest, dying in 274 or shortly thereafter.[1]

The outlines of Zenobia's short but luminous reign (267–272) are manifested throughout Palmyra's opulent monuments, coins, and inscriptions. Our knowledge of her person and policy comes principally from the *Historia Augusta*, covering 117–284 CE, but otherwise a fourth-century compilation of debatable facts and disputed origin. The Latin sources paint her as a rebel vanquished by the Roman emperor Aurelian (d. 275). And finally she is known for her extreme beauty and chastity.[2]

---

1 See Andrade, *Zenobia*, 209; Hoyland, *Arabia and the Arabs*, 75, 193; al-Fassi, "*al-Awdaʿ al-siyasiyyah*," 455.
2 Andrade, *Zenobia*, 225.

Zenobia

The whimsical stories of pre-Islamic Arabian battle folklore about her come from the Nestorian Christian court poet 'Adi b. Zayd (d. *ca.* 600) and the Muslim historian Hisham b. al-Kalbi (d. 204/819), otherwise preserved in later medieval Arabic histories. The Arabic sources introduced in Chapter 2, virtually bereft of historicity, tell of the vulgar advances and bloodthirsty wiles of the queen called al-Zabba' as she is known in Arabic, owing to her hairy, demonic legs. The legend goes that she fought and killed a king by the name of Jadhimah b. Malik (d. *ca.* 268), nicknamed al-Abrash or al-Waddah in Arabic on account of his alleged leprosy. He was king of Tanukh in al-Hirah and lower Mesopotamia during the third century.[3] To explain the origins of the animosity between Iraqi and Syrian Arab kingdoms in the sixth century, the literary figure of the Palmyrene queen of Syria, al-Zabba', was constructed and projected into the past as the first arch-enemy of the Lakhmids and their Tanukhid kindred.[4]

A similar report by Ibn Ishaq claims Shahpur I (d. 270) conquered Hatra after an unnamed daughter of Sanatruq II (d. *ca.* 241) seduced the

---

3 Muhammad b. Jarir al-Tabari, *Tarikh al-tabari: tarikh al-rusul wal-muluk wa man kan fi zaman kul minhum*, ed. Sidqi al-'Attar, Beirut: Dar al-Fikr, 2017, 1:364.
4 Cf. Toral-Niehoff, *al-Hira*, 49–50.

Sasanian king of kings with wine, won his favor, and betrayed her own people.[5] The fictional episode and various *topoi* were woven by men. They probably sought to sully the reputation of princess Dushfari bt. Sanatruq II, whose life-sized statue (see Chapter 2), still standing today, testifies that she was a noblewoman of commanding power and beauty.

Historically, the Tanukhids were likely allies of emperor Aurelian (d. 275) who probably vanquished Palmyra and its empress.[6] The next generation of Lakhmids and Tanukhids would form an alliance, creating the character of another great queen, Mawiyah bt. 'Afzar or the legendary version of Mavia, to whom we will turn in the next chapter. But far from history, the literary drama recalls the scandal of David and Bathsheba in 2 Samuel 11. Moreover, it "foretells" the story of Muhammad and Zaynab in Q 33.[7] Let us not forget that the Arabic name Zaynab is itself the translation of the Greek name *zenobia*. So clearly the Palmyrene empress had a singular impact upon the religious and political culture of Arabian society.

Several specialists have given the source material the meticulous attention it deserves; and yet this material remains hotly contested.[8] Be that as it may, what little we know of Zenobia's regnal years is yet far greater than what we know of her birth or death, which is essentially nothing. The paucity of reliable evidence about one of antiquity's greatest queens has not reduced but rather amplified all manner of storytelling about "one of the most romantic figures of history."[9] Nor is there any shortage of attentive study or artistic production concerning Zenobia's life and her contribution to Roman and Near Eastern civilization.

Our concern here is how holy men antagonized by Rome or Persia—especially Paul of Samosata (d. 275)—found safe haven under Zenobia. After extrapolating biographical nuggets from the sources about Zenobia and Paul vis-à-vis female power, our examination moves on

---

5 Ibn Ishaq, *Sirah*, 57–58.
6 Andrade, *Zenobia*, 203.
7 Cf. David Powers, "Demonizing Zenobia," 128–129; "Sinless, sonless and seal of prophets: Muhammad and Kor 33, 36–40, revisited," *A* 67, 2020, 333–408.
8 Powers, "Demonizing Zenobia," 127–182; Andrade, *Zenobia*, 1–13, 223–225.
9 Shahid, *Byzantium and the Arabs in the Fourth Century*, 141.

to how they helped shape the late antique religious and political culture of Arabian society. This includes the theology of the earliest Arabian churches and its contribution to the milieu of the Qur'an.

Goddess-Queen of the Earth

Zenobia belonged to the proud heritage of queenship in the Arabian sphere, and beyond. Scholars have debated the extent to which she saw herself as heir to a global imperial legacy, and the extent to which the impressive female statues filling the city of Palmyra were connected to her.[10] Her Palmyrene name, Bathzabbai, or "merchant's daughter," suggests her family roots lay in trade. And she is said to have spoken Aramaic and Egyptian well, while learning Greek and Latin.[11] She adopted the Latin *gentilicum* Septimia, meaning "born in September" or "seventh born" from her husband. His full name was Septimius Odenathus b. Hairan b. Vaballathus b. Nasor. His family inherited the title Septimius from the Roman emperor Septimius Severus. The emperor, who emerged from Semitic and North African origins, granted the kindred family of Odenathus Roman citizenship. And so both husband and wife appear to be of heterogenous Palmyrene ancestry, i.e. mixed Arab-Aramaean ethnicity; and their sons simply carried the names of their forefathers. These are namely Hairan, or Arabic *hayran* meaning "good, prosperous"; and Vaballathus, or Arabic *wahb allat*, meaning "gift of Allat." The latter was a common theophoric name in Syro-Arabian communities at the time, and only serves to underscore the pervasiveness of the goddess Allat in the affairs of society.

The Palmyrene empress was heir to the Emesan queen regents of Rome under the Severan dynasty (193–235 CE). Her rise to power came shortly after the reigns of Julia Domna, Julia Maesa, Julia Soaemias, and Julia Mamaea. Zenobia was highly cognizant of her place in history. She counted herself among the luminaries of ancient Near Eastern and North African civilization, claiming descent from the last Macedonian queen of Egypt, Cleopatra VII (d. 30 BCE), and the

10 Cf. in relation Krag, *Funerary Representations of Palmyrene Women*, 111–114.
11 Andrade, *Zenobia*, 51, 171.

semi-legendary Phoenician queen and founder of Carthage, Dido (fifth century BCE).[12] Zenobia's matriarchal pedigree, undoubtedly contrived, makes three unequivocal assertions vis-à-vis female power and its Arabian context.

First, extending her ancestry to include the celebrated dynasties of Ptolemaic and Punic origins is a brazen repudiation of Roman hegemony. It may be understood as an assertion of protest against Roman destruction of ancient Near Eastern civilization. Its devastation of Carthage, and its conquest of Egypt and Nabataea left deep scars in Zenobia's consciousness as a leader.[13]

Second, as pretender to the Ptolemaic throne Zenobia considered herself heiress to the pharaohs of Egypt and monarchs of Macedonia, at least symbolically. But why? By laying claim to this dual legacy she asserted her right to be "queen of the earth." This no doubt echoes the epithet given to Inanna herself. Otherwise, it follows the prodigious example of Alexander of Macedon (d. 323 BCE) and his larger-than-life reception by later cultures as "Alexander the Great," the "two horned conqueror" (Q 18:83–101).[14]

Third, Dido and Cleopatra were not merely queens. Their antiquated grandeur gave them a divine aura. They were prototypes for the deification of queens and the development of female power in ancient Near Eastern cultures, including Arabian society.

However, there remains one final note concerning Zenobia as a deity. This comes from the famous historian and exegete Tabari (d. 310/923) who, reporting from his Muslim predecessor Ibn al-Kalbi, and his Christian predecessor 'Adi b. Zayd, calls Zenobia by the name Na'ilah.[15] Tabari furnishes no details about this ostensibly innocuous and rather unassuming name. However, the intrepid scholar can hardly fail to miss that this name belongs to the purported mother

---

12 Richard Stoneman, *Palmyra and Its Empire: Zenobia's Revolt against Rome*, Ann Arbor: University of Michigan Press, 1992, 120; Andrade, *Zenobia*, 171; Hoyland, *Arabia and the Arabs*, 76.

13 See further David Potter, *The Roman Empire at Bay, AD 180–395*, London: Routledge, 2004, 266–268.

14 Cf. in relation Ghaffar, *Der Koran in seinem religions- und weltgeschichtlichen Kontext*, 15–44.

15 al-Mallah, *al-Wasit fi tarikh al-'arab qabl al-islam*, 167.

goddess of Quraysh in Mecca. Indeed, Ibn al-Kalbi's *Book of Idols* reports that the Arabian divine couple in the Hijaz—Isaf and Na'ilah—performed the ancient Near Eastern cultic practice of sacred marriage within the very sanctuary of the Kaabah of Mecca. Some consider the divine pair merely another imported set of deities from further north (Syria). I would contend that we should consider the possibility of their origins and worship as ancient king and queen, or high priest and priestess of Mecca or its environs. In other words, the name Na'ilah—whether associated with Mecca or Palmyra—could preserve the echoes of yet another deified Arabian queen. My point here is that one of the medieval Islamic received traditions of Zenobia is her association with the Hijazi mother goddess and perhaps queen, Na'ilah. This observation, while speculative, fits perfectly within the literary and theological framework of Abrahamic traditions condemning female power in sexual and idolatrous terms, as I have demonstrated earlier.

It is debatable whether Zenobia *actually* considered herself a goddess by virtue of queenship. But she certainly ruled as one, making genealogical claims to a regal pedigree of famed goddess-queens before her time. Her reception among the Qurashis of Mecca was also associated with, I argue, queenship and divinity. Never before, and never again, would any Arabian queen wield so much power.

Counter-Matriarch to Abrahamic Tradition

Zenobia was not merely the foil to Rome. She was the opposing matriarch to the servile queens and docile noblewomen portrayed by the growing tide of Abrahamic traditions. Generations of medieval Christian and Muslim authors adapted her—diminishing her power—into merely another biblical, Christian or Islamic matriarch. Modern researchers have examined the literary mechanisms of the Arabic story connecting her with ancient biblical queens Bathsheba and the queen of Sheba, Lakhmid queen Hind bt. al-Harith (sixth century CE), and Zaynab bt. Jahsh (d. 9/641).

Some consider Zenobia's adoption of the Latin title Septimia a recollection of Bathsheba, whose name in Hebrew means "seventh daughter." She was wife to king David, mother of king Solomon, and queen regent of ancient Israel.[16] Unlike her scorned Phoenician successor Jezebel, Bathsheba's roots were close enough to David's inner circle to win his blessing (2 Samuel 11:3; 23:34; 1 Chronicles 3:5; 11:36). However, we cannot determine the exact relationship of Zenobia to Bathsheba.

Zenobia's connection to the matriarchs of Ethiopia, Lakhm, and Quraysh concerns her Arabic name al-Zabba', meaning "long haired, hairy." In the legendary battle between Palmyra and Lakhm, Ibn al-Kalbi claims that in the heat of combat al-Zabba' the queen lifted her dress and exposed herself to Jadhimah the king. Of course, a dress is not clothing appropriate for warfare. al-Kalbi continues, "Lo and behold, her genital hair was braided." She further taunted the king who once longed for the beautiful queen's hand in marriage, "do you think this is the handiwork of a bride?"[17] Besides its blatant affront to common decency in the heat of combat, moreover, this report places Zenobia in the same realm of literary representation of the four women under consideration here, and decisively subjugates their regal authority through crude sexualization. A *topos* within this storyline is that a man desirous of a particular woman is confronted by her or her surrogate in the nude.[18] This seems a rather obvious psychological insecurity made plain by its male authors. Thus:

- al-Zabba' deliberately exposes herself to Jadhimah.
- Bathsheba bathes nude before the prying eyes of David.
- Hind's covetous maidservant has sex with her mistress's soon-to-be husband, 'Adi b. Zayd.
- Zaynab's body is exposed by a gust of wind before Muhammad takes an interest in her.

The fact that the name Zaynab was given to the prophet Muhammad's own daughter bears witness to the fact that Zenobia's legacy persisted

---

16 Zeev Maghen, "Davidic Motifs in the Biography of Muhammad," *JSAI* 35, 2008; David Powers, *Muhammad is Not the Father of Any of Your Men: The Making of the Last Prophet*, Philadelphia: University of Pennsylvania Press, 2009, 48, 123–124, 145.
17 Powers, "Demonizing Zenobia," 152. See further Andrade, *Zenobia*, 225.
18 See further Streete, *The Strange Woman*, 93–95.

in the memory of the Arabian communities of the Hijaz. Her name remained suitable for Hijazi female nobility. The Arabic word *zaynab* is derived from the empress's Greek name *zenobia*, "life of Zeus." This is striking. Among all her names four have come down through posterity:

- al-Zabba'
- Na'ilah
- Bathzabbai
- Zenobia

It is the clearly pagan Greek appellation which was Arabized and which rose to the prominence of Qurashi nobility and medieval Islamic piety. These signs reinforce the Roman sphere of influence under which the Hijaz operated.[19] To sum up this point, the story of Zaynab bt. Jahsh may be one of many patriarchal *topoi*, but her name bespeaks a powerful legacy of female power, nobility, and queenship.

The shared motif described above says more about its male authors then the women they malign. Their misogyny, no matter how creative in form, is unmistakable. The power of queenship threatened the very foundation of Abrahamic faith—one male god—and they were demoted time and again by association with the basest desire of men—sex.[20] Furthermore, this process suggests the demotion of Arabian goddesses to angelic demons or mere idols.

The historical Zenobia stands as a bulwark against the sexual, servile, and sinister matriarchs of the Bible, Qur'an, and medieval Christian and Muslim orthodox traditions. Her ambitious genealogical claims to the throne asserted her authority as the earth's terrestrial sovereign and as a goddess by virtue of queenship. Like her predecessors and successors alike, her power and independence made her the subject of *demonization* by men, who, I have argued, had recourse to the purely male-oriented discourses of Abrahamic tradition and Roman political norms.

19 Bowersock, *The Crucible of Islam*, 15. Toral-Niehoff, *al-Hira*, 55 cites the name Tamadur as another possibility.
20 Cf. in relation Streete, *The Strange Woman*, 65, 75, 104–105, 148.

And yet Zenobia fostered certain varieties of Abrahamic cultic practice as well as Roman imperial politics. What can explain this apparent anomaly?

Roman, Greek, or Semitic?

Palmyra was a complex web of indigenous Semitic cultures, Greek colonists, and Roman imperialists. The full range of Palmyrene ethnic, religious, and civic diversity is beyond our scope here, and otherwise given the nuanced scrutiny it deserves elsewhere.[21] Late antique Near Eastern identity was a mélange of local societies often sharing a Semitic language, infused with varying layers of Hellenic influence. Greek language, religion, and culture mixed with the Aramaean and Arab foundation of Palmyra, and its wider Syro-Arabian cultural sphere. This came about through waves of ancient Greek maritime colonies, Alexander's Greco-Macedonian conquest, and then Roman conquest. The spread of the Greek *polis* or "city" and especially Syrian, Phoenician, and Arab *ethnoi* or "nations" developed simultaneously.[22]

These kindred identities were fluid, unstable, and often interchangeable, especially when viewed through the lens of privileged Roman authors, and equally privileged modern orientalists parroting the myth of mighty, near-universal Greco-Roman identity. "Arabs" are believed to have been an integral part of the major metropolises of Palmyra, Dura Europos, Bosra, Gerasa, and Apamea, all of which housed civic councils harkening back to the Seleucid era. Secular codes of law, governance, and commerce were written and publicly available. Long after the Athenians and much before Islam, and for better or for worse, Arabian communities became seasoned practitioners of urban democracy, public law, and mercantile enterprise.[23]

---

21 Nathaniel Andrade, *Syrian Identity in the Greco-Roman World*, Cambridge: Cambridge University Press, 2013.

22 Ibid., 23.

23 Ibid., 32, 126, 147–165, 261, which the classical orientalist trend of Millar, "Ethnic identity in the Roman Near East," 383–385 seems to ignore. See further al-Fassi, "*al-Awda' al-siyasiyyah,*" 470–471.

The Palmyrene Empire was more than merely the sum of its prosperous towns and vibrant ethnicities. Zenobia trod the path of her predecessor, Julia Domna, by becoming matron of the arts and sciences. Palmyra became a regional capital of Greek *paideia*, attracting philosophers from far and wide, including Longinus (d. 273) who was a Syrian hailing from Emesa. He tutored the queen before being executed by the Romans upon the city's reconquest. The realm would go on to produce philosophers of great repute, including the Syro-Arabian Iamblichus of Calchis (d. 325), who argued that Greek philosophy acquired its wealth of knowledge from the ancient Mesopotamians and Egyptians.[24] He certainly had a point.

But change was afoot, namely Christianity. At the turn of the fourth century, Near Eastern ethnic identity became increasingly defined by church rather than city.[25] Its fruit was not so much the philosophers as it was the clergy. The latter included most notably the bishops of burgeoning congregations and communities.[26] This is where the unique nature of Zenobia's mandate comes into focus. Starting with the reign of emperor Septimius Severus (193–211), husband of Julia Domna, and throughout the third century, Palmyra served as an empire of transition, between the region's classical and pagan past, on the one hand, and its Christian destiny, on the other.[27] Growing sects of Jewish and Gentile Christianity had not come into full bloom and were sporadically persecuted by the emperor in Rome.

However, Rome itself soon became engulfed in political crisis, mired in war with Germania in the West, and unable to protect its vast holdings from the Persians in the East. Only faintly in the grasp of

---

24 Ibid., 337.

25 Millar, "Ethnic identity in the Roman Near East," 394. See further B. T. H. Romney, *Religious Origins of Nations? The Christian Communities of the Middle East*, Leiden: Brill, 2010.

26 Cf. Philip Wood, *"We Have No King but Christ": Christian Political Thought in Greater Syria on the Eve of the Arab Conquest (c. 400–585)*, Oxford: Oxford University press, 2010.

27 Xavier Teixidor, "Palmyra in the third century," *A Journey to Palmyra: Collected Essays to Remember Dilbert R. Hillers*, ed. Eleonora Cussini, Leiden; Boston: Brill, 2005, 181; cf. in relation Edward Watts, *The Final Pagan Generation*, Berkeley: University of California Press, 2015.

Rome, and outside of Persia's altogether, heterodox and syncretic religious groups thrived in Palmyra and its Syro-Arabian environs. Zenobia played no small part in their rise and efflorescence.

Jewish, Christian, or Manichaean?

Before we explore Zenobia's matronage of her holy man and his faithful following, we must delve into the religious landscape of her realm. The point here is not to enumerate the many gods of the Palmyrene pantheon, nor encompass all its Judeo-Christian or Gnostic sects. We will examine the influx of Judaism, heterodox Christianity, and nascent Manichaeanism, in anticipation of Zenobia's matronage.

There is sufficient evidence from a synagogue and funerary inscriptions attesting to a small Jewish community in the environs of Palmyra, although the Babylonian Talmud is generally hostile to the city. Its king Odenathus is said to have hindered Jewish trade.[28] Among Zenobia's building restorations in Egypt, on the other hand, is a synagogue.[29] While the extent to which Jewish communities thrived in Palmyra is debated, the existence of Christian communities there is even more unclear.

All the evidence for Christianity in Palmyra comes after the reign of Zenobia. One reason for this apparent anomaly could be the gravitation of converts towards the oldest Christian communities on earth. These were located in neighboring cities throughout greater Syria, but outside Palmyra proper. Antioch is where the Jewish sect of Jesus became "Nazarenes" and then "Christians" throughout the first century CE. Dura Europos was home to one of the world's oldest churches, founded *ca.* 230. In nearby Edessa, the Syriac Christian astrologer and philosopher Bardaisan (d. 222) had introduced the dualist worldview of light versus darkness, commonly held by Gnostic circles harkening back to Marcion of Sinope (d. *ca.* 160) and Persian Zoroastrianism before that, to the

---

28 Philippe Berger, "Les inscriptions hébraïques de la synagogue de Palmyre," *MSLP* 7, 1889, 65–97; Teixidor, "Palmyra in the third century," 208–210.
29 Stoneman, *Palmyra and Its Empire*, 151; Andrade, *Zenobia*, 183.

debate on fate and free will.[30] Still, Christianity remained techni-
cally outlawed and Roman governors persecuted those professing
the faith as a matter of policy, including in Syria.[31] So long as it
enjoyed independence Palmyra remained a syncretic pagan
stronghold.

While the status of Christians in third-century Palmyra was dubious, Manichaeans coming from Persian Mesopotamia flourished.
Their founder, the prophet Mani (d. 274), had ties to the Jewish-
Christian sect known as the Elchasaites. This was a baptismal sect
influenced by Mandaneanism, Gnostic dualism, Zoroastrianism, and
Indian religions. His eclectic faith preached the coming of a great
apocalypse, witnessing one final battle between good and evil. This
fiery doctrine found fertile ground in neighboring Syria, where the
crisis of the third century had brought about widespread turmoil. This
period witnessed fighting and fractiousness which threatened the
integrity of the Roman Empire.

Mani delegated his missionary work to his chief disciples: Thomas,
Hermas, and Addas. Manichaean texts claim the latter visited Egypt
and Syria, and was welcomed by the household of Zenobia who is
known by the Syriac name Nafsha. There he is said to have cured her
so-called sister, Tadi.[32] Although the encounter is hotly debated,
Zenobia is said to have been deeply moved, to the point of religious
conversion. But conversion to what?

There is no consensus. Neither the sources nor the scholarship agree
as to which religion the empress belonged. Some suggest that after the
episode described above she converted to Manichaeism.[33] Others
claim the very same encounter shifted her curiosity towards Judaism,

30 Cf. generally H. J. W. Drijvers, *Bardaisan of Edessa*, Assen: Van Gorcum & Co.,
1966.
31 Cf. in relation Andrade, *Zenobia*, 185–186.
32 Teixidor, "Palmyra in the third century," 208.
33 J. Vergote, "L'Expansion du Manichéisme en Égypte," *After Chalcedon: Studies in
Theology and Church History Offered to Professor Albert Van Roey for His Seventieth
Birthday*, ed. Carl Laga et al., Ann Arbor: University of Michigan press, 1985, 472–475;
Samuel Lieu and Mary Boyce, *Manichaeism in the Later Roman Empire and Medieval
China: A Historical Survey*, Manchester: Manchester University Press, 1985, 74; Amin
Maalouf, *Les jardins de lumière*, Paris: J. C. Lattès, 1991, Ch. 17.

and that she fostered good relations with Jews in Antioch and Alexandria.[34] This claim was first made by the firebrand Christian patriarch Athanasius of Alexandria (d. 373), and can hardly be taken at face value.[35] Coming a century after the fact and by the chief proponent of Trinitarian Christianity no less, Zenobia's supposed Jewish sympathies appear to be an accusation made by a male author in defense of his masculine god, and maligning the power of a female monarch in the process. This accusation of Zenobia was made because of her association with the Christian bishop of Antioch, Paul of Samosata (d. 275), who denied the divinity of Christ, among other more colorful beliefs and practices. Their partnership suggests that they had "Jewish-Christian" leanings.[36] However, this complex matter deserves our full attention now.

Jewish-Christianity and the Semitic Churches

To fully comprehend the historic significance of the relationship between empress Zenobia and Paul of Samosata vis-à-vis female power, and to clearly document its impact on the late antique religious and political culture of Arabian society, we must embark on a long journey putting Paul in the wider context of:

(1) "Jewish-Christianity" and subsequent "nativist theology"
(2) The subsequent conflict between "Semitic churches" versus a "Greek church"
(3) The disbanding of pre-Nicene Semitic congregations I dub the "Nativist church," addressed shortly

This task, while considerable, is neither to explore the full semantic and historical range of Jewish-Christianity, nor its contribution to

---

34 Teixidor, "Palmyra in the third century," 209; Southern, *Empress Zenobia*, 12; cf. also Millar, "Paul of Samosata, Zenobia and Aurelian," 265.

35 Cf. in relation Teixidor, "Palmyra in the third century," 217; Stoneman, *Palmyra and Its Empire*, 71.

36 Andrade, *Zenobia*, 187.

Islam,[37] nor is it to argue the existence of Semitic churches—speaking Aramaic (mainly Syriac)—and the antagonism of the Greek church towards them.[38] There is a plethora of scholarship on the development of Christianity in its first three centuries, laying this foundation for our current analysis. The term "Jewish-Christianity," at times pejoratively constructed and academically perpetuated, has everything to do with Greek and then Roman cultural domination of Semitic cultures. The following units of examination offer us the requisite explanation in this vein.

37 Cf. generally Adolf von Harnack, *Die Mission und Ausbreitung des Christentums in den ersten drei Jahrhunderten*, Leipzig: J. C. Hinrichs, 1902; Walter Bauer, *Rechtgläubigkeit und Ketzerei im ältesten Christentum*, Tübingen: J. C. B. Mohr, 1964; Bart Ehrman, *Lost Christianities: The Battles for Scripture and the Faiths We Never Knew*, Oxford; New York: Oxford University Press, 2005; Jacques Giri, *Les nouvelles hypothèses sur les origines du christianisme: Enquête sur les recherches récentes*, Paris: Karthala, 2010; Millar, "Ethnic identity in the Roman Near East," 381. On a range of views by von Harnack, Roncaglia, Haddad, Azzi, Gnilka, Hawting, DeBlois, Crone, Griffith, and Zellentin see Emran El-Badawi, *The Qur'an and the Aramaic Gospel Traditions*, London: Routledge, 2013, 25–30.

38 See F. C. Burkitt, *Early Christianity Outside the Roman Empire: Two Lectures Delivered at Trinity College, Dublin*, Glasgow: Cambridge University Press, 1899; Gustave Bardy, *La question des langues dans l'église ancienne*, Paris: Beauchesne et ses fils, 1948; Ighnatyus Ya'qub, *al-Kanisah al-suryaniyyah al-antakiyyah al-urthuduksiyyah*, Damascus: Alif Ba' al-Adib Press, 1974; Robert Murray, *Symbols of Church and Kingdom: A Study in Early Syriac Tradition*, London: Cambridge University Press, 1975; H. J. W Drijvers, "East of Antioch: Forces and Structures in the Development of Early Syriac Theology," *East of Antioch*, ed. H. J. W. Drijvers, London: Variorum, 1984; Sebastian Brock, *An Introduction to Syriac Studies*, Piscataway: Gorgias Press, 2017; Fergus Millar, "Paul of Samosata, Zenobia and Aurelian: The Church, Local Culture and Political Allegiance in Third-Century Syria," *JRS* 61, 1971, 1–17, reprinted in *Rome, the Greek World, and the East: Volume 3: The Greek World, the Jews, and the East*, eds. Hannah Cotton and Guy Rogers, Chapel Hill: University of North Carolina Press, 2006, 243–274; Sebastian Brock and Susan Harvey, *Holy Women of the Syrian Orient*, Berkeley: University of California Press, 1998; Wassilios Klein, *Syrische Kirchenväter*, Stuttgart: Kohlhammer, 2004; Wolfgang Hage, *Das orientalische Christentum*, Stuttgart: Kohlhammer, 2007; Jeanne-Nicole Mellon Saint-Laurent, *Missionary Stories and the Formation of the Syriac Churches*, Berkeley: University of California Press, 2015; *The Syriac World*, ed. Daniel King, London: Routledge, 2018.

Jewish Monotheism and Aramaic Language

At its minimum Jewish-Christianity refers to a sect that accepts both Jesus as Messiah and maintains some recognition of Jewish Law. As such, several disconnected Jewish-Christian groups arose throughout late antiquity, some would add, culminating in Islam itself.[39] In basic historical terms, Jewish-Christianity refers to the early church formed by the apostle Peter (d. *ca.* 68) in the first century. Peter was the apostle Jesus personally entrusted in Jerusalem to be the "rock" for the building of his future church (Matthew 16:18). His small flock was:

(1) Ethnically Jewish
(2) Linguistically Aramaic

One of the church's earliest converts, Paul of Tarsus (d. *ca.* 67), disputed with Peter at the Council of Jerusalem in 50 CE over the requirement of keeping the Jewish Law. The greatest matter of contention was the practice of circumcision for the multitude of Gentiles (Greeks and others) throughout the Roman Empire. Paul's missionary zeal and Roman citizenship promoted "Gentile Christianity" across the empire (Acts 16:37–38; 22:25–28). The apostle Peter is said to have moved to Antioch for a while, becoming its first bishop, where his flock remained Jewish and Aramaic. This celebrated history is marred by its less publicized dark underbelly. The imperial Greek culture of the *polis* frequently blotted out the native Aramaic cultures of the countryside.

The sociologist Max Weber suggested that only Judaism and Islam were "strictly monotheistic," while Christian trinitarianism and the Catholic cult of saints came close to polytheism.[40] This observation, while blunt and lacking nuance, merits some analysis. The Semitic churches negotiated theological positions between their monotheistic and polytheistic interlocutors. In this vein, a number of local cities and church fathers maintained nativist, Semitic customs similar to the apostle Peter, including:

---

39 Cf. generally Mustafa Akyol, *The Islamic Jesus: How the King of the Jews Became a Prophet of the Muslims*, New York: St. Martin's Press, 2017.
40 Teixidor, *The Pagan God*, 35.

(1) Theologies that adhered more closely to Jewish norms—especially strict monotheism
(2) Aramaic language

In the words of Syriac Church historian Arthur Vööbus, "the transition of the Christian message from the Aramaean Jewish community to the native Syrian communities is also quite natural."[41] Syriac was the dialect of Aramaic adopted by the Semitic churches. The nationalist undertones of these communities stood in clear opposition to the privileged Greek power structure, offering an alternative. The different theologies adopted by Syriac church fathers to express Semitic beliefs and customs require more explanation and are intrinsically linked to the religious and political culture of Arabian society, its biblically imbued audiences, and the Qur'an.

Nativist Theologians

Nativist theologians came primarily from among the non-Greek, non-Italic "barbarian" tribes of the periphery.[42] They were nationalist heroes at home, but rebels to Rome and Byzantium. And they were outcasts to the growing imperial church. Their local congregations were, therefore, held together by a theologically conversant and connected set of congregations located throughout Syro-Arabia, dubbed the "Nativist church."

Nativism

This terminology is in the spirit of Patricia Crone's study on *The Nativist Prophets of Early Islamic Iran*, which examines the "Iranian response to the Muslim penetration of the Iranian countryside, the

---

41 Arthur Vööbus, *History of Asceticism in the Syrian Orient: A Contribution to the History of Culture in the Near East*, Louvain: Secrétariat du Corpus SCO, 1958, 9.
42 Hoyland, *Arabia and the Arabs*, 150 refers to Christian Arab chiefs joining a "provincial creed," while Shahid, *Byzantium and the Arabs in the Fourth Century*, 154 alludes to Moses of Sinai having "principles of religion" outside the church hierarchy.

revolts that the Muslims triggered there, and the religious communities that these revolts revealed."[43] The Syro-Arabian response to Roman penetration of their countryside both antagonized as well as roused various nativist Christian religious communities there. The force of their response is felt in the military revolt of Zenobia, and the theological discourse to which Paul and his predecessors contributed. As the coming discussion demonstrates, the nativist response was slandered by the patriarchs of the pro-establishment church, historians, and heresiologists as "pro-Jewish" and "anti-Roman." Indeed, Peter Brown finds the social struggles of the Roman Near East more complex than merely a tug of war between "resistance" and "assimilation."[44] Indeed, for the simplistic, heresiographical characterizations, while true at crudely basic level, were little more than a polemical caricature of reality. The following discussion introduces the Nativist church as Semitic, pre-Nicene, and exhibiting qualities some late antique heresiologists and modern historians may describe as Jewish-Christian or Gnostic.

Christian Heresy or Strict Monotheism?

Judaism quite simply forged the *earliest* church. It shared many of the qualities of Syro-Arabian nativist theology as a parallel expression of Semitic beliefs and customs. The lofty qualities of divinity promoted by nativist theology segregated God from mortals, even if He loved them sufficiently to sacrifice his son (as did Abraham!). Strict monotheism was therefore prioritized by design. This is why Nativist church fathers frequently denied completely Christ's consubstantiation, the hypostatic union of his so-called natures, or his pre-existent divinity.[45]

In the second–third centuries their ranks included Syriac-speaking Nativist church fathers. Among them is the first known author of the Gospel harmony, the *Diatessaron*. The Syriac text was purportedly translated from Greek. Its author, Tatian of Adiabene (d. 180), is

---

43 Patricia Crone, *The Nativist Prophets of Early Islamic Iran: Rural Revolt and Local Zoroastrianism*, Cambridge; New York: Cambridge University Press, 2012, vii.
44 Brown, *Society and the Holy in Late Antiquity*, 155.
45 Ehrman, *Lost Christianities*, 163–164, 185.

otherwise a mysterious figure about whom little is known. He was, evidently, a pugnacious opponent of Greco-Roman culture.[46] Among his teachings he insisted on the "strict monotheism" of God.[47]

Bardaisan of Edessa (d. 222), introduced earlier, believed in the transcendence of God. Like the Babylonians, he surmised that the heavenly constellations were "beings" under His service. Otherwise, his dualist worldview is sometimes credited with influencing nativist theologies of a Gnostic variety, especially Manichaeism and Isma'ili Shiism.[48]

Beryllus of Bosra (d. *ca.* 250) is known for teaching what scholars call "dynamic Monarchianism," or the doctrine that God the Father is indivisibly one, and that the Son was temporarily granted divinity during the life of Jesus. Jesus was, therefore, quite plainly neither pre-existing nor co-equal with the Father. Beryllus was said to have sparred with Origen of Alexandria (d. 253) at the Councils of Arabia in 238 and 244. Church histories claim Beryllus made sizeable compromises with his adversary. Whatever the case may have been, Beryllus was the nearest contemporary to Paul of Samosata and the latter's teachings built directly upon those of his predecessor. Paul elaborated on the doctrine of dynamic Monarchianism, further diminishing Jesus' divinity by claiming that he was merely "adopted" by God the Father at his baptism.[49]

Paul's students are also credited (or blamed!) for influencing Arius of Alexandria (d. 336), to whom we return in Chapter 5. There is more to Paul than the smear of "Adoptionism." Paul worked within the distinctly Semitic rather than Greek institution of prophecy. His prophetic ministry would have appeared an abomination to the Byzantine Greeks who enjoyed the privilege of molding their classical heritage into the perceived Eastern Orthodox and Catholic churches of medieval times. To state this plainly, Greek-speaking Byzantine holy

46 Vööbus, *History of Asceticism in the Syrian Orient*, 34–38.
47 Emily Hunt, *Christianity in the Second Century: The Case of Tatian*, London: Routledge, 2003, 105, 132, 180–185.
48 Cf. Garth Fowden, *Before and after Muhammad: The First Millennium Refocused*, Princeton; Oxford; Princeton University Press, 2014, 200–201.
49 Bardy, *Paul de Samosate*, 152–156.

men replaced Hellenic philosophers as intermediaries between the people and their emperor. They expressed their power in populist rather than aristocratic circles.[50] There was no room for prophets.

These men—Tatian, Bardaisan, Beryllus, and Paul—were the Syro-Arabian nativist theologians par excellence. They became the first architects of strict monotheism within the early church.[51] Their origins stemmed from the Jewish and Aramaic foundations of the apostle Peter in Antioch during the first century. And their trajectory founded the Semitic churches of the second–third centuries, including the ancient congregations of Antioch, Osrhoene, Adiabene, and the Bosra. Leading up to and following the Council of Nicaea in 325, these ancient churches would evolve in different trajectories. Therefore, Antioch increasingly became Greek-Chalcedonian territory. Osrhoene and Bosra fell under the sway of the West Syrian Church. And Adiabene came under the control of the East Syrian Church.

Wonder and Mystical Gnosis

Nativist theology embodied the intense experience of *wonder*, which shaped varieties of gnostic mysticism in later centuries. Wonder is a quality of devotion at the very heart of the religious mysticism shared by Syriac-speaking Christians and Arabic-speaking Muslims throughout the fourth–eighth centuries. During this time, varieties of gnostic mysticism thrived in the provinces of Mesopotamia and Bahrayn, and along the Persian Gulf. So, what is wonder?

Wonder informs the single-minded devotion and ecstatic poetry of the wisdom writings in the Hebrew Bible, Syriac verse homilies, the Qur'an's poetic speech, and early Sufism. God's wonder manifests itself within this world in the form of signs and symbols. These include the "signs and wonders" unveiled before: Moses and Pharoah (e.g. Exodus 7:3; Q 20:22–24), Daniel (Daniel 4:2–3; 6:27), Jesus and the Apostles (e.g. Acts 2:22–43; cf. 2 Corinthians 12:12; Q 2:87; 3:49–50; 5:110–114), or those describing the miraculous beauty of gardens in paradise

---

50 Brown, *Society and the Holy in Late Antiquity*, 135.
51 Vööbus, *History of Asceticism in the Syrian Orient*, 37 makes a similar point.

and on earth, celebrated by Ephrem the Syrian (d. 373) and Q 55–56.[52] Indeed, Islamic tradition received all Qur'anic verses as wondrous "signs" or *ayat*.

Wonder is behind the "light" of God envisioned by Ephrem. It is behind the "transcendence" of God safeguarded by Jacob of Serugh (d. 521). It is behind the "mysteries, symbols" known as in Syriac as *raze*, not to be confused with the ancient Greek Eleusinian mysteries which are genealogically distinct. The greatest proponent of wonder in the Syrian churches was Isaac of Nineveh (d. *ca.* 700). In fact Isaac, originally hailing from Beth Qatraye (Qatar) in eastern Arabia, is recognized by scholars as the compiler, architect, and theoretical founder of "wonder and astonishment."[53] It is little surprise that these qualities of nativist theology—luminosity, transcendence, and revealing mystery—define the quintessence of the qur'anic God and His divine revelation (Q 2:255; 22:74; 24:35; 25:61; 33:46; 50:22; 53:58; 78:13; 58:21; 85:12–16). The mystical qualities of the Syriac fathers seem to resurface among the earliest generation of Sufi masters.

Wonder is also the ecstatic emotion and vivid psychological state associated with prophecy. That is to say, when God "reveals" His mysteries or essence to the prophets of Semitic cultures, the recipient appears overwhelmed by wonder. This is true for the Hebrew prophets (e.g. Ezekiel 3:14; 33:22), Syriac fathers—especially Jacob and Isaac—and Arabic prophetic figures—notably Muhammad—whose experience is often compared to that of ecstasy or nirvana.[54]

None of this discussion implies in any way that Nativist church fathers were one and the same. Nor does it intimate that they were untouched by the prevailing winds of the Byzantine Church or its pragmatic emperor. Far from it. Their members wrestled with crafting several different Christologies and ecclesiastical structures as did their imperial, so-called "orthodox," counterparts. In the context described

---

52 Emran El-Badawi, "Syriac and the Qur'ān," *EQ*, ed. Jane McAuliffe, Leiden: Brill, 2018.
53 See generally Jason Scully, *Isaac of Nineveh's Ascetical Eschatology*, Oxford: Oxford University Press, 2017.
54 Cf. Abdolkarim Soroush, *Bast-i tajrubay-i nabavi*, Tehran: Moasese Farhangi Serat, 1999, English trans. Nilou Mobasser, *The Expansion of Prophetic Experience*, Leiden: Brill, 2008, 1–25.

here, the varieties of nativist theologians, known to the sources as "heretics," were not deviants from an artificial Christological standard, but rather, perfectly normal spokespeople of widespread Semitic beliefs and customs.[55]

Mary as Mother Goddess and Queen of Heaven

Concurrent with the activism and dogma of nativist theologians was the veneration of Mary not just as virgin, but also as mother goddess and queen of heaven in Syro-Arabia, especially between Palestine and Transjordan. The extent to which this veneration is a continuation of pagan custom or internal church developments is a matter of intense debate. Some have proposed that a wide array of Near Eastern and Hellenic goddesses influenced the cult of Mary in the early church.[56] Others have gone further, stating "Marian piety" and devotion originally constituted a distinct institution, separate from the church itself.[57] Still others walk upon a middle ground, arguing that pagan fertility cults were gradually assimilated into the Christian symbology of Mary.[58] More recent scholarship calls some of these proposals into question given the difficulty of dating literary evidence and the problem of Catholic apology versus Protestant polemics, especially among Western scholars today.[59] And finally, some have cast doubt on the "rhetorical bluster" of the church fathers, namely Epiphanius, whose work is examined shortly.[60]

---

55 Cf. in relation Bart Ehrman, *How Jesus Became God: The Exaltation of a Jewish Preacher from Galilee*, San Francisco: Harper One, 2014, 150–166.

56 See generally Stephen Benko, *The Virgin Goddess: Studies in the Pagan and Christian Roots of Mariology*, Leiden: Brill, 1993.

57 Ashe, *The Virgin*, 242; Michael Carroll, *The Cult of the Virgin Mary: Psychological Origins*, Princeton: Princeton University Press, 1986, 43–48.

58 See generally Marina Warner, *Alone of All Her Sex: The Myth and the Cult of the Virgin Mary*, New York: Vintage Books, 1986.

59 Cameron, "The Cult of the Virgin in Late Antiquity," 1.

60 See Stephen Shoemaker, *Mary in Early Christian Faith and Devotion*, Newhaven; London: Yale University Press, 2016, 149 vs. Millar, "Ethnic identity in the Roman Near East," 391–392.

Women petitioners before Mary, Dayr al-Suryan

Native Women vs. Foreign Men

It is not my goal to adopt any one of these perspectives per se, as much as it is to add my voice to a diverse scholarly quorum, acknowledging the changing views of scholars themselves over the years. The greatest point of scholarly contention concerns the cult of Mary in Arabia known as the Collyridians or Kollyridians. The Greek word *kollyris* refers to "bread cakes" offered to deities. Epiphanius describes this group or sect in fantastical terms, as we will see.

After initially dismissing Epiphanius' dubious portrayal of "women priests," Stephen Shoemaker later concedes the existence of female "liturgical leaders" who may have "led prayer."[61] As he demonstrates "Marian piety" was finally "embraced" as "god bearer" at the Council of Ephesus in 431. She was "fused with the Christian empire and its church," which I may add was an overwhelmingly male cast of characters crafting orthodoxy on behalf of their god. Prior to this, the origins of her veneration within the church are unclear. True, this practice "developed organically from within the early church tradition ... as simply one popular variant of the nascent cult of the saints." But this does not tell the whole story. It seems a rather patriarchal fallacy to pit

---

61 Shoemaker, *Mary in Early Christian Faith and Devotion*, 160 both agrees with and debates Ally Kateusz, "Collyridian Déjà Vu: The Trajectory of Redaction of the Markers of Mary's Liturgical Leadership," *JFSR* 29.2, 2013, 75–92.

this insight against a "straw woman" argument. This is namely that of the "intrusion of pagan goddess worship ... or ... other foreign impulse."[62]

Here Shoemaker goes too far. The cults of the saints and early church tradition are *fundamentally* built upon pagan origins. The many nuances of this truism have garnered abundant scholarly atten-tion.[63] Furthermore, goddess worship may indeed have been a *foreign* impulse to Nicene holy men molding a church in their image. But it was *native* to the faithful multitudes in Syro-Arabia since ancient antiquity. This was the case especially for its priestesses and female petitioners, as I have shown.

The rich Dormition and Assumption traditions, though imprecisely dated from the third–fifth centuries, offer insights into the long-stand-ing cult of the mother goddess and queen of heaven.[64] Within this body of apocrypha is a work believed to have been written in Syriac known as the *Six Books Dormition Apocryphon*, which corroborates some of what Epiphanius writes. There is other documentary evidence also validating his claims.[65]

The Native Cult of Mary

We should not stray much further from our focus on female power in late antique Arabia by delving too deeply into this tradition. A handful of striking details stand out for our purposes. In this tradition, Mary is clearly venerated or worshipped as the queen of heaven. Like her predecessor Asherah:

62 Shoemaker, *Mary in Early Christian Faith and Devotion*, 29.

63 Stephen Wilson, "Annotated bibliography," *Saints and their Cults: Studies in Religious Sociology, Folklore and History*, ed. Stephen Wilson, Cambridge: Cambridge University Press, 1985, 325; Teixidor, *The Pagan God*, 135, 160; Peter Brown, *The Cult of the Saints: Its Rise and Function in Latin Christianity*, Chicago: University of Chicago Press, 2009, 5–6.

64 See further Stephen Shoemaker, *Ancient Traditions of the Virgin Mary's Dormition and Assumption*, Oxford: Oxford University Press, 2002.

65 Millar, "Ethnic identity in the Roman Near East," 392; Macdonald, "Arabs, Arabias, and Arabic before Late Antiquity," 308.

(1) Her cult is frequented by female pilgrims from across the lands.
(2) She is associated with healing, fertility, and intercession.
(3) Her cult is associated with agricultural feast days.
(4) Her petitioners bake bread cakes for her.[66]

Should the sum of these cultic practices be considered "foreign," this says more about the external perspective and polemical malice held by the observer, and the persistent hegemony of a false "orthodox" narrative, than it does anything substantive about the native cult of Mary as mother goddess and queen of heaven.

Nativist Church Doctrine and Ecclesiology, *ca.* 220–320

What little we know about the Nativist church comes from neither Paul nor Zenobia. It comes rather from their fiercest adversaries. These problematic sources call for a close, critical eye. As the architects of Trinitarian theology and canon law, the "orthodox" Nicene church fathers disparaged their Syro-Arabian nativist predecessors as heretics. In some cases, modern Christian apologists and partisan orientalists have uncritically, or worse, deliberately, accepted the prejudice of the sources attributing all manner of "heresy" to pre-Islamic Arabian society.[67] Even today scholars are at pains to come to a consensus while wearily debating the "heretical" extent of Muhammad's prophecy and of qur'anic teachings.[68] There is no denying things are complicated. They should be.

In what follows, every measure has been taken to describe the shape and content of the Nativist church in "positivist terms," i.e. not as heresy but as a natural, coherent set of doctrines and sound ecclesiology. This task entails reading *against* late, foreign, and thoroughly

---

66 Shoemaker, *Ancient Traditions of the Virgin Mary's Dormition and Assumption*, 44–45, 301, 303, 323, 386, 401–409.

67 Cameron, "The Cult of the Virgin in Late Antiquity," 1.

68 Darren Slade, "*Arabia Haeresium Ferax* (Arabia Bearer of Heresies): Schismatic Christianity's Potential Influence on Muhammad and the Qur'an," *ATI* 7.1, 2014, 43–53 merely lists "heresies" he observes. Gabriel Reynolds, "On the Qur'an and Christian heresies," *The Qur'an's Reform of Judaism and Christianity: Return to the Origins*, ed. Holger Zellentin, London: Routledge, 2019, 318–323 is more skeptical and nuanced.

patriarchal sources—especially the fourth-century *Historia Augusta*, Eusebius of Caesarea (d. 340), Epiphanius of Salamis (d. 403), Jerome (d. 420), and Augustine of Hippo (d. 430). It is little surprise that the heresiographical tendencies of such imposing men took female power in Arabia as their target.

The Nativist church conceived here merged the cultic site for the queen of heaven worshipped in Syro-Arabia, examined in the first three chapters, with the nativist theology of Syro-Arabian church fathers introduced in this chapter. I argue that its doctrine and ecclesiology flourished in greater Syria *ca.* 220–320. This context hosted the spread of non-canonical apocryphal Syriac writings such as the *Protovangelium of James* and the *Dormition and Assumption* traditions. These writings helped shape the church, until its disbanding under emperor Constantine. I contend that the church was loosely organized between three cities already introduced:

- Mamre
- Bosra
- Antioch

Each city carried within its congregation an indigenous, local teaching. This teaching privileged strict monotheism and melded it with the vestiges of pagan female power. Recalling the deification of kings and queens examined in Chapter 3, the doctrines presented here are those of:

(1) The mother goddess and counter-ecclesiology
(2) The eternal father and mortal sons
(3) The son of sacred marriage

The Mother Goddess and Counter-Ecclesiology—Mamre

The cult of the mother goddess was a staple of societies throughout Near Eastern antiquity and therefore *native* to early Semitic churches, prior to Greco-Roman supremacy. It left an indelible mark on all churches through the veneration of the Virgin Mary, and medieval

Mariolatry and Mariology.[69] Like the next rung on a ladder, she was incrementally added to a long list of Near Eastern mother goddesses, including al-'Uzza, Atargatis, Asherah, Ishtar, and Inanna, whose cults thrived in Syro-Arabia.[70]

The New Asherah

There is no telling how early Mary was promoted to the rank of mother goddess. Her cult flourished throughout late antiquity. By the third century the "mother of God" was venerated by the nascent Syrian Church. She was connected to the *Protovangelium of James* and the liturgy of Mari and Addai.[71] Mary's petitioners were women. They baked bread cakes to beseech their mother goddess, the "queen of heaven"—supplanting the cult of Asherah in Mamre—an ancient practice bemoaned by the Hebrew Bible centuries prior and subsequently by Sozomen.

The female cultic practices of Semitic peoples, including Phoenician and Arabian communities, offended the male sensibilities of the rising Byzantine clergy. In their xenophobia and misogyny, Greek-speaking church fathers dedicated whole tracts to denigrating the cultic practices of neighboring cultures as heresy and, more importantly, associated them with "motherhood." To the objective outsider heresiology in this context appears as much about denigrating colonized people and women, as it was about imposing empire and masculinity.

Collyridianism and Bread Offering in Arabia

In his informative yet problematic treatise against so-called heresies, the *Panorion*, Epiphanius of Salamis attacks dozens of fourth-century groups as "mothers of heresy." Among them he identifies the

---

69 Benko, *The Virgin Goddess*, 5.

70 Cf. in relation al-Qimani, *al-Usturah wal-turath*, 259; al-Mallah, *al-Wasit fi tarikh al-'arab qabl al-islam*, 403.

71 See further Murray, *Symbols of Church and Kingdom*, 314–331; Miguel Ariño-Durand, "La Vie de la bienheureuse Vierge Marie dans les traditions apocryphes syro-orientales," PhD thesis, Université Paris-Sorbonne/Institut Catholique de Paris, 2014.

"Collyridians" of Arabia, introduced earlier. He argues that they originated among the Scythian or Thracian cultures of the Balkans.[72]
Similarly, the worship of the goddesses Rhea and Demeter figures
prominently in the Roman Balkans, almost in parallel with analogous
cults in Arabia. In any case, Epiphanius describes the cultic practices
of the Collyridians as follows:

> For some women decorate a carriage or a square by covering it
> with fine linen, and on a certain definite day of the year [on certain
> days] they set forth bread and offer it as sacrifice in the name of
> Mary.[73]

We know very little about the "bread-baking" cult of Arabia. They are
considered by some modern researchers a mysterious sect whose
existence and connection to Q 5:73–115 centuries later is debated.[74]
The debate is overstated and uninformed, because its focus is the
assessment of Epiphanius's reliability, rather than thoughtful examination of a millennium's worth of mother worship in the region.

This brings us to the Latin church father Theodoret of Cyrrhus (d.
457), to whom some attribute the infamous condemnation, "Arabia
the mother of heresies."[75] Although he does not refer to the Collyridians
by name, there can be little doubt this affront targets them at some
level. The pervasiveness of mother worship on its native soil, its organ-
ization into the Nativist church structures with female clergy of
Arabian (and Thracian) communities, and its growing influence
throughout the empire, infuriated foreign holy men. They called for a
tribunal, in large part to condemn and co-opt its power into the
masculine Christian imperium.[76] The Council of Ephesus in 431

72 Cf. generally Stephen Shoemaker, "Epiphanius of Salamis, the Kollyridians, and the
Early Dormition Narratives: The Cult of the Virgin in the Later Fourth Century," *JECS*
16, 2008, 369–399.
73 Benko, *The Virgin Goddess*, 171.
74 Corrie Block, *The Qur'an in Christian–Muslim Dialogue: Historical and Modern
Interpretations*, London: Routledge, 2013, 186.
75 Shahid, *Byzantium and the Arabs in the Fourth Century*, 278.
76 Cf. in relation Vasiliki Limberis, *Divine Heiress: The Virgin Mary and the Making of
Christian Constantinople*, London: New York; London: Routledge, 1994, 118–139.

Women baking bread, nineteenth-century Syria

disputed the semantic range and theological significance of Mary as the "god bearer," a term probably originating in correspondences between Dionysus of Alexandria (d. 264) and Paul of Samosata during the third century. The council served only to fracture the church further, and paved the way for the Nestorian schism.

The Arabian congregation of the mother goddess centered near Mamre carried with it an ecclesiological structure fundamentally independent from, outside of, and against the ecclesiology of holy men typified elsewhere. Its clergy were women. They embodied how "devotion to Mary reached the height of organized worship."[77] But there was more to this counter-ecclesiology than female priestesses and Marian cakes.

Ecumenism Prior to Emperor Constantine

Mamre was the site where Jews, Christians, and adherents of the mother goddess Mary (and previously Asherah) worshipped together

---

77 Ibid., 120.

until their disbanding under Constantine *ca.* 320. We ought to remember that for centuries prior to Roman encroachment, early Abrahamic traditions coexisted side by side with mother goddess traditions. But it was not to last, and when the imperial axe fell on interconfessional worship in Mamre, the Arabian congregation of the mother goddess was no more. The religious and political culture of Arabian society was changing. With the breaking of the congregation of the mother goddess it was slowly but surely deprived of female power, which from here on was deliberately excluded by church men as heresy and idolatry.

The Arabian adherents of the Mamran congregation did not vanish into thin air. But we have no record of them after Sozomen. Surely, many among them were absorbed into existing structures of Judaism, Christianity, and the gradual tide of Hanifism (pre-Islamic monotheism) and proto-Islam swelling their ranks throughout Arabia in later centuries. The relationships between late antique Abrahamic monotheism in Arabia and subsequent qur'anic Islam, while debated ceaselessly by scholars, could not be more obvious. But within this rich and complex genealogy, there also rests the overlooked cult of the mother goddess in Mamre.

Yet Mary remained a devotional figure in the church as powerful as she was divisive. While the Collyridians saw her as a goddess, the Antidicomarianites saw her as human. Meaning they saw her as merely the mother of Jesus, conceived with her husband Joseph the carpenter, and virgin no longer.[78] Yet as contentious as Mary was, just as polarizing were the roles of the Father and the Son in the Nativist church, which we address next.

The Eternal Father and Mortal Sons—Bosra

The Christian Trinity represented the highly patriarchal, imperial Roman triple deity. It belonged to a long tradition of trinitarian models of worship prevalent throughout Near Eastern antiquity. Behind the Trinity was the divine couple and child introduced in the preceding chapter and made plain in the three persons of the Father, Son, and Holy Spirit.

78 Ibid., 119.

Following this genealogy, the Holy Spirit, itself conceived as a female being, replaces the "Mother" or Virgin Mary. This is how she is celebrated in Syriac Christian tradition and as Q 5:116 implies.[79] It also follows that, as the ancient Canaanite ritual of offering bread cakes to Asherah continued with the Jewish Palestinian figure of Mary, so too would the worship of the divine couple and child—El, Asherah and Baal—continue in the form of the Father (formerly El), Mary (formerly Asherah), and Jesus (formerly Baal).[80] Both cults emerged from the same geographical location, namely Canaan-Palestine. From there they were inherited by their Arabian neighbors and spread to Rome during the Severan dynasty and under Philip the Arab in the third century, as elucidated in Chapter 7.

The third century was also the time of a thriving Christian Arab congregation in Bosra under the leadership of the nativist theologian Beryllus of Bosra, whose teachings were introduced earlier. The community may have been known to the famed Byzantine Church historian of Syrian origin, Eusebius of Caesaria, and his Latin successor Jerome, as the *Arabici* owing to their Arabic-speaking origins.[81]

It appears Beryllus believed quite simply that God (the Father) was eternal in nature while humankind remained hopelessly mortal. In other words, the soul of the Father lived forever, while those of human mortals ceased at death, and would be resurrected at the final Judgment. Jesus was a mortal, who thanks to the Father's grace alone was "promoted", so to speak, to the status of the Son until his death. After this he was, like all mortals, no more.

Say what you will about Beryllus' doctrine, it was entirely conventional in his Syro-Arabian context, resembling that of his Jewish predecessors and his Hanafite successors almost to the letter (cf. further 1 Timothy 6:16; Q 40:16). The charge against him of heresy, and the labeling of his doctrine "dynamic Monarchianism" says more about the

---

79 Susan Harvey, "Feminine imagery for the divine: The Holy Spirit, the Odes of Solomon, and early Syriac tradition," *SVTQ* 37, 1993, 111–139.

80 Cf. in relation Bardy, *Paul de Samosate*, 344, 370.

81 See Eusebius of Caesaria, *The Fathers of the Church*, 58–59; Jerome, *On Illustrious Men*, trans. Ernest Richardson, Buffalo: Dalcassian Publishing, 2017, 26 is not explicit about this.

ulterior motives of his foreign critics than it says anything remotely irregular about his ordinary beliefs or customs. It is unclear what the fate of the *Arabici* was after his excommunication around 244, but their absorption into alternate Jewish and Christian congregations can be assumed. Like their Mamran neighbors, the ranks and doctrine of the *Arabici* likely contributed to subsequent Hanifism and proto-Islam.

This brings us to the most contentious person of the Christian Trinity, the Son.

The Son of Sacred Marriage—Antioch

Paul of Samosata was a student of Beryllus, whether in person or indirectly. His influence by Theodotus of Byzantium (late second century) is less clear.[82] In any case, by claiming the Father adopted the Son at his baptism, he was merely continuing the work of his nativist predecessor. Naturally, subsequent Greek and Latin church historians and heresiologists would caricature Paul and his ideas.

I argue that Adoptionism, while in principle preserving the strict monotheism of God, is originally based on the sacred marriage of the divine couple, particularly that of El and Asherah, whose cults significantly shaped the Hebrew Bible and religion in Rome, as we shall see in Chapter 7. As was the case in neighboring Palestine, sacred marriage was a staple of pagan religion throughout late antique Arabia, including the union between the divine couple who "founded" the Kaabah in Mecca, Isaf, and Na'ilah.

With time the divine couple lost the physical characteristics of creators, becoming instead an "ethical-spiritual" Father and "childless-virgin" Mother, who adopted rather than procreated.[83] Ditlef Nielsen expounds upon the evolution of the sacred marriage couple into "ethical, merciful, adoptive parents of human beings," stating:

This marriage eventually transforms the married couple into the ethical, merciful, adoptive parents of human beings in religious culture. It is regarded with great respect. Like creation, it is the

82 Millar, "Paul of Samosata, Zenobia and Aurelian," 272–273.
83 Nielsen, "Die altsemitische Muttergöttin," 524, 538.

original, sacred principle of existence. And it is reflected in the sexual rites and fertility ceremonies of the cult.[84]

By arguing that the Son was adopted, i.e. temporarily divine, Paul was at once acknowledging and attenuating Jesus being the son of a sacred marriage between two gods. Adoption, I argue, was a negotiated theological position, a middle way between two positions. At one extreme was unbridled, ancient, pagan sacred marriage. At the other was newly mandated strict monotheism.

The Nativist church, I argue, culminated in the belief and customs of Paul. His congregation in Antioch is *genealogically* linked to that of Bosra, on the one hand, and Mamre, on the other. Evidence for this link is discernable in the refutations of Paul's interlocutors, who associate his "heresy" with that of his predecessor Beryllus and other Monarchianists.[85] His interlocutors similarly force a Christological reinterpretation upon the patriarch Abraham's "theophany at Mamre" (Genesis 8:1–15), diminishing its original meaning altogether.[86] To rearticulate this point in positive terms, Paul's doctrine with respect to the Son built upon the premise of sacred marriage between the eternal Father and divine Mother.

Tyranny and the Proto-Byzantine Church, *ca.* 246–325

The "ecumenical church councils" and their subsidiary synods ravaged nativist theology and strict monotheism among the faithful multitudes. This fueled animosity and division between the churches and nations. The Syro-Arabian Nativist church fathers were not its only victims, and their grievances with the Roman emperor were not merely on theological grounds. *Race* and *culture* played an ominous

---

84 Ibid., 542, translated by the author.

85 Allen Brent, *Hippolytus and the Roman Church in the Third Century: Communities in Tension before the Emergence of a Monarch-Bishop*, Leiden; New York; Köln: Brill, 1995, 394–395.

86 Bogdan Bucur, *Scripture Re-Envisioned: Christophanic Exegesis and the Making of a Christian Bible*, Leiden: Brill, 2018, 42–70; Henry Chadwick, *The Church in Ancient Society: From Galilee to Gregory the Great*, Oxford; New York: Oxford University Press, 2001, 166–167.

role too.[87] The nascent Christian empire's fiercest heretics, discussed further below, were conveniently, though not always, from the "barbarian" periphery. They were, in other words, varieties of nativists, nationalists, and rebels who resisted the imposition of a centrally mandated foreign orthodoxy, by force sometimes.[88]

Race and Culture

It is not without reason that the nativist North African church fathers Cyprian of Carthage (d. 258), Donatus Magnus (d. 355), and Arius of Alexandria (d. 336) became the arch nemeses of the imperial Greek church of Byzantium. Their ministries were interrupted by Roman execution, or imperially rigged trials and church councils.[89] Arius was famously condemned at the Council of Nicaea in 325. Despite his condemnation he was joined by Ulfilas (d. 383), a part-Gothic church father who spread Arianism throughout the tribes of Germanic Europe. They served as Rome's fiercest military adversary. The Arian versus Byzantine church divide during the fifth century only contributed to increased hostilities between the Romans and Germanic Goths. This division contributed directly to the Gothic conquest of the western Roman empire by *ca.* 476 and their subsequent war with the Romans during 535–554, under emperor Justinian (d. 565). Similar to their Germanic Arian counterparts, the Donatists controlled the churches of North Africa for centuries, only falling to the Arab conquests *ca.* 647–709.

With the gradual Christianization of Byzantium and Rome in the early fourth century a number of Nativist church fathers abandoned insurgency and gravitated ever closer to imperial compromise. Some went on to become staples of the medieval Greek Orthodox and Latin Catholic churches. A full excursus on the damage caused by the

---

87 Millar, "Ethnic identity in the Roman Near East," 391 makes this point citing Epiphanius as evidence.

88 See Millar, "Ethnic identity in the Roman Near East," 392.

89 Cf. discussion on "theology becomes politics" in Gale Heide, *Timeless Truth in the Hands of History: A Short History of System in Theology*, Eugene: Wipf and Stock Publishers, 2012, 48–67.

Christological controversies and the fall of Rome is beyond our scope of investigation. What matters here is that these councils failed to build consensus, because ecumenism was merely a cover for the "tyranny of the many" and the pragmatic will of a precariously placed and often impatient emperor. Fostering ecumenism became, in effect, a pretext for its diametrical opposite, exclusion and intolerance.[90]

From Nativism to "Heresy"

Orthodoxy was shaped by the manufacture of heresy. Nativist theologies were labeled "anathema" and nativist theologians suffered "excommunication." What is more, for the non-Greek Asian and African metropolises of the empire, Greek was imposed upon the natives as the official language of ecumenical negotiation.

It appears that post-Nicene bishops of Antioch, Jerusalem, Alexandria, and other Hellenized cities produced theological and ecclesiastical power structures in *opposition* to local, pre-Hellenic, often Semitic beliefs and customs throughout the Near East. In other words, the Christological controversies disputed *race* and *culture* as much as they did theology and law. The task of Christian clergy formulating "orthodoxy" through consensus building clearly favored Greco-Roman norms and empowered an expedient Greek-speaking emperor in Byzantium.

The Nicene Greek- and Latin-speaking church fathers condemned Judaizing practices, and referred to Jewish-Christian groups pejoratively. In doing so they disparaged, whether consciously or incidentally, earlier generations of largely Aramaic-speaking Christian groups clinging stubbornly, as it were, to Jewish norms. That these polemics were motivated largely by racial motives within the church is demonstrated in the works of Egeria (d. 384) and Jerome, who indicate the use of Syriac as a subordinate language to Greek in Near Eastern churches. Thus, "orthodox" church fathers unfairly deemed several local, nativist groups from the second–third centuries "heretical,"

---

90 For more on the complexities of Christian orthodoxy and heresy in the Near East, see Jack Tannous, *The Making of the Medieval Middle East: Religion, Society, and Simple Believers*, Princeton: Princeton University Press, 2020, 29–30.

including the official Syriac- and Coptic-speaking churches no less. In what may be described as late antique Christian imperialism, the ecumenical councils forced foreign policies down the throat of an increasingly disaffected Near Eastern countryside, labeling their nativist heroes "heretic." Paul of Samosata and his near contemporaries were precisely this kind of heretic.[91]

The tyranny of the Greek-speaking proto-Byzantine Church struck its hardest blow against the Syro-Arabian Nativist theologians and their strict monotheism three times. First, the Councils of Arabia (246–247) condemned Beryllus of Bosra and his nascent church. Roman Arabia became known thereafter by the Latin fathers of late antiquity as the "mother of heresies"—a phrase introduced already. Second, the Synods of Antioch (264–269) condemned Paul of Samosata for his teachings. And third, the Council of Nicaea in 325 condemned Arius of Alexandria. While himself a Nativist of Libyan-Cyrenaican origin, Arius was actually a student of Paul of Samosata's Nativist protégés in Syria, Lucian of Antioch (d. 312) and Eusebius of Nicomedia (d. 341).[92] In what would become a cycle of ironies in early church history, emperor Constantine (d. 337), who backed the Council of Nicaea condemning Arius, was himself baptized on his deathbed by none other than Arius' mentor, Eusebius of Nicomedia.

Bishops Behaving Badly

Constantine's maturity as a leader was overpowered by the malice and corruption of the very church fathers whose power he sought to appease, or at least moderate. Despite his imperial concessions, Constantine had ample reason to back down, on a personal level at least, from the contentious ramifications of the Nicene creed. His antithesis was Athanasius of Alexandria, a spiteful fundamentalist and

---

91 See Millar, "Ethnic identity in the Roman Near East," 393, although pp. 382–390 overstate the Greek influence on the Semitic, especially Syriac-speaking, landscape; Patrick Gray, "The Legacy of Chalcedon: Christological Problems and Their Significance," *The Cambridge Companion to the Age of Justinian*, ed. Michael Maas, Cambridge, Cambridge University Press, 2006, 215–238.

92 Bardy, *Paul de Samosate*, 407.

firebrand who used the Nicene Church as a weapon against his personal adversaries—namely Arius. Before him came the firebrand bishop Donatus Magnus, who rejected outright the sacraments of Christian submitters under the Roman persecution in Carthage. The conflict pushed Constantine to call the Council of Arles in 314. It was to no avail.[93] In 333, a few years before his passing, the famed emperor expressed his agony and regret about the destruction wrought by vindictive bishops, who used the church to settle scores and spoil the faith:

> Even the barbarians now through me, the true servant of God, know God and have learned to reverence him … [while bishops] do nothing but that which encourages discord and hatred and, to speak frankly, which leads to the destruction of the human race.[94]

But it was too late. Constantine had created a monster. His own soul sought refuge not in the Nicene Church which he first convened, but rather in the Arian Church which it condemned. This irony was thanks in large part to the influence of Eusebius of Nicomedia, who was in fact his distant cousin and loyal adviser. In an unlikely twist of fate, Arianism survived several more centuries before being finally extinguished.

The ramifications of divisive church councils on the Semitic churches were dire. They were increasingly squeezed between a rock and hard place: compromise with Byzantium, or departure.

Compromise after Nicaea

The nativist theologians would be overwritten on their native soil by the great "poet theologians" of the fourth century and their successors. Their immense contribution to the West and East Syrian churches coincided with the Christianization of the Roman Empire. This was also the time its emperor mandated the Nicene doctrine ("orthodoxy")

---

93 Hal Drake, *Constantine and the Bishops: The Politics of Intolerance*, Baltimore: Johns Hopkins University Press, 2002, 217–228.
94 Ibid., 4.

through the purported "consensus building" of clergy from across the empire, to which we return shortly. In other words, Syriac church fathers began adopting the qualities of their Nicene, often Greek-speaking, interlocutors, despite the theological rift between both camps.[95]

By way of example, we may consider the adoption of teachings against Jewish Law, first established by Paul of Tarsus and his Gentile flock from the first century, returning deep within "Semitic territory." Aphrahat the Persian Sage (d. 345) planted the seeds of what we may describe as anti-Semitism throughout his many *Demonstrations*, a sentiment upon which his successors eagerly built.[96] Consider furthermore that Ephrem the Syrian (d. 373) broke with his nativist predecessors and—like his Greek contemporary Epiphanius of Salamis—attacked them directly in his prose heresiography, *Refutations of Mani, Marcion and Bardaisan*.[97]

My point here is twofold. First, nativist theologians were deliberately and systematically ejected from the proto-Byzantine Church starting in the third century. Second, as the Semitic churches and their Coptic and Ethiopian peers negotiated Christology and ecclesiology with their imperial Greek counterparts, they increasingly compromised their own nativist positions for a theological discourse alien to their own culture, but absorbed by them nonetheless. In this respect, no bishop embodied Nicene fundamentalism and intolerance more than the Egyptian Athanasius, already introduced.

And thus the flame of Syro-Arabian nativist theology and strict monotheism was extinguished. Or was it?

---

95 Cf. in relation Millar, "Ethnic identity in the Roman Near East," 383.

96 See Jacob of Serugh, "Homélies contre les Juifs," *PO* 38, 1976, 44–181; S. Kazan, "Isaac of Antioch's Homily against the Jews," *OC* 45, 1961, 30–53; Susanna Drake, *Slandering the Jew: Sexuality and Difference in Early Christian Texts*, Philadelphia: University of Pennsylvania Press, 2013, 78–98 on John Chrysostom's sermon against the Jews.

97 Ephrem the Syrian, *S. Ephraim's Prose Refutations of Mani, Marcion, and Bardaisan*, ed. Charles Mitchell, Farnborough: Gregg International Publishers, 1969.

The Disbanding of the Nativist Church, *ca.* 320–337

The Nativist church, as defined earlier, included the congregation of Arabian tribes and adjacent communities who gathered annually at the feast and marketplace at the Oak of Mamre in Hebron, Palestine. It also subsumed nativist theologies from neighboring Arabian congregations in Bosra and Antioch. And some would say it recrystallized subsequently as Hanifism on the margins of official churches discussed below. The shrine venerating Mary as the mother goddess and queen of heaven has its origins in the Asherah groves of ancient Canaan, and in the evolution of the religious landscape of "pagans" of Arabian and Phoenician communities who were joined in communal worship by Jews, and later Christians.[98] The site exemplifies the meeting point between ancient mother goddess worship, on the one hand, and the late antique worship of a father god in the image of the biblical patriarch Abraham, on the other. Having learned of this holy site's interconfessional or ecumenical festival and marketplace, emperor Constantine attempted to eradicate pagan practices there. He built a basilica enclosing the sacred tree within it instead. I argue that the emperor's confiscation of Mamre from the so-called pagans in *ca.* 320, and his transforming it into a basilica, constitutes the expulsion and disbanding of the Nativist church.

Christians, Jews, and Pagans in Arabia

Readers may find puzzling the prospect of a Nativist church serving the Arabian masses so early, and prior to the existing Syrian or Greek churches.[99] We have virtually no evidence of an Arabic-speaking church prior to the spread of Islam. What we have are early Arabic inscriptions demonstrating that by the fifth–sixth centuries, Christianity had reached truly remote fringes of Arabian society. These include Hima, Yemen, and Zabad, Syria. However, the brief honorific

---

98 Arieh Kofsky, "Mamre: A Case of Regional Cult?" *Sharing the Sacred Religious Contacts and Conflicts in the Holy Land: First–Fifteenth Centuries CE*, ed. Guy Stroumsa, Jerusalem: Yad Izhak Ben Zvi, 1998, 19–30.
99 Millar, "Ethnic identity in the Roman Near East," 382–383.

or funerary nature of these writings do not divulge to what church those communities belonged. The absence of explicit sectarian leanings in those texts has led scholars to speculate broadly about the influence of provinces and cities supporting a sizeable Christian community: Roman Arabia, al-Hirah, or Najran.[100] Furthermore, the avalanche of scholarship on pre-Islamic Christian Arabs posits Syriac or Greek as their liturgical language. This state of affairs is certainly true for their ranks among the West Syrian, East Syrian, and Melkite churches to which Arabian communities largely belonged. However, what liturgical or ecclesiastical space did Arabic-speaking Christians occupy, if any, both *before* the fruition of these official churches and *outside* the Christian auspices of the Tanukhids near Aleppo, the Lakhmids in al-Hirah, the Ghassanids in Bosra, or the enclave in Najran?

There is evidence for the rise of:

(1) Arab national consciousness founded upon the *biblical* patriarch Ishmael, which appears in the writings of Josephus (d. 100 CE)

(2) Arabian tribes worshipping *alongside* Jews and Christians before the fifth century near Hebron, housing the shrine to Abraham known as the Oak of Mamre, according to Sozomen (d. 450)

(3) Religious and military alliance of Arabian tribes with Palestinian Jews *against* Byzantine Christians at the Sasanian conquest of Jerusalem in 614, according to Sebeos (d. *ca.* 670)[101]

By contrast, sixth-century Jewish–Christian alliances in South Arabia were merely an extension of Persian–Roman rivalry, rather than interconfessional ecumenism.[102] What the specific evidence from the north

---

100 Greg Fisher, *Rome, Persia, and Arabia: Shaping the Middle East from Pompey to Muhammad*, London: Routledge, 2019, 186–187.

101 Cf. in relation Sean Anthony, "Why Does the Qur'an Need the Meccan Sanctuary? Response to Professor Gerald Hawting's 2017 Presidential Address," *JIQSA* 3, 2018, 25–41. See further Fathiyyah 'Iqab, "*al-'ilaqat al-siyasiyyah bayn al-anbat wa-l-yahud fi filastin wa mawqif al-dawlah al-rumaniyyah minha: min awakhir al-qarn al-thani qabl al-milad ila al-qarn al-awwal al-miladi*," PhD diss., Abd al-Aziz University, 2000.

102 Sergius, *The Book of the Himyarites*, lxix–lxx.

demonstrates is that there was a dynamic Arabic-speaking community subscribed to Abrahamic monotheism around Palestine. That being said, the extent to which Arabic-speaking Christians formed a critical mass in the north, while borne out in these particular sources, is however a matter of ongoing scholarly debate.[103]

Whatever the case may have been, Sozomen describes the Jewish, Christian, and pagan cultic practices of the site in detail, stating:

> I consider it necessary to detail the proceedings of Constantine in relation to what is called the oak of Mamre. This place is now called Terebinthus, and is about fifteen stadia distant from Hebron, which lies to the south, but is two hundred and fifty stadia distant from Jerusalem. It is recorded that here the Son of God appeared to Abraham, with two angels, who had been sent against Sodom, and foretold the birth of his son. Here the inhabitants of the country and of the regions round Palestine, the Phoenicians, and the Arabians, assemble annually during the summer season to keep a brilliant feast; and many others, both buyers and sellers, resort thither on account of the fair. Indeed, this feast is diligently frequented by all nations: by the Jews, because they boast of their descent from the patriarch Abraham; by the Pagans, because angels there appeared to men; and by Christians, because He who for the salvation of mankind was born of a virgin, afterwards manifested Himself there to a godly man. This place was moreover honored fittingly with religious exercises. Here some prayed to the God of all; some called upon the angels, poured out wine, burnt incense, or offered an ox, or he-goat, a sheep, or a cock. Each one made some beautiful product of his labor, and after carefully husbanding it through the entire year, he offered it according to promise as provision for that feast, both for himself and his

---

103 See several reviews of recent scholarship: Aziz Al-Azmeh, "Pagan Arabs, Arabia, and monotheism," *Marginalia: LA Review of Books*, 1 March 2019 debates recent scholarship; Philip Wood, "Peter Webb, Imagining the Arabs: Arab Identity and the Rise of Islam," *AUW* 25, 2017, 178–183. David King, "The Petra fallacy: Early mosques do face the sacred Kaaba in Mecca but Dan Gibson doesn't know how," 2018, 1–54 debates recent pseudo-scholarship.

dependents. And either from honor to the place, or from fear of Divine wrath, they all abstained from coming near their wives, although during the feast these were more than ordinarily studious of their beauty and adornment. Nor, if they chanced to appear and to take part in the public processions, did they act at all licentiously. Nor did they behave imprudently in any other respect, although the tents were contiguous to each other, and they all lay promiscuously together. The place is open country, and arable, and without houses, with the exception of the buildings around Abraham's old oak and the well he prepared. No one during the time of the feast drew water from that well; for according to Pagan usage, some placed burning lamps near it; some poured out wine, or cast in cakes; and others, coins, myrrh, or incense. Hence, as I suppose, the water was rendered useless by commixture with the things cast into it.[104]

This passage summarizes crucial details about cultic practices originating in ancient Canaan, later Phoenicia, and adopted by Arabians of the Levant and greater Syria, including Emesa. Petitioners ostensibly cast cultic objects into the well. The "coins, myrrh and incense" situate the site along the network of Arabian spice trade. More importantly, the casting of "cakes" is a signature practice for the cultic worship of the "queen of heaven," and it points to the worship of the Canaanite goddess Asherah and her groves, which evolved into the cult of Mary the mother goddess.

Mother Goddess vs. Mother-in-Law

Sozomen then adds how at the behest of his mother-in-law, the emperor destroyed the site's symbols of pagan idolatry and erected a church basilica in its place—ultimately likening emperor Constantine to "good king Josiah" who torched the Asherah groves during the temple's purported restoration (2 Kings 23:4–14).

---

104 Sozomen of Gaza, *The Eccelesiastical History of Sozomen, Comprising a History of the Church from A. D. 323 to A. D. 425*, trans. Chester Hartranft, London: Bohn, 1855, 261.

Once whilst these customs were being celebrated by the Pagans, after the aforesaid manner, and as was the established usage with hilarity, the mother-in-law of Constantine was present for prayer, and apprised the emperor of what was being done. On receiving this information, he rebuked the bishops of Palestine in no measured terms, because they had neglected their duty, and had permitted a holy place to be defiled by impure libations and sacrifices; and he expressed his godly censure in an epistle which he wrote on the subject to Macarius, bishop of Jerusalem, to Eusebius Pamphilus, and to the bishops of Palestine. He commanded these bishops to hold a conference on this subject with the Phoenician bishops, and issue directions for the demolition, from the foundations, of the altar formerly erected there, the destruction of the carved images by fire, and the erection of a church worthy of so ancient and so holy a place. The emperor finally enjoined, that no libations or sacrifices should be offered on the spot, but that it should be exclusively devoted to the worship of God according to the law of the Church; and that if any attempt should be made to restore the former rites, the bishops were to inform against the delinquent, in order that he might be subjected to the greatest punishment. The governors and priests of Christ strictly enforced the injunctions contained in the emperor's letter.[105]

Sozomen illustrates here the raw power of Roman hegemony upon the heterodox Nativist church. However, we can hardly speculate about the existence of a disbanded ancient church without recourse to its beliefs and customs. These I argue flourished in tandem with the nativist theologies of Beryllus of Bosra and Paul of Samosata. My proposal is that three congregations—Mamre, Bosra, and Antioch—were loosely connected and complemented one another.

Remnants of a Nativist Church?

On a more general level, should the doctrines of the Nativist church be genealogically interconnected, as I argue, they account for the

105 Ibid.

blending of traditions favoring the queen of heaven, on the one hand, and those favoring the male Abrahamic god, on the other. From the three angles of Mamre, Bosra, and Antioch one can glimpse the very outlines of an ancient Nativist church at its height during the third century. The three sites come together, furthermore, to paint a complete picture of the doctrines followed by the faithful multitudes, with the cult of Mary the mother goddess thriving in Mamre, while theologies of God the eternal Father in Bosra and the Son of sacred marriage in Antioch complemented one another.

Although he was excommunicated and deposed from his post as bishop of Antioch around 269, Paul's doctrine lived on among the Christian faithful of Arabian society and certainly had some impact on subsequent Arianism, Monophysitism, and the shape of Christianity as a whole. Paul and his nativist peers are tied to so-called heresies which thrived in the Roman Oriens for centuries to come. Among these are the Messalians or "the praying order" of the Syrian churches and the Paulicians of Armenia.[106] The former group, condemned by all from Ephrem the Syrian to John of Damascus, were associated with sleepless night vigils, travel, begging and iconoclastic tendencies. They believed the persons of the Trinity were reducible to one substance which was physically perceivable through the senses.[107] The warning, "woe unto the praying folk" (Q107:4), while retelling Jesus' condemnation of the Pharisees in Matthew 23 and Luke 11,[108] may stand as a criticism of the relentless prayer and asceticism of the Messalians in later times. However, this point requires further examination. Elsewhere the Qur'an clearly attests to competing Adoptionist (Q 2:116; 10:68; 18:4),

106 Cf. Carlos Segovia, "Messalianism, Binitarianism, and the East-Syrian Background of the Qur'an," *Remapping Emergent Islam: Texts, Social Settings, and Ideological Trajectories*, ed. Carlos Segovia, Amsterdam: University of Amsterdam Press, 2020, 111–128; Christine Ames, *Medieval Heresies: Christianity, Judaism, and Islam*, Cambridge: Cambridge University Press, 2015, 121.
107 Cf. in relation Vladimir Baranov, "The iconophile fathers," *The Wiley Blackwell Companion to Patristics*, ed. Ken Parry, Chichester: John Wiley & Sons, 2015, 348; Wood, "*We Have No King but Christ*," 57–58.
108 El-Badawi, *The Qur'an and the Aramaic Gospel Traditions*, 129.

Dualist (Q 5:116), Trinitarian (Q 6:101; 19:90–91; 43:81), and Tritheist Christologies (Q 4:171; 5:73).[109]

I contest, finally, that remnants of the three erstwhile congregations of the Nativist church, once disbanded, may have remained intact and restored under the banner of the "middle community" between kindred Jews and Christians (Q 2:143). This was the recreation of Abrahamic monotheism in its Arabian context. Abraham was not its father, but rather its faithful "exemplar" (Q 2:130–135; 3:95; 4:125; 6:161; 16:123). Jewish Law and probably circumcision as well were viewed favorably but critically (Q 3:50, 78; 5:66–68). The abuse of power by an emboldened church hierarchy was viewed skeptically (Q 9:31–34; 57:25–27). And with time, strict monotheism, the signature doctrine of nativist theology, flourished among Arabian communities both within and on the periphery of the Syrian churches.[110] Throughout the fourth–seventh centuries these churches disparaged adherents belonging to the church but *still* abiding by nativist doctrine, that is Jewish laws and counter-ecclesiastical sensibilities. They were called "heathen, pagan," which in Syriac is *hanpa* and in Arabic *hanif*. One final detail about the counter-ecclesiology of this group is their rooted-ness, not in the urbanized church episcopate, but rather in the poetic and legal traditions handed down by ascetics, prophets, and charismatic holy men. The practice of strict monotheism according to prophetic tradition was known as *mashlmanuta* in Syriac and *islam* in Arabic—only later becoming the name of Islam as a global religion.[111]

---

109 Cf. Corrie Block, *The Qur'an in Christian–Muslim Dialogue*, 39–43.

110 Holger Zellentin, *The Qur'an's Legal Culture*, Tübingen: Mohr Siebeck, 2013, 163–164; El-Badawi, *The Qur'an and the Aramaic Gospel Traditions*, 216–217; Shari Lowin, *The Making of a Forefather Abraham in Islamic and Jewish Exegetical Narratives*, Leiden: Brill, 2006; Hamza Zafer, *Ecumenical Community Language and Politics of the Ummah in the Qur'an*, Leiden: Brill, 2020.

111 See full discussion by El-Badawi, *The Qur'an and the Aramaic Gospel Traditions*, 62–74, and further examples in the Peshitta, Ephrem the Syrian, Jacob of Serugh; the *Julian Romance*; and John of Ephesus. See response by Juan Cole, "*Paradosis* and monotheism: A late antique approach to the meaning of *islam* in the Quran," *BSOAS* 82.3, 2019, 405–425.

Paul under Zenobia

Having thoroughly situated Paul of Samosata's nativist doctrine in its Syro-Arabian context, his political and personal praxis deserve equal attention. By way of reminder, Paul was bishop of Antioch *ca.* 261–272. He was a well-paid procurator of Roman emperor Aurelian at first, and later for empress Zenobia of Palmyra. About his controversial role in the church and government Fergus Millar states:

> Paul, coming from Samosata, was the champion of the "native" (Syriac- or Aramaic-speaking) element in the Antiochene Church. His opponents were the representatives of Greek culture ... Thus a conflict of cultures becomes intimately linked to a political conflict. Paul owes his position to Zenobia, and his opponents' appeal to Aurelian will have taken place when the latter recaptured Antioch from the Palmyrenes in 272 ... [this case] also serves what appears to be the necessary function of explaining how the synod of Antioch could have petitioned a pagan emperor, and how that Emperor found it worthwhile to attend to their request, and to give it a favorable response.[112]

Millar hesitantly opens the door to the historical rise of late antique Syrian "nationalism" in the time of Paul, then firmly slams the door shut by arguing that Paul and his Syriac-speaking predecessors—Mara bar Serapion (d. after 73 CE), Tatian, and Bardaisan—were thoroughly bi-cultural, writing in both Syriac and Greek. The author is overly fraught by the "ambiguities" of Syrian-Greek cross-pollination by framing Paul's otherwise quite natural beliefs and practices in a Syrian context as "deviations" from an arbitrarily more robust orthodox set of beliefs and practices of Greek origin.[113]

Setting aside the tired scholarly routine of extricating Syriac beliefs and practice from underneath the oppressive weight of Greek "orthodoxy," we return to Paul. Besides his nativist doctrine, what did he practice, and why did his Greek- and Latin-speaking peers so fiercely

---

112 Millar, "Paul of Samosata, Zenobia and Aurelian," 244–245.
113 Ibid., 248–251, 273.

reject him? How did he fall out with Rome, who paid his wages at the time, and then find favor with Palmyra?

Paul's simultaneous role as procurator and bishop made him a lightning rod for the resentment and envy of later church historians and heresiologists. The caricature of Paul painted by Eusebius as a corrupted holy man, associating with women inappropriately and fattened by worldly riches and otherworldly illusions, can hardly be taken seriously.[114] But where there is smoke there is fire.

After leaving the service of emperor Aurelian, insofar as it is true, he likely held fast to the title of procurator rather than bishop given his outright rejection of the growing influence of the Greek-speaking church fathers and their imperial Latin patron in Rome. This rejection is evident in Paul's refusal to step down after being deposed as bishop in 269, leading to his forcible eviction by Aurelian in 272. The pagan emperor of Rome sided unequivocally with the Greek and Latin church fathers closing in on Paul in Antioch, and purging the city of Palmyrene loyalists.[115] The preference for his political title may also reflect his loyalty to the new leader and employer of the Roman Oriens, empress Zenobia.

Complementing this was likely Zenobia's need for Paul. As a wealthy Roman official of Syrian origin, she relied on his valuable political prowess as she did that of her other advisers. Certainly, Paul's office in Antioch planted loyalty to Palmyra among the population there. The symbiotic relationship between these two figures sets the precedent, I argue, for the pattern of delegating power by the female sovereign onto the holy man in subsequent Arabian communities, especially with the spread of Christianity.

Zenobia grew close to Paul sometime in the 260s, but certainly by the final Synod of Antioch condemning him in 268 when she frequented that city. As the preceding examination makes clear, the sources associate her with Judaism, either through Paul himself or Addas the

---

114 Eusebius of Caesaria, *The Fathers of the Church, Eusebius Panphili, Ecclesiastical History, Books 6–10*, trans. Roy Deferrari, Washington, D.C.: The Catholic University of America Press, 1955, 7:30 or 138–153; Millar, "Paul of Samosata, Zenobia and Aurelian," 263.

115 Millar, "Paul of Samosata, Zenobia and Aurelian," 262, 267.

Manichaean—neither of whom was Jewish in the first place! I contend here that Zenobia simply belonged to the Syro-Arabian nativist tradition of Paul's Christian congregation, which resembled Judaism in some ways and diverged from it in others. To this end Paul's congregation denied the divinity of Christ, but did not observe the Sabbath or circumcision.[116] This is not why the great empress would have submitted to the teachings of Paul, as the sources may imply. There are other reasons why such a powerful woman would find Paul's ideas appealing.

Prophet and Ladies' Man?

According to Eusebius, Paul was guilty of:

> Putting an end to the Psalms addressed to our Lord, Jesus Christ, on the theory that they are modern and the compositions of modern men, but in the middle of the church, on the great day of the Pasch, training women to sing psalms to himself, which one would shudder to listen to … But those who sing psalms to him and praise him among the people declare that their impious teacher is an angel come down from heaven … And his women, the *subintroductae* as the Antiochenes call them, and those of the presbyters and deacons among his followers … he has even made them rich, for which cause he is loved and admired by those who covet such things.[117]

Setting aside all polemics, this tract lists several nativist Semitic religious practices. First, clearly Paul's congregation considered him a prophet receiving angelic revelation. Prophecy was a signature of ancient Near Eastern religion, and it was inherited by the Syrian church fathers and subsequent Hanafite or proto-Muslim separatists.[118]

Second, the congregation sang local "psalms," which presumably in Syriac belonged to a more ancient, locally rooted tradition. This was

---

116 Ibid., 261–266.

117 Eusebius, *Ecclesiastical History*, 145–146.

118 Patricia Crone, *The Qur'anic Pagans and Related Matters: Collected Studies in Three Volumes, Volume 1*, Leiden: Brill, 2016, 318.

instead of the "modern" presumably foreign psalms imported by Greek-speaking church fathers. The potency of Syriac hymns or *memre* and Arabic prophetic speech or *saj'*, was manifested in the recitation verses in the original language, not in translation. Furthermore, this type of recitation may have influenced Greek hymnography.[119]

Third, there was the matter of "spiritual marriage" between celibate men and celibate women. Sacred marriage, as introduced already, originated with the sexual union of divinities in the depths of pagan antiquity. It was dramatized by the priest and virgin. And then it evolved with the patriarchal influence of Christianity into an institution of spiritual union throughout Syria and Egypt.[120] Sacred marriage became encoded in various biblical and Gnostic references to the temple's inner sanctum, the holy of holies or bridal chamber, where only freemen and virgin women were welcome (e.g. Philip 68–73).[121] The institution evolved by the fourth century into the monastic order of "solitary ones" and celibate order of Syrian "members of the covenant." The latter lived together, formed a choir and sang the hymns of Ephrem.[122] It is believed that some of Ephrem's hymns were in fact taken from the very women who organized and led choirs.[123] Despite the prevalence of this sort of "celibate relationship" as good ascetic practice, it was condemned by Athanasius of Alexandria, John Chrysostom (d. 407), and others.[124]

There is some evidence for wealthy widows practicing spiritual marriage or celibacy among both late antique Roman and Arabian

119 Vööbus, *History of Asceticism in the Syrian Orient*, 64.

120 Millar, "Paul of Samosata, Zenobia and Aurelian," 273.

121 Cf. Barker, *The Mother of the Lord*, 305–308.

122 See further Wood, "*We Have No King but Christ*," 52–54. See further Sidney Griffith, "Monks, 'Singles,' and the 'Sons of the Covenant': Reflections on Syriac Ascetic Terminology," *Eulogema: Studies in Honor of R. Taft*, eds. E. Carr et al., Rome: Pontificio Ateneo S. Anselmo, 1993, 141–160; Sebastian Brock, *Spirituality in the Syriac Tradition*, Kerala: St. Ephrem Ecumenical Research Institute, 2005, 52–54.

123 Susan Harvey, "Revisiting the Daughters of the Covenant: Women's Choirs and Sacred Song in Ancient Syriac Christianity," *HJSS* 8.2, July 2005.

124 Bardy, *Paul de Samosate*, 227 cannot contain his confessional objections. See further Patricia Miller, *Women in Early Christianity: Translations from Greek Texts*, Washington, D.C.: The Catholic University of America Press, 2005, 118–119.

communities.[125] It does not require much of an imagination to see how the most powerful widow at the time—Zenobia—would have found such a practice appealing. This is not at all to suggest that Zenobia herself was officially a "spiritual wife" or "daughter of the covenant." But there is evidence that this celibate order was composed of lay people, not nuns.[126]

Nevertheless, some may see in Zenobia's abstinence an echo of Thecla of Iconium (d. *ca.* 30 CE), who stood as a rare yet generic example of female power in the early church, and whose celibacy was celebrated in the second-century *Acts of Paul and Thecla*.[127] Actual marriage meant ceding or sharing power with a husband and was, therefore, a liability for so powerful a woman, fighting with Rome to her last breath. Be that as it may, my point here is that precisely what so-called "orthodox" church fathers found heretical about Paul's beliefs and practices, female monarchs like Zenobia clearly found quite attractive.

A Short-Lived but Profound Legacy

And so the story of empress Zenobia and Paul of Samosata is more than a tale of a ravishing queen and a gluttonous holy man as the sources may suggest. Their story, rather, is an integral link in the chain of stories about female power in late antique Arabia. The story, while complex, demonstrates vividly the religious and political culture of Arabian society during the height of its Hellenic and Roman influence.

125 Dyan Elliot, *Spiritual Marriage: Sexual Abstinence in Medieval Wedlock*, Princeton: Princeton University Press, 1995, 51; Nader Masarwah, "Marriage in Pre-Islamic Arabia as Reflected in Poetry and Prose: The Social and Humane Relations between Husband and Wife," *SS* 3.11, 2013, 850.
126 Menachem Macina, "Les bnay et bnat qyama de l'Église syriaque: Une piste philologique sérieuse," *PS2* 6, 1999, 13–49.
127 Polymnia Athanassiadi, *Mutations of Hellenism in Late Antiquity*, London; New York: Routledge, 2017, 125. See also Catherine Burris and Lucas Van Rompay, "Thecla in Syriac Christianity: Preliminary Observations," *HJSS* 5.2, 2002; Stavroula Constantinou, "Thekla the Virgin: Women's Sacrifice and the Generic Martyr," *The "Other" Martyrs: Women and the Poetics of Sexuality, Sacrifice, and Death in World Literatures*, ed. Alireza Korangy and Leyla Rouhi, Wiesbaden: Harrassowitz Verlag, 2019, 73–86.

Zenobia relied on the loyalty and service of great men to execute her will. In addition to Paul, they included the philosopher Longinus, as well as her generals in battle against Rome, Zabbai and Zabdas.

The Syro-Arabian realm during the third century was a time of great transition. In cities such as Antioch, Bosra, and Mamre—where I have argued an ancient Nativist church was constituted for some time—the nativist theologians blended the cult of the ancient mother goddess, Jewish monotheistic sensibilities, and local Semitic expressions of Christianity. Zenobia and Paul were architects in that world in transition. Their political and religious mastery was short-lived but left a profound legacy. The twilight of Rome's pagan emperors and the rising tide of Greek and Latin church fathers had vanquished the most powerful woman recalled in Arabian battle folklore. But she was not the last of her kind.

5

Mavia, Moses, and Arab Christendom (375–500 CE)

Jewish Arabia Meets Christian Arabia, Fourth Century

The elimination of Palmyra created a regional power vacuum, and disruptions to long-range international trade.[1] It also opened the way to Christian and Jewish missions who profoundly shaped the construction of "Arabias" in the north and south during the fourth century.

Zenobia had fallen, and the Nativist church promoted by Paul of Samosata was disbanded soon thereafter. Arabian rulers—imperial phylarchs, tribal chieftains, and regent queens—succumbed to Arian or Nicene forms of Christianity, as well as rabbinic Judaism. Beginning in 275 and throughout the fourth century, two blocs within Arabian society began to form simultaneously. One of these centered on the Roman-serving *foederati*, starting with the Tanukhids in Syria. The other centered on the Himyarites of Yemen. Around them, subsequent tribal and urban structures coalesced for the next two centuries. In particular, Christian communities in the north converted en masse through the partnership of tribal leaders, typically a king or queen, on the one hand, and a priestly holy man, on the other.[2]

Through conquest and diplomacy the Himyarite–Kindite alliance further absorbed tribes into their fold. Not least among them were the formidable Bakr and Taghlib in Mesopotamia, and the kingdom of

---

1 Emanuele Intagliata, *Palmyra after Zenobia, 273–750: An archaeological and historical reappraisal*, Havertown, PA: Oxbow Books, 2018, 98, 113. Cf. in relation al-Fassi, "al-Awda' al-siyasiyyah," 470.

2 On the rise of Arabian monotheism see Hoyland, *Arabia and the Arabs*, 146–150.

Maʿadd in the center of the peninsula, making that bloc the most powerful state in all Arabia at the time.[3] Tanukh spurred the northern alliance of Qudaʿah, whose members, including Salih and Kalb, would serve the Roman and Umayyad empires subsequently. The allegiances of both camps were diametrically opposed to one another. This was not by mere happenstance but by deliberate policy. And so the religious and political culture of Arabian society convulsed yet again.[4]

Maʿadd became increasingly subjugated under Jewish kings starting *ca.* 380. The founders of Jewish Arabia, so to speak, may be considered the Himyarite king Asʿad Abu Karib (d. 430) or alternately the Kindite king Hujr b. ʿAmr (fourth–fifth century). On occasion this realm found itself subjugated under the thumb of the Romans as well.[5]

Qudaʿah primarily served Byzantium as *foederati* and increasingly converted to Christianity by the fourth century.[6] The founders of Christian Arabia arose out of this realm. Mavia (d. 425) and her bishop, Moses of Sinai (d. late fourth century), became the matriarch and architect of Arabian Christianity respectively. This is their story.

The Historical Mavia of Tanukh

What we know of Mavia's war with Byzantium and her elevation of Moses to bishop comes primarily from the Latin and Greek church fathers. They were astonished by the likes of such a powerful woman, but relieved nonetheless by her rejection of Arianism and commitment to Nicene Christianity.[7] Her choice was more likely motivated by political if nationalist sentiment than it was any religious conviction—and we will analyze this too.

In the account of her contemporary Tyrannius Rufinus of Aquileia (d. 411), Mavia looms large. As our main source for the historical Mavia, Rufinus documented the Christian conversion of the three

3 Cf. in relation Hoyland, *Arabia and the Arabs*, 79.
4 al-Fassi, "*al-Awdaʿ al-siyasiyyah*," 455.
5 See further Webb, *Imagining the Arabs*, 70–71; Robin, "Les religions pratiquées," 231, 234.
6 Cf. further Sergius, *The Book of the Himyarites*, xlviii–l; Hoyland, *Arabia and the Arabs*, 157, 234.
7 Cf. Fisher, "From Mavia to al-Mundhir," 190–200.

great monarchs during his day: the king of Ethiopia, the king of Georgia, and the queen of the Saracens—Mavia. The sources also include her near contemporaries Socrates Scholasticus (d. 439), Sozomen of Gaza (d. 450), Theodoret of Cyrrhus (d. 457), and their imaginative compiler Theodorus Lector (d. *ca.* 543).

While good Arabic, the name Mavia rarely appears in later centuries,[8] making our heroine stand out all the more. Like her predecessor Zenobia, virtually nothing is known about the origins or fate of Mavia, leading her male chroniclers at times to substitute fact for confusion or conjecture. She was known to be queen of the powerful Arabian tribe of Tanukh between Mesopotamia and greater Syria. Her husband, the king, died without an heir, bequeathing his kingdom to his wife and queen. Beyond these barest details, about which there is no real disagreement, some narratives place her precise locale in Umm al-Jimal, just south of Bosra, while others place her in the desert of Paran, nestled between Sinai, Palestine, and Transjordan. The region is, at any rate, a coherent and contiguous body of land between Roman Arabia and the northern Hijaz. Outside of these literary references is a little-known place in the central Arabian desert of Najd, known as "Mavia's settlement," located on the trade route between Mecca and Basrah. The kings of Lakhm, Ghassan, and al-Harrah are said to have used its grounds for hunting and other outdoor activities in the spring.[9]

The very notion that a Tanukhid king betrothed Mavia as a slave, however, and that she dramatically climbed the social ladder to the rank of queen and conqueror cannot be entertained—it is a fantasy on the part of male authors. Her birth date is unknown, though we may generally posit the middle of the fourth century. She enjoyed a long life it seems. However, her death date is a matter of dispute centered on the person of one Mavia cited in the Greek funerary inscription dated 425 in Anasartha (Khanasir), south of Aleppo.[10] If this dating is correct

8 Sergius, *The Book of the Himyarites*, xcii.
9 'Abd al-Rahman, *Tarikh al-'arab qabl al-islam*, 112.
10 Cf. Fisher et al., "Arabs and Christianity," 311; Shahid, *Byzantium and the Arabs in the Fourth Century*, 190, 222.

then, following the death of her husband in 375, queen Mavia reigned for half a century *ca.* 375–425. And her resting place may lie there.

The Arabic sources name a handful of Tanukhid kings in service to Byzantium: al-Nu'man (thought to have lived in the third century), Malik b. Fahm (d. *ca.* 231), Jadhimah b. Malik (d. *ca.* 268), and al-Hawari (d. 375), most of whom are believed to have been Christian and the last of whom was reportedly married to Mavia.[11] Could one of these kings be the Saracen chief known as Zocomus, or the king Baslios named elsewhere?[12] It is unclear. At any rate, the Tanukh tribe were at the center of powerful alliances. al-Nu'man is believed to be the eponymous founder of Ma'arrat al-Nu'man in Syria, as well as Hirat al-Nu'man in Mesopotamia, thereby connecting them to the Lakhmids.

Alternatively, Mavia's origins likely come from the tribe of Kalb. Its settlements stretched from Palmyra in Syria to Tabuk in northern Hijaz.[13] The Kalbids were arguably the most numerous and powerful of the Quda'ah coalition. This mostly explains how Mavia secured so many allies prior to her military triumphs against the Romans.

Her biographical details are only part of why her legacy endures. Like all great conquerors, Mavia is most renowned for her victories on the battlefield and how she altered the face of religion. In this respect she was both a warrior-queen and a bishop-maker.

Warrior-Queen

Mavia conquered Arabia, Palestine, and parts of Egypt. Till the end of her life she remained undefeated against a series of Roman legions and garrisons. Her relatively short war with Byzantium was over her desire to install an Arab monk named Moses as bishop. Rufinus recounts the moment Mavia burst into history:

> While Lucius was behaving thus with all arrogance and cruelty, Mavia, the queen of the Saracens, began to rock the towns and cities on the borders of Palestine and Arabia with fierce attacks,

11 Shahid, *Byzantium and the Arabs in the Fourth Century*, 196.
12 Hoyland, *Arabia and the Arabs*, 148; al-Fassi, "*al-Awda' al-siyasiyyah*," 456.
13 Shahid, *Byzantium and the Arabs in the Fourth Century*, 197, 377.

and to lay waste the neighboring provinces at the same time; she also wore down the Roman army in frequent battles, killed many, and put the rest to flight. Sued for peace, she said she would agree to it only if a monk named Moses were ordained bishop for her people. He was leading a solitary life in the desert near her territory and had achieved great fame because of his merits and the miracles and signs God worked through him. Her request, when presented to the Roman sovereign, was ordered to be carried out without delay by our officers who had fought there with such unhappy results.[14]

Far from the palace splendor for which Zenobia was recalled in the sources, Mavia is remembered as a rugged fighter and an able military general. She had peers across the late antique world. Her predecessors in this regard included the Celtic revolutionary of Roman Britain, Boudica (d. 61 CE). And her successors included the Berber warrior-priestess of Numidia, known to the Arabic sources as al-Kahinah Dihya (d. *ca.* 703), who fought the Umayyads till the end. For her peers the humiliation of defeat and suicide (typically ingesting poison) became the norm, and perhaps especially so for female insurrections. Mavia, however, seems to have lived a long and triumphant life.[15]

The Egyptian hermit Ammonius (d. 357) was her contemporary. While he does not name her explicitly, his *Relatio Ammonii* attests to the uprising of the Saracens, and their attack of monasteries in the Sinai. He relates that they killed numerous monks, except a handful who held out under siege and ostensibly lived to tell the tale. The evidence suggests that Mavia's revolt was a major military engagement, amassing a "broad Arab confederation and … a large number of imperial units," ultimately engulfing the provinces of Phoenicia, Arabia, and Sinai.[16]

---

14 Rufinus of Aquileia, *The Church History of Rufinus of Aquileia: Books 10 and 11,* trans. Philip Amidon, New York; Oxford: Oxford University Press, 1997, 11:6 (67).

15 Shahid, *Byzantium and the Arabs in the Fourth Century,* 223.

16 Noel Lenski, *Failure of Empire: Valens and the Roman State in the Fourth Century* A.D., Berkeley; Los Angeles; London: University of California Press, 2002, 205–206.

But something is wrong with this picture. Why would a good Christian woman attack monks at a monastery in her quest for theological orthodoxy? It does not take an expert to recognize the egregious duplicity of such an action. Furthermore, historians do not doubt the hostilities in question. So it would seem, as historians rightly deduce, that Mavia was neither Christian nor particularly bothered by the minutiae of orthodoxy. In other words, throughout her confrontation with the Romans she was not interested in pandering to the squabbling gang of imperial holy men. She brought her own! Mavia was in fact pagan till only after hostilities ended. If she converted at all it was likely after the cessation of hostilities.[17] The nationalist impulse behind Mavia's revolt and her insistence upon Moses specifically, both of which are recognized by historians, I take for granted. Arabism animated every fiber of her political and religious calculations.

I argue further, that since the decline of nativist theology following the disbanding of what I dubbed the Nativist church by 320, and the exclusion precipitated by the Council of Nicaea in 325, Christian Arabs sought both vengeance and self-determination against their Roman adversaries. In this context Mavia was *not* the champion of an imagined orthodox or catholic doctrine, as the ecclesiastical sources lead us to believe. Since her adversary—Valens (d. 378) and the emperors of the fourth century—was Arian, it seems the Arab queen *merely* preferred Nicene Christianity in opposition to those men.

Another justification for war proposed by some is that emperor Valens provoked Mavia when requesting Arab troops to aid in the Balkan campaign against the Goths.[18] Mavia was supposedly unwilling, and the Romans once again had two insurrections to contend with simultaneously. The menace of Arabian and Germanic rebellion ignited a century earlier would continue unabated for generations to come. By the seventh century, barbarian wars on the periphery of Roman territory helped produce the caliphate and Franco-Gothic kingdoms. In this vein emperor Valens was tested not only against Mavia, but against Gothic king Athanaric (d. 381) as well.

---

17 See Lenski, *Failure of Empire*, 207 *contra*. Shahid, *Byzantium and the Arabs in the Fourth Century*, 154.

18 Ibid., 208.

Others consider Mavia's war an act of asserting authority, especially as a woman following her husband's death.[19] About this there can be little doubt. While the precise motivation for her military insurrection may be debated, none of the sources or scholarship dispute that Mavia's conquests were a show of raw, brazen power by a female general and monarch in the face of foreign male conquerors. Rufinus counted Mavia's conversion among her kingly peers, and Sozomen claimed she "regarded not the sex which nature had given her and displayed the spirit and courage of a man."[20]

The scholar would be remiss should she fail to consider how the "masculine" image of the warrior-queen fits within the motif of Arabian iconography. That is, the classically "male" characteristic of courage and chivalry, often represented as riding off to battle, evokes the images of the goddess Allat the warrior and her many counterparts (Athena, Ishtar, or Inanna), brandishing her lance and shield. Did Mavia fight on camel-back, did she hunt or keep lions, did she wield a lance and shield during combat? While we may never know precisely how Mavia appeared in battle, such details we would take for granted when speaking of male warriors, and kings.

Chasidat: Arab Martyr and Roman Noblewoman

Queen Mavia demanded and offered terms no different to a king once her war was won. She was now bound to Valens by peace treaty. Once Moses was ordained bishop and the future of her people secured, she agreed to dispatch Tanukhid military auxiliaries in support of the Romans in Thrace, desperately fighting for their lives against the emboldened and more numerous Goths. Before sending her people into battle, she first gave her daughter Chasidat in marriage to a Roman officer named Victor. Chasidat is said to be the Syriac name *hasidta*,

19 Cf. Glenn Bowersock, "Mavia, queen of the Saracens," *Studien zur zur antiken Sozialgeschichte: Festschrift F. Vittinghoff*, eds. Werner Eck et al., Köln; Vienna: Böhlau, 1980, 477–495.

20 Sozomen of Gaza, *Historia ecclesiastica*, ed. Edward Walford, London: S. Bagster, 1846, 4:20.

referring to Mary "full of grace." This may demonstrate the normative custom of Christian Arabs adopting Syriac names.[21]

Chasidat's marriage to Victor, and Mavia's alliance with Valens, built genuine bridges between the Romans and the Arab *foederati*. Chasidat is believed to have been a warrior and martyr of Mavia's revolt, and, after her marriage to a Roman officer, to have become a Roman citizen. This is why Victor erected a *martyrium* to his beloved wife in Anasartha, within Roman lands. And so peace between Byzantium and its Arab *foederati*—lasting some three centuries—was sealed by the first marriage ever attested in history between an Arab woman and a Roman man.[22]

Bishop-Maker

Mavia's motivation for war may well have been as much political as it was religious, the distinction between the two being largely artificial. According to Sozomen's retelling of events:

> Mawia, the widow of the late monarch, after attaining to the government of her race led her troops into Phoenicia and Palestine as far as the regions of Egypt lying to the left of those sailing up the Nile and which are generally denominated Arabia. This war was by no means a contemptible one, although conducted by a woman … as the war was still pursued with vigour, the Romans found it necessary to send an embassy to Mawia to solicit peace. It is said that she refused to comply with the request of the embassy unless consent were given for the ordination of a certain man named Moses who practiced asceticism in a neighboring desert, as bishop over her subjects. This Moses was a man of virtuous life and noted for performing divine and miraculous signs … he reconciled them to the Romans and converted many to Christianity, and passed his life among them as a priest.[23]

---

21 Shahid, *Byzantium and the Arabs in the Fourth Century*, 236–237.
22 Ibid., 232–233.
23 Sozomen, *Historia ecclesiastica*, 6:38.

Mavia knew what she was doing. And Moses was worth fighting for. Following hostilities with the Romans, Moses mended bridges between them and the "many," presumably Arabian peoples, converting them and living among them as their ecumenical leader. He did not merely become her bishop. He became bishop to a new generation of semi-nomadic Arabs who now entered history.

Unlike his predecessors, the urban Beryllus of Bosra or aristocratic Paul of Samosata, Moses was a desert hermit, little more than an ascetic monk treading the path of Egyptian "Desert Fathers." His origins better resemble Paul of Thebes (d. 341) or Anthony the Great (d. 356). According to Sozomen, Moses was the first *ethnically* Arab bishop ministering to the believing multitudes of Arabian society.[24] He paved the way for Arab holy men operating under the Nicene churches. These included his West Syrian successor, Maras of Anasartha, named in the Synod of Antioch 445; and his East Syrian successors, Barhadbshabba of Hulwan/Beth 'Arbaya (d. seventh century) and George, Bishop of the Arabs (d. 725), whose bishopric starting 686 served the Arabs of Tanukh, Tayyi', and 'Uqayl under Umayyad rule. Moses pioneered the movement of desert fathers turned bishops, the language of which is palpable in the "priests and monks" extolled in Q 5:82.[25]

One final detail about Mavia's choice of Moses as bishop is in order. Beyond the political struggle between Romans and Arabs, the entire Near East was beset by schism and sectarian conflict between Arian and Nicene camps. The early fourth century was a sea of Arianism largely thanks to its patronage by Roman emperors beginning with Constantine himself. The only local population to take up arms to combat Arianism—to fight Byzantium—and turn the tide in the latter part of the century were the Arab *foederati* governed by Tanukh. This historical fact raises the question: for better or for worse, to what extent

---

24 Shahid, *Byzantium and the Arabs in the Fourth Century*, 156–157.

25 Emran El-Badawi, "From 'clergy' to 'celibacy': The development of *rahbaniyyah* between Qur'an, Hadith and Church Canon," *AB* 11.1, 2013, 1–14; Holger Zellentin, "Ahbar and Ruhban: Religious leaders in the Qur'an in dialogue with Christian and Rabbinic literature," *Qur'anic Studies Today*, eds. Michael Sells and Angelika Neuwirth, London; New York: Routledge, 2016, 262–293.

would all the peoples of the Near East have accepted Nicene Christianity and rejected Arianism were it not for Mavia's revolt or Moses' mission? We will never know the answer to this question, but we can scrutinize the person of Moses.

Moses and the Arabian Flock

Virtually nothing is known of Moses beyond his service to Mavia's cause. He exhibited the qualities of late Roman holy men throughout Syria and Egypt. He was possibly born in Palestine, but lived as a hermit in Sinai before his rise to bishop for his great queen's realm.[26] He may have been the second Moses, after his biblical namesake (Exodus 34:29), to descend from the mountains of Sinai onto the pages of history. But he was the first Arab desert father.

After conquering most of the Roman East, Mavia entrusted her Arabian flock to Moses. In this respect, Moses typifies the rising "local power" of the Arabs, and the "usurped authority" of their queen Mavia.[27] His reported humility and reluctance to accept the office of bishop shone, in stark contrast to the power-hungry urbanites who acceded to the bishoprics of Alexandria, Carthage, or Rome. Many of them, in the words of emperor Constantine, wrought "discord and hatred" in the wake of the Council of Nicaea. At least this is how Moses is represented in the sources. In his exposition on him, Rufinus states:

> Moses was taken and brought to Alexandria, as was usual, to receive the priesthood. Lucius, to whom the ceremony of ordination was entrusted, was present. Moses, when he saw him, said to the officers who were there and were anxious to make haste, and to the people, "I do not think that I am worthy of such a great priesthood, but if it is judged that some part of God's providence is to be fulfilled in me, unworthy as I am, then I swear by our god, the Lord of heaven and earth, that Lucius shall not lay on me his hands, defiled and stained as they are by the blood of the saints." Lucius, seeing himself branded with so heavy a reproach in the eyes of the

26 Shahid, *Byzantium and the Arabs in the Fourth Century*, 185.
27 Cf. Brown, *Power and Persuasion in Late Antiquity*, 5.

multitude, said, "Why, Moses, do you so easily condemn one whose faith you do not know? Or if someone has told you something different about me, listen to my creed, and believe yourself rather than others." "Lucius," he replied, "stop trying to assail even me with your delusions. I know well your creed, which God's servants condemned to the mines declare, as do the bishops driven into exile, the presbyters and deacons banished to dwellings beyond the pale of the Christian religion, and the others handed over some to the beasts and some even to fire. Can the faith be truer which is perceived by the ears than that which is seen by the eyes? I am sure that those with a correct belief in Christ do not do such things." And thus Lucius, now loaded with even more disgrace, was forced to agree that he might receive the priesthood from the bishops he had driven into exile, since the need to look to the welfare of the state was so pressing. Having received it, he both preserved the peace with that fiercest of peoples and maintained unimpaired the heritage of the catholic faith.[28]

Moses' adamant rejection of Alexandria's Arian bishop, Lucius, stands out. He is accused of persecuting Nicene Christians, driving their bishops, presbyters, and deacons into exile. The story goes that Moses ultimately came to accept his post as bishop, but only through the ordination of the righteous bishops returned from exile. The passage almost suggests the sectarian animosity outweighed any political calculation, but may otherwise be attributed to the fact that our sources on Mavia are "ecclesiastical histories" whose point it was to tell the story of the victorious so-called "orthodox" or "catholic" faith.[29] In any case, the most salient credentials of Moses as a Near Eastern holy man are, however, his threefold role as:

(1) Miracle worker
(2) Mediator
(3) Missionary

28 Rufinus, *The Church History of Rufinus of Aquileia*, 11:6 (68).
29 Cf. in relation Lenski, *Failure of Empire*, 205; Wood, *"We Have No King but Christ,"* 27.

Miracle Worker

Sozomen mentions his "divine and miraculous signs." We are not told what these miracles are specifically, but we may speculate by examining the *topoi* of Syriac hagiography. Theodoret expounds upon the ideal "type" of bishop in greater Syria, which is where Arabian holy men were forged. They were bolstered by ascetic practice and given divine approval through miracles. The charismatic and flamboyant qualities of rather wild ascetics conflicted at times with Theodoret's heresiographical propensities, which is a matter on its own.[30]

Be that as it may, in the fourth century the most rudimentary miracle attributed to the "missionary bishop" was healing, which may well be what believers saw in Moses. The miracles increase in sophistication over the course of the fifth–seventh centuries, as holy men presented the miracles of "doctrinal clarity, rhetorical skills, and epistolary persuasion."[31] In other words, eloquent speech came to be viewed as miraculous. During this time, Syro-Arabian communities were home to ever more monks, nuns, and various monasteries and nunneries situated amid the biblical deserts of Sinai, Midian, and beyond, reaching deep into the Hijaz.[32]

The evolution of Near Eastern miracles during this time is telling. For it is worthy of note that the shift in appealing to believers through emotion—healing—to the intellect—clarity, rhetoric, and persuasion—distinguishes Moses of Sinai from his successor, Muhammad, to whom we turn in the next chapter.

Mediator

Sozomen also credits Moses with reconciling his people to the Romans. In so doing he embodied the role of the bishop as a mediator for the people of later generations, interceding for the forgiveness of sins, but

30 Wood, *"We Have No King but Christ,"* 39, 47–49.
31 Saint-Laurent, *Missionary Stories and the Formation of the Syriac Churches*, 87.
32 Shahid, *Byzantium and the Arabs in the Fifth Century*, 405–409.

also keeping the peace.[33] By the fifth century, precisely when bishops and emperors fractured Near Eastern Christendom into its three major churches, they had amassed unparalleled political power, and become "senators of the church."[34] Nevertheless, as mediator between his people on the one hand and great empires on the other, Moses anticipated the function of "protector of the people." During times of crisis, Christian populations routinely looked to their bishop for protection and mediation. One example of bishops playing this role came after the sectarian violence between Jews and Christians in the South Arabian city of Najran. The conference of Ramlah in 523 was attended by mediators and monarchs who cooperated in liberating the Christian population there.[35] Moses also anticipated the hagiographies of Islamic tradition, or Sirah, where among other functions the youthful Muhammad was viewed as a mediator among Arab factions, namely the tribes of Aws and Khazraj in Yathrib.[36]

Missionary

The final detail Sozomen shares with respect to Moses is that he "converted many to Christianity," thereby fulfilling his role as a missionary to the Arabs. His mission paved the way for future waves of Syriac-speaking bishops and Arabic-speaking prophets for generations. As discussed earlier, Moses was the first missionary of his kind. He was the architect of what some consider the beginnings of an "Arab

33 Claudia Rapp, *Holy Bishops in Late Antiquity: The Nature of Christian Leadership in an Age of Transition*, Berkeley: University of California Press, 2013, 88, 269, 301. See further Greg Fisher, "Reflections on Arab leadership in Late Antiquity," *To the Madbar and Back Again: Studies in the Languages, Archaeology, and Cultures of Arabia Dedicated to Michael C.A. Macdonald*, ed. Laïla Nehmé et al., Leiden: Brill, 2018, 489–521.

34 Rapp, *Holy Bishops in Late Antiquity*, 301. See further Rafal Kosinski, *Holiness and Power: Constantinopolitan Holy Men and Authority in the 5th Century*, Berlin: De Gruyter, 2016.

35 Cf. Wood, *"We Have No King but Christ,"* 222–223; Irfan Shahid "Byzantino-Arabica: The Conference of Ramla, A.D. 524," *JNES* 23, 1964, 115–131.

36 F. E. Peters, *Muhammad and the Origins of Islam*, Albany: SUNY Press, 1994, 192.

national church," lending cohesion to the *foederati* identified with Quda'ah and the rumblings of a unified North Arabia.[37]

The Legendary Mawiyah bt. 'Afzar

Mavia joined the constellations of pre-Islamic Arabian battle folklore and poetry. Sozomen claims the Saracens celebrated the victories of their queen Mavia in songs.[38] And she is both remembered and reimagined by posterity. For the medieval Arabic sources, I argue, the historical Mavia of Tanukh was refashioned as the sixth-century literary heroine of Arabic poetry, Mawiyah bt. 'Afzar, "queen of the Arabs." This identification is contemplated by Irfan Shahid in passing. However, this is only one in a series of names attested in the sources, some of which he tries to forcibly harmonize with Mavia.

The Arabic sources offer little conclusive evidence pointing to our Mavia. In his *Comprehensive Genealogy* Ibn al-Kalbi lists two women with this name: Mawiyah bt. Ka'b b. al-Qayn and Mawiyah bt. Julayy b. Ahmas. Mawiyah bt. 'Awf b. Jusham, nicknamed Ma' al-Sama' or "waterfall of heaven" on account of her beauty, was wife to king Nu'man II b. al-Aswad (d. 503) and mother to al-Mundhir III b. Nu'man (d. 554). The latter, whose notorious paganism and persecution of "Romans" or "Christians" is addressed later, was famously known in matrilineal terms. In other words he is identified as the son of his mother. The Arabic sources call him al-Mundhir b. Ma' al-Sama'. Her descendants were known as Banu Ma' al-Sama'.[39]

The Greek-speaking hagiographer, Cyril of Scythopolis (d. 559), lamented the lawless raid on Palestine in 503 by "al-Mundhir son of Sikika," known as "Mundhir son of Zaqiqa" in the Syriac *Book of the Himyarites*.[40] There may or may not be any connection between the names Sikika/Zaqiqa and Ma' al-Sama'. Whatever the case, she was

---

37 Cf. Shahid, *Byzantium and the Arabs in the Fourth Century*, 92, 158, 290, 339.
38 Webb, *Imagining the Arabs*, 242.
39 See Ibn al-Kalbi, *Jamharat al-nasab*, 23, 189; Ibn Sa'd, *Tabaqat*, 1:33.
40 Cyril of Scythopolis, *The Lives of the Monks of Palestine*, trans. R. M. Price, Collegeville: Cistercian Publications, 1991, 230; Sergius, *The Book of the Himyarites*, ciii.

evidently a prominent Lakhmid queen whose name was worthy of recording.

Otherwise, Mawiyah appears as: a tribal bloc or *batn* of the Azd tribe; Mawiyah bt. Malik b. Zayd-Manat b. Hubal;[41] two of the martyrs in Najran;[42] and finally as the matronymic to the Banu Mawiyah of the Kalb tribe.[43] Shahid's efforts to synchronize the disparate women with our protagonist, while valiant, are too noncommittal and inconclusive. Ibn Saʿd lists only Mawiyah the slave of Hujayr whose life in the seventh century is too far removed for consideration.[44]

That being said, it may be accepted, as Shahid suggests, that echoes of the historical Mavia of Tanukh are preserved in more than one of the source references. I assert they are namely: (1) the Banu Mawiyah which appears to be a matrilineal label, (2) and Mawiyah bt. ʾAfzar to whom we turn now. The stories and poems surrounding Mawiyah bt. ʾAfzar are the only lengthy narrative among the Mawiyahs found in the Arabic sources, and thus the right starting point for this examination. But we need to analyze them with care.

Critical Analysis of the Arabic Sources

First, the patronymic Banu ʾAfzar is not attested in the genealogical collections and should be, therefore, understood symbolically rather than historically. This legendary figure possibly developed, in part, from the more fantastical stories in the existing fragments of Theodorus Lector (d. *ca.* 543), who perpetuated the narrative of a romance between a young slave girl and a wealthy Arab king introduced earlier. Her story of choosing a suitor among the finest poets in particular underscores her wealth and freedom before the *crème de la crème* of Arabia's most eligible bachelors. The story is cobbled together from different sources, but principally told in the famous *Book of Songs*

---

41 Ibn al-Kalbi, *Nasab maʿadd wal-yaman al-kabir*, 289.
42 Sergius, *The Book of the Himyarites*, cxxi.
43 Shahid, *Byzantium and the Arabs in the Fourth Century*, 196–197.
44 Ibn Saʿd, *Tabaqat*, 10:285, and see further 8:354; 9:235.

(*Kitab al-aghani*) by the Persian historian and poet Abu al-Faraj al-Isfahani (d. 356/967).[45]

Second, Mawiyah bt. 'Afzar is primarily known in the Arabic sources for her marriage to the wealthy nobleman and poet of the Tayyi' tribe, Hatim al-Ta'i (d. 578), for whom the city of Ha'il is famous.[46] He also typifies the Arab norms of generosity and hospitality.[47] I contend that the marriage of Mawiyah and Hatim is not historical, but represents rather the competition between male power and female power, and the demonization of the latter. The sources extol Hatim's generosity and faith, while Mawiyah is depicted as a rash woman, fretful of her children going hungry—qualities rather unbecoming of a powerful monarch or chieftain.[48]

Third, the stories use literary mechanisms and *topoi* like those preserved in the story between al-Zabba' and Jadhimah narrated by 'Adi b. Zayd via Ibn al-Kalbi, explored in the preceding chapter. Both storylines situate their locus of narration amid the grandeur of the royal court in al-Hirah in Mesopotamia, and its great Christian kings, queens, and poets. However, placing Mawiyah bt. 'Afzar in al-Hirah indirectly speaks to the power of her queenship, as the city was the abode of Arabia's great Christian monarchs on the eve of Islam.

Fourth, Mavia's absolute power is buttressed by her lofty title in the sources, "queen of the Arabs." This title suggests her uncontested sovereignty over the realm. It equates her with the men attested to in the sources as "kings of the Arabs," which intriguingly list al-Zabba' (Zenobia) as a king not a queen.[49] This title applied to monarchs who controlled Arabian communities stretching from Syria to deep within the peninsula. They include the Lakhmid king Imru al-Qays b. 'Amr

45 Abu al-Faraj al-Isfahani, *Kitab al-aghani*, ed. Muhammad Ibrahim, Cairo: al-Hay'ah al-Misriyyah al-'Ammah lil-Kitab, 1993, 17:387–392. See further 'Umar Kahalah, *A'lam al-nisa' fi 'alamay al-'arab wa-l-islam*, Beirut: Mu'assasat al-Risalah, 2008, 5:13–20.

46 'Abd al-Rahman al-Ansari and F. Yusuf, *Ha'il: dayrat hatim*, Riyadh: Dar al-Qawafil, 2005; Hatoon al-Fassi, "*Mintaqat al-ha'il qabl al-islam*," *Mawsu'at al-mamlakat al-'arabiyyah al-su'udiyyah/Encyclopedia of Saudi Arabia*, vol. 14, Riyadh: Maktabat al-Malik 'Abda al-'Aziz al-'Ammah, 2007, 117–131.

47 *Diwan hatim al-ta'i*, ed. Ahmad Rashad, Beirut: Dar al-Kutub al-'Ilmiyyah, 2002, 3–6.

48 al-Fassi, "*Mintaqat ha'il qabl al-islam*," 125a, 127b.

49 Ibid.

according to the Namarah Inscription dated 328 CE,[50] and the Qedarite king Hazael (d. *ca.* 676 BCE) explored in Chapter 2. The medieval Arab chroniclers struggled to locate a legendary queen named Mawiyah in the regal landscape of Arabian history. Writers situated her in different eras of Arabian prominence and memory beyond al-Hirah. Some place her in Damascus, harkening back to an Umayyad or Ghassanid context, while others place her in the royal house of Yemen and its earlier glory days.[51]

These testimonies warrant reflection, as I am not aware of any woman given this honor in the medieval Arabic sources. In this respect, her regal significance is paralleled by her Nabataean predecessors in the epigraphic record.[52] The sovereignty of a Tanukhid queen in the Lakhmid capital, while ahistorical, may serve as evidence of the alliance between both tribes after the fall of Palmyra in the late third century CE.[53]

Fifth and lastly, al-Isfahani's account represents the literary figure of Mavia as the archetype of pre-Islamic female power, to which we return in subsequent chapters.

All the Queen's Men—Hatim, al-Nabighah, and al-Nabiti

The stories of Mawiyah bt. 'Afzar, queen of Arabia, are first and foremost situated within the many stories about Hatim al-Ta'i. The stories confuse or conflate Mawiyah bt. 'Afzar with one Mawiyah bt. Hujr bt. Nu'man of Ghassan, along with various other unnamed wives of Hatim.[54] Their saga together was celebrated over a century after his passing, among the storytellers of caliph Mu'awiyah b. Abi Sufyan (d. 60/680) at his court in Damascus.

Hatim was the chivalrous knight of Tayyi', a tribe whose Syriac name *tayyaye* was synonymous with other appellations for Arabic-speaking peoples. They include the Ishmaelites or Saracens leading up

50 Bowersock, *Roman Arabia*, 138–143.
51 al-Fassi, "*Mintaqat ha'il qabl al-islam*," 125a–b.
52 al-Fassi, "*Malikat al-'arab*," 24.
53 Bowersock, *Roman Arabia*, 132–133.
54 al-Fassi, "*Mintaqat ha'il qabl al-islam*," 125a.

to the Arab conquests of Syria and Mesopotamia.[55] The Greek name for them *tayenoi* was yet more generic, signifying the Saracens at the Council of Nicaea in 325. They were likely from Tanukh rather than Tayyi'. The term presumably also referred to the Lakhmid assassin of emperor Julian the Apostate (d. 363).[56] While there is no denying genealogical confusion of the Tayyites in the Greek and Syriac sources, they seem squarely positioned between their Lakhmid and Tanukhid *foederati* rivals in the fourth century. This timing is precisely after the demise of Zenobia and leading up to the rise of Mavia.

In this context the "memory of Hatim," if it may be considered so, harkens back to a time earlier than the Arabic sources claim. It fits in more closely with that of the historical Mavia. In any case, Hatim is portrayed as a prodigious man of esteemed origin. As such, he is said to have visited the greatest courts in Arabia, including those of the Ghassanids and Lakhmids.

Male Courtesans

The queen Mawiyah bt. 'Afzar is portrayed as sexually covetous, seducing her male prey with wine—behavior which could signify female power were it not such a blatant *topos* by repressed male storytellers.[57] Be that as it may, the queen demands of her officials to bring her "the handsomest men they find in al-Hirah." They summon Hatim. He arrives in the city, but she is unable to have her way with him as he resists entering the queen's chambers or drinking her wine—another *topos*. At the palace he is startled to find so many young male servants toiling in service of the powerful queen. He asks two of the youths if they prefer herding the queen's sheep or death by her command, to which they express indifference. The queen was allegedly a tyrant who, furthermore, "married whomever she wished."[58]

The impartial reader may glean from the narrative, thus far, the presence of a "male harem" belonging to the great queen. Had the

---

55 Retso, *The Arabs in Antiquity*, 97–98.
56 Shahid, *Byzantium and the Arabs in the Fourth Century*, 127, 332.
57 Streete, *The Strange Woman*, 65.
58 *Diwan hatim al-ta'i*, 3.

genders been reversed—meaning young female slaves in service of a great king—the presence of a harem would be taken for granted without recourse to further evidence. Hatoon al-Fassi surmises, more generally, that the queen had "a number of marriages" without further specification.[59]

Male Suitors

We return to the story. Hatim has a change of heart and returns to ask for the queen's hand in marriage. He finds two worthy rivals already waiting at the queen's court. The first is al-Nabighah al-Dhubyani (d. *ca.* 604), the "genius" of pre-Islamic Arabia, renowned for his poetry about the battles between Lakhm and Ghassan, and those between 'Abs and Dhubyan. The second is al-Nabiti, a little-known poet from a tribe linked to the Ansar of Yathrib called al-Nabit. Mawiyah instructs the three fine noblemen to depart and prepare for a poetry contest. The winner of the contest will win the queen's hand in marriage. She states, "for I will marry the most generous and eloquent among you."[60]

No sooner do the eligible trio leave for their respective camps to slaughter camels in honor of their great queen, than Mawiyah devises a secret test. The queen dresses as a maidservant—a *topos* possibly connected to the fanciful tales of Theodorus—visiting each of the three camps. She beseeches each nobleman to give her something to eat. Her true identity unbeknownst to them, al-Nabiti gives the slave girl worthless intestines. She fares no better with al-Nabighah who gives her fat leftovers. Hatim—true to his generous reputation—gives her the finest cuts of meat from three different parts of the camel. Mawiyah stores each of their food contributions in a pot to spring upon each nobleman when the time is right. The next day, the poetry contest commences before the court of Mawiyah, who has now returned to her queenly grace upon the throne. al-Nabiti goes first, reciting an eloquent poem and receiving the queen's praise. al-Nabighah goes second, reciting a similarly sturdy poem and receives praise. Hatim goes last and recites the following poem:

---

59 al-Fassi, "*Mintaqat ha'il qabl al-islam*," 126b.
60 *Diwan hatim al-ta'i*, 4.

Oh Mawiyah! Too long has been my escape and exile
    For just vindication prevented my seeing you
Oh Mawiyah! Wealth comes and goes
    And what remains of wealth but stories and memories?
Oh Mawiyah! I say not to the seeker
    who comes one day, "our wealth is meagre"
Oh Mawiyah! One is either stingy before the world
    Or generous, not even repulsing the wicked
Oh Mawiyah! What good are riches to a prince
    If his soul is crushed and his heart is miserable?
When those whom I love lower me
    into the dusty corner of my tomb
Then they flee hastily releasing their palms
    They say our fingers have bled from digging
Oh Mawiyah! When my corpse lies beneath
    the wasteland, no water nor wine will there be
You shall behold what I spent did not ruin me
    And that my hands kept nothing out of greed
Oh Mawiyah! I am merely a man seeking the refuge
    Of his mother, who can be neither killed nor taken captive
And the clans know if Hatim
    desired wealthy riches, he had it abundantly
And I do not hold back giving charity
    For it first abounds to be saved up later
To free the slave or to feed the noble
    otherwise stripped naked by wagering and gambling
Nor do I wrong my kinsman, even if my brethren were
    witnesses. For fate extinguishes all brethren
We lived long between poverty and wealth,
    Just like fate, in its days of difficulty and ease
We clothed the bareness of fate with clemency and hardship
    And to both have we given fate to drink in their cups
For harming our kinsfolk does not
    enrich us, nor does our miserliness ward off poverty
I have heeded not the blame of women
    While my ten fingers could grasp the finest possessions
Nor does it harm an ally, oh daughter of the clan know this,

who protects me, that he may not have refuge
My eyes see not the allies of my people
and my ears hear not what they say.[61]

Once Hatim has showered the queen with musical, enunciate wisdom, Mawiyah knows he would be her man. She invites the three suitors to lunch, at which each of them is presented with the same food they had given the slave girl the night before. The queen declares Hatim the most generous and the most eloquent; and the other two men go on their way.

But there is a problem. Hatim is already married! So Mawiyah agrees to marry Hatim on the condition he leave his current wife. This is a rather important liability we only come to learn about at the end of the story. He refuses. So she expels him from the palace. While galloping upon his steed heading back home, Hatim has another change of heart, conveniently coinciding with the death of his wife. So he returns to Mawiyah—one final *topos*—and the couple are wed, producing 'Adi b. Hatim al-Ta'i (d. 68/688), a prominent companion of Muhammad. But like all good love stories, it was not to last.

Divorcing Hatim

Another story, still more fanciful, is told about Mawiyah bt. 'Afzar and Hatim al-Ta'i many years into their now ripened and ostensibly fatigued marriage. Our heroine here is far removed from any semblance of power or palace splendor and is, for all intents and purposes, no longer a queen. She has been reduced to the life of a downtrodden and impatient housewife with little children. Their home is little more than a fur hut. This was otherwise a signature of tent-dwelling nomads.[62] It is said that Hatim's nemesis among his tribe was his cousin Malik, who was miserly and covetous. Above all he coveted his cousin's wife— Mawiyah. Malik approaches her, promising not to be a "spendthrift" on guests like her erstwhile husband Hatim. He promises to look after her, her children, and their collective wealth. Malik persuades Mawiyah

---

61 *Diwan hatim al-ta'i*, 5, 23–24, translated by the author.
62 al-Fassi, "*al-Awda' al-siyasiyyah*," 462.

with his repeatedly stingy advances, coaxing her. She is conflicted by this choice but eventually comes around.

She divorces Hatim, expelling him from their home. She then marries Malik. The two are wed and shortly thereafter a delegation of fifty guests arrives to visit Hatim. Not knowing he has been expelled from his own home, the guests become Mawiyah's burden. At this point the story resummons the *topos* of the slave girl, whom Mawiyah sends frantically to fetch food and milk for guests, first from Malik the miser and then Hatim the hero. Malik sends word to Mawiyah: "This is why I told you to divorce Hatim!"—meaning he would not give generously like his wife's ex-husband. He turns the slave girl away empty-handed. She then predictably makes her way to Hatim. He is a new bachelor, and his single life has him tending his herds in far-flung pastures. Upon hearing the request for help, he immediately releases two camels to satiate the hunger and thirst of his guests. Mawiyah is not satisfied. She is, rather, incensed by the ceaseless hospitality of her ex-husband, exclaiming, "This is why I divorced you; you leave nothing for your children!" Hatim does not flinch, but rather suavely breaks into poetry once again, instructing the audience about the virtues of hospitality and the iniquity of miserliness.[63]

The traditional lesson of this story flatters the chivalrous generosity of Hatim, and is not the primary subject of examination. But one detail is critical—the divorce itself. Mawiyah decides to leave Hatim for Malik, a decision the narrator implies she will later regret. She divorces Hatim according to the following pre-Islamic custom:

So women—or at least some of them—used to divorce their husbands in the *jahiliyyah*. And if they lived in a fur home, they flipped the hut around. So if the door faced east they flipped it towards the west. Or if the door faced Yemen [south] they flipped it towards Syria [north]. So when the man sees it he learns that she has divorced him, and he does not enter upon her.[64]

---

63 al-Isfahani, *Kitab al-aghani*, 17:387–390.
64 Ibid., 17:386–387.

This description is a startling revelation. It would seem some women exercised the right to divorce their husbands with great impunity in pre-Islamic Arabian society.[65] They did so independently, without consulting their husband or a counsellor, and indefinitely kept possession of the home and children in the process. The story only stipulates that "some women" practiced this form of what we may call "unilateral separation," and that Mawiyah was one of these women. Perhaps this qualification refers to Arabian women of a particular tribe or region, or just noblewomen. The latter seems more likely, given the portrayal of Mawiyah as the "finest woman of the people" in the very same story,[66] and her reputation as "queen of the Arabs" in the preceding tale.

The narrator's astonishment allows us to grasp the extent of the freedom enjoyed by pre-Islamic women. After all, Mawiyah both "*married* whomever she wished" and served as an example of women who "used to … *divorce* their husbands in the *jahiliyyah*." These valuable nuggets diametrically conflict with the patriarchal norms of traditional Christian or Islamic marriage. They corroborate, I argue, the far-reaching power enjoyed by Arabian queens and noblewomen on and off throughout antiquity, and the prospect of polyandrous marriage and matrilineal descent, which is the subject of future investigation.

Defenders of Constantinople

Meanwhile, our discussion returns to writings on the historical Mavia of Tanukh, and the army of fighters she dispatched to assist Valens in his Balkan campaign in 378, a fateful year. The dust had barely settled in the Oriens when Thrace erupted into war. Mavia's peace with the Romans was anything but free. And if its first phase was the marriage of her daughter Chasidat to the Roman officer Victor, then dispatching Tanukhid auxiliaries to fight for Valens was certainly its second phase. The Germanic Goths were on the move again, crossing the Danube River, south into Roman territory, driven out of their settlements in Eurasia by the rising tide of the Turkic Huns. Gothic–Roman skirmishes escalated to the brink of war, and Valens was desperately short

65 Masarwah, "Marriage in pre-Islamic Arabia," 848.
66 al-Isfahani, *Kitab al-aghani*, 17:387.

on manpower. The power of Mavia and her men had come to the rescue.

A century after the demise of Zenobia, the empire was once again in jeopardy. And once again its Arabian allies would come to its aid. Following the same route as his predecessor Aurelian, Valens made the fateful trek from Antioch to Constantinople through the mountain passes of Asia Minor. Mavia's "Saracen cavalry" then fought successfully in multiple battles alongside their newfound Roman allies throughout the Thracian Balkans south of the Danube.[67] This much we know from Greek historians, namely the soldier who lived in Antioch by the name of Ammianus Marcellinus (d. *ca.* 400), and the chronicler Zosimus (d. *ca.* 520) writing some generations later.

In light of Mavia's military consolidation as both Roman *foederatus* and her later reputation as queen of the Arabs, the Saracen cavalry may have come from a broader coalition beyond its Tanukhid core. They were, in any case, the successors of Syro-Arabian mounted archers who had served the Romans as auxiliaries in the past. These include the Osrhoenian mounted archers of the *Ala Nova Firma Cataphractaria* under the Severan dynasty (193–235) who fought in both Germania and Arabia in the third century, and the Itureans of the *Cohors I Augusta Ituraeorum* in the first century.[68] The "barbarianization" of the imperial military and bureaucracy reached its height, in fact, under Valens. And Mavia's Roman son-in-law was said to have facilitated the integration of her army into that of the legionary ranks in Thrace.[69] Mavia's warriors were, thus, the climax of a diverse and storied military tradition going back centuries.

Their renewed solidarity did not, however, save them from the furious Gothic multitude amassed against them in Thrace. The Goths all but massacred the Roman legions at the battle of Adrianople in 378,

---

67 Samuel Parker and John Betlyon, *The Roman Frontier in Central Jordan: Final Report on the Limes Arabicus Project, 1980–1989*, Washington, D.C.: Dumbarton Oaks Research Library and Collection, 2006, 539.

68 Shahid, *Byzantium and the Arabs in the Fourth Century*, 55; Salah Said, "Two New Greek Inscriptions with the name YTWR from Umm al-Jimal," *PEQ* 138.2, 2006, 125–132; Yann Le Bohec, *The Imperial Roman Army*, London; New York: Routledge, 1989, 23.

69 Shahid, *Byzantium and the Arabs in the Fourth Century*, 175, 266.

killing emperor Valens in the process, though Mavia's army mostly lived to fight another day. Smelling blood, the Goths advanced on the Roman capital of Constantinople later that year. Outside the great walled city one barbarian host repulsed another, as the Arabs finally confronted the Goths in an organized Arabian wedge formation (*Saracenorum cuneus*), this time breaking their ranks. Ammianus adds the rather grotesque hyperbole that the Goths were horrified by the sight of a bare-chested Saracen who severed the head of his enemy and drank his blood.[70] Setting aside the role of barbarian vampire propaganda in the service of Roman military history, Constantinople was saved. This was in part thanks to the ferocity of the Arab *foederati* and their formidable queen.

Arab Church Nationalism

Some of Mavia's troops may have remained in Constantinople even after the conclusion of the Gothic War (376–378). An increased Arab population in the city would be a logical conclusion. However, there is not a single Arab signatory to the next ecumenical council held in Constantinople during 381. Discontent may have grown among Christian Arabs, who, having pledged their faith to the Nicene Church and forged their identity in the blood of Roman battle, mistrusted emperor Theodosius I (d. 395), who assembled the First Council of Constantinople. Theodosius was, at the time, taking a significant risk by reintroducing Constantinople, which at the time was a sea of Arianism, to the Nicene Church. He invited prominent persons from among the Goths. These included their Arian representative Ulfilas (d. 383), and the anti-Christian Athanaric (d. 381) in his call to the council. It is plausible that Theodosius' imperial magnanimity towards the erstwhile Gothic enemy was lost on the Arabs, whom they had fought ferociously just years prior, and who were unbelievers in any case. In this respect Irfan Shahid claims that

> The Arab *foederati* were uncompromisingly orthodox and in this
> respect were intransigent, possibly even truculent, in their

---

70 Parker and Betlyon, *The Roman Frontier in Central Jordan*, 539.

Holy men with Mavia, Dayr Mar Musa

relations with the imperial government … A telling indication of the possibility that the Arabs were discontented might be the fact of their nonparticipation in the Council of Constantinople in 381. After their wars in behalf of orthodoxy and their victories over the Arians both in Oriens and in Thrace, it was expected that they would send a representative to the council, which, moreover, was composed almost exclusively of the Oriental bishops; but they did not, and the name of a bishop of the Saracens does not appear among the signatures.[71]

Mavia's men may well have been "uncompromisingly orthodox." This was not on account of any theological position, but for the mere fact that they fought and died to defeat the heathen Goths. It just so happened their costly sacrifice meant they were committed to Nicene Christianity. Their queen similarly fought to install Moses as bishop of the Arabs. Compromise was never part of the deal. In fact, it was uncompromising orthodoxy which united their tribes, defeated the legions of Byzantium in the Near East, and drove their armies to fight

71 Shahid, *Byzantium and the Arabs in the Fourth Century*, 205–206.

in far-flung Roman territories. Successive generations of *foederati*, including the Ghassanids, operated as cohesive "soldiers of the cross" whose loyalty to clergy kept the flame of their Monophysite zeal alive.[72] In this respect the conquests of Mavia and conversions of Moses served as not only predecessors of Khadijah and Muhammad, but also to generate an Arabian nationalist project through the church during the intervening two centuries.

Religious Unity before Islam?

Modern scholars dispute the moment of Arabia's genesis as a cohesive ethnos or national unit. At the heart of this dispute is the question, did "Arab identity" manifest itself before or after the galvanizing force of Islam? Among the scholarly cacophony introduced in Chapter 1 are anthropological studies, which despite erudite analysis and careful examination, come out on diametrically opposing ends of this critical question. Aziz Al-Azmeh argues "Paleo-Islam" was a force of late antique religious cohesion uniting pagan Arabs prior to the arrival of Muhammad.[73] Against this position is Peter Webb who, adopting the approach of "ethnogenesis," ascribes the "stirring of Arab communal consciousness [as] a consequence of Islam's spread."[74] Despite the apparent gulf between the two positions, there is a certain valence to both views envisaged around the weighty locus of Islam, either immediately before or after it. The former does not go far enough when considering the "scatterings of creed" before a backdrop of rather indeterminate paganism.[75] The latter's assertion that pre-Islamic Arabian communities did not share a common creed goes too far, because it denies the communion of many (if not most) Arabs with Near Eastern Christendom on the eve of Islam.

Even Webb acknowledges, as many before him, the role of religious creed—Christianity—in shaping West Syrian identity and community,

---

72 Shahid, *Byzantium and the Arabs in the Sixth Century*, 1:34.

73 Aziz Al-Azmeh, *The Arabs and Islam in Late Antiquity: A Critique of Approaches to Arabic Sources*, Berlin: Gerlach Press, 2014, 1–14.

74 Webb, *Imagining the Arabs*, 12.

75 Al-Azmeh, *The Emergence of Islam in Late Antiquity*, 368–369.

despite their lack of political independence.[76] Why Christianity has not been more seriously considered by scholars as a galvanizing force for Arab identity prior to Islam remains problematic. It seems probable—almost *inevitable*—given the sizeable list of Arabian monarchs who adopted evolving forms of Christianity for themselves and their people between the first and fourth centuries, that the institution of the church helped shape pre-Islamic Arab identity and community (and vice versa). In this respect the claim that "previously divided Arabian groups had banded together under a religious creed with a militarized outlook" starting in the second/eighth century is highly problematic given such a late crystallization.[77] There is no denying the sheer scale and unprecedented magnitude of the Umayyad conquest of the known world. It was an astounding era of disruption and creation. But it had lesser historical precedents. What of the Christian and Jewish sensibilities of the bellicose Quda'ah and Ma'add after Mavia? In other words, Islam was neither the first nor the only "militarized creed" in service of carving out a national, communal identity for the Arabs.

The possible beginnings of an Arab national church coincide with the *terminus ad quem* of North Arabian pagan inscriptions and South Arabia's turn towards monotheism, as well as a "high degree of Arab self-awareness" during the fourth–fifth centuries.[78] One of the architects of Arab self-awareness may have been Moses, the monk turned bishop. Its monarch may have been none other than queen Mavia. Their story compels the researcher to consider "Arab church nationalism" when scouring for the origins of pre-Islamic Arab identity and community.[79]

Historians formerly concerned with piecing together late antique Arabian masculinity have grown weary of repeating the words of clearly patriarchal, partisan and polemical Christian or Muslim men

76 Webb, *Imagining the Arabs*, 139.
77 Ibid., 155.
78 Grasso, "The gods of the Qur'an," 314 suggests these changes took place as early as the fourth century; Shahid, *Byzantium and the Arabs in the Fourth Century*, 157; Shahid, *Byzantium and the Arabs in the Fifth Century*, xxvi.
79 Cf. discussion in Fisher, "From Mavia to al-Mundhir," 200–215.

because they meet some standard of "authenticity." Their scholarly forays have thankfully considered piecing together a more comprehensive picture of late antique Arabian society. However, they are yet to come to terms with the centrality and complexity of female power. Should they search for a *historical* matron of Arabian Christianity, or a *historical* matriarch to an Arab ethnos, Mavia will be waiting for them.

Christian *Foederati*: The Legacy of Queen and Bishop

Given our examination of queen Mavia, she may be considered quite simply the matriarch of Christian Arabia par excellence. Her story stands out as an edifice of female power in late antique Arabia, both *against* and *in spite* of Roman hegemony. The imposition of her will upon great men—including emperor Valens, his officer Victor, and her handpicked bishop Moses—place her above them. Her stunning conquests came at huge personal cost, sacrificing her daughter Chasidat twice, first in marriage to the enemy and second in her martyrdom on the battlefield. Mavia ascended to greatness as a master of war, genius of diplomacy, and protector of her people, who were known to Greek and Syrian contemporaries as Saracens and Ishmaelites. To her Arab successors she was both recorded among the greatest monarchs of Arabia and disparaged as the lowly wife of the poet Hatim al-Ta'i.

Quda'ah's alliance was forged not only in the blood of Christ, so to speak, but in the bloodshed of Roman battle. The origins of this alliance are not entirely clear and its constituent parts are disputed. Much of the uncertainty is due to mythical, if not wholly political, genealogies marred by the 'Adnan versus Qahtan rivalry during Umayyad rule, to which we return in Chapter 7. Medieval as well as modern historians debate precisely which tribes belonged therein. What can be said with some confidence is that at the core of Quda'ah were the tribes of the protagonists of pre-Islamic Arabian battle folklore:

(1) al-Hawari (Tanukh)
(2) Mavia (Kalb)
(3) Hatim (Tayyi')

And their *foederati* kindred, including smaller tribes:

(1) Salih
(2) Juhaynah
(3) 'Udhrah
(4) Bali
(5) Bahra'
(6) Banu al-Qayn
(7) Jarm and others[80]

The invocation, indeed intrusion, of Ma'add or Himyar as grandfather of Quda'ah is, I argue, not a genealogical but political sentiment to which we will return later. For much of its history the kingdom of Ma'add was clearly more powerful than the Quda'ah alliance. Medieval Arab genealogists and historians, at the head of whom is none other than Ibn al-Kalbi, were acutely aware of the power dynamic between northern and southern Arabia. They sought to hard code the dominance of the latter within the "DNA of Arabia" as a whole.[81] The reader should not forget, while Ibn al-Kalbi was an invaluable source of knowledge of pre-Islamic Arabian society, he was, as his name professes, a proud member of the Kalb tribe.

The foregoing pages have demonstrated that while the warrior queen Mavia propagated the parallel causes of Arabism and Christianity, there is no evidence that she or her predecessor Zenobia practiced Christianity, whatever that may have looked like at the time. This dichotomy may appear curious at first glance. At second glance the reader will not be surprised at the reluctance of independent female Arabian monarchs to relinquish their hard-won power. As was the case with other Abrahamic traditions, any subservience to a masculine church hierarchy could scarcely have appealed to them on a personal level, not least given the sometimes misogynistic undertones of its clergy and scripture.

Despite her disregard for the theological disputes of holy men, and living the duration of her life ostensibly as a pagan for reasons already

---

80 M. J. Kister, *EI²*, "Kuda'a."
81 Cf. Retso, *The Arabs in Antiquity*, 475.

discussed, her legacy of "uncompromising orthodoxy" on behalf of her people lasted for centuries after her. However, the status of queen, or more precisely female phylarch and *foederata*, within Christian Arabia would not last beyond Mavia herself.[82] The power enjoyed by queens in pagan times was, as demonstrated in the preceding chapters, doomed under the thumb of holy men who crafted a church in their image.

Be that as it may, by the turn of the fifth century, Arabian society was (re)forged through the formidable forces of Christianity and Byzantium. Indeed, the Arab *foederati* tradition stands firmly upon the shoulders of Mavia—the pinnacle of female power in Christian Arabia.

The Missing Link between Nabataea and 'Adnan?

Could the tribes which merged into the Christian *foederati*, Quda'ah, have emerged from the scattered remains of the Nabataean Arabs after Roman conquest, and serve as the historical foundation of the imagined patriarch of North Arabia, 'Adnan? The matter is worth investigating, not least because Mavia—monarch over a newly Christian Arabia—played an integral role in the formation of the Quda'ah alliance as examined throughout this chapter.

There is no denying the Roman conquest of the Near East fundamentally rearranged the makeup of local communities, giving birth to new ones. In the three centuries prior to Islam, ancient kingdoms typically described by the sources as Nabataean, Qedarite, or Ishmaelite disappear from the record. They are replaced by new communities tied to the two dominant blocs introduced already: Quda'ah and Ma'add.[83] Modeled after the biblical table of nations, which transforms whole nations into legendary forefathers (Genesis 10), they were imagined as individuals forming the basis for all Arabian tribes. Quda'ah's genealogy, imagined no doubt, is fraught with contradictions between medieval Arab genealogists and historians. Some claim he was a descendant

---

82 Shahid, *Byzantium and the Arabs in the Fifth Century*, 152–153.
83 Webb, *Imagining the Arabs*, 5.

of 'Adnan, while others Qahtan.[84] The genealogical inconsistencies are the direct result of inter-Arab tribal conflict under the Umayyads, and Persian versus Arab ethnic rivalry under the Abbasids. Most common is the lineage Quda'ah b. Ma'add b. 'Adnan, which immediately appears suspect to the critical examiner because it reinforces the subservience of Quda'ah, and all Arabs, to Ma'add.[85]

Beyond the faintest cultural memory manipulated for political purposes, how much of Quda'ah's lineage is historical? Evidently not much. But still there are historical nuggets tucked away in the Arabic sources, hinting at the barest outline. Let us consider two cases in this vein.

First, there is a series of imprecise, anecdotal, and altogether unruly reports that Ma'add b. 'Adnan lived during the time of the biblical leader Moses, prophet Jeremiah, or Babylonian king Nebuchadnezzar.[86] What comes through these folk stories, however, is that the imagined patriarch of the Arabs—Ma'add—lived at the time of the Neo-Babylonian conquest of Arabia, and therefore vaguely recalls the Nabataeans.

Second, the Arab authors were troubled by the inconsistencies in the lineage of Quda'ah. We must not forget this was the very lineage of Muhammad the prophet. It carried, therefore, immense weight. Medieval scholars were reluctant to speculate about the lineage above Ma'add himself; though they did this anyway! The philologist Ibn Durayd (d. 321/933) ascribed this hesitation to the assertion that the names of generations prior to Ma'add were in Syriac and could not, therefore, be studied utilizing the Arabic conventions of the time.[87] This assertion, largely accepted by modern scholars, reveals two important details:

84 Hoyland, *Arabia and the Arabs*, 255.
85 Cf. Webb, *Imagining the Arabs*, 70–71. See further al-Fassi, "*al-Awda' al-siyasiyyah*," 459; Masarwah, "Marriage in pre-Islamic Arabia," 856.
86 Jawad 'Ali, *Tarikh al-'arab qabl al-islam*, Baghdad: al-Majma' al-'Ilmi al-'Iraqi, 1950, 18.
87 Webb, *Imagining the Arabs*, 210.

(1) Ibn Durayd does not dispute the Arabness of Maʿadd's ancestors, despite their use of Syriac.

(2) The ancestry of Maʿadd is located among the Christian Arabs of the late antique Syriac-speaking churches originating in the north.

This brings us back to the historical alliance of Qudaʿah, whose nobility often had Syriac names,[88] and at the center of which was its queen Mavia and its bishop Moses. They began the process of widespread Arab conversion to Christianity.

If the preceding analysis is accurate, then ʿAdnan (or Maʿadd) cannot seriously be considered the historical ancestor of the Arab people. He was more likely a symbol for a reified late antique Arab identity—a myth. There can be no single historical ancestor to such people. However, the historical actors who played a founding role in their solidarity, given what little evidence we have, is more than likely the bringer of both Syriac and Christianity to Qudaʿah and beyond. Among these historical actors was Arabia's most powerful Christian Arab queen, Mavia.

Qudaʿah in Pre-Islamic Times

Following their Tanukhid kin, in 410 the Kalbids raided the Roman Oriens from Phoenicia through Egypt, following the same route and strategy taken by Mavia it seems. And during the early fifth century, the Salihids became the next Arab *foederati*. The historian al-Masʿudi (d. 345/956) recalls their accession to power, claiming that after converting to Christianity the Romans made them "kings over the Arabs of Syria."[89] The Salihids were succeeded by a new influx of Arabs into greater Syria, namely the tribe of Ghassan, whose eponymous founder was reported to be Jafnah I b. ʿAmr (d. *ca.* 265 CE).

Tyranny turned to failure in the fifth century as the nascent Chalcedonian Church actively alienated heterodox and nativist branches of Christianity. These included the Arian Goths and the

---

88 For example, Shahid, *Byzantium and the Arabs in the Fifth Century*, 268–269.
89 See Shahid, *Byzantium and the Arabs in the Fourth Century*, 24, 411.

Syrian churches of the Near East. Like so many church councils before and after them, the first Council of Ephesus (431) severed ties that would bring about the rise of the Nestorian or East Syrian Church; while the Council of Chalcedon (451) severed ties with the future bloc of Monophysite or West Syrian, Coptic, and Ethiopic churches.

Some Arab converts accepted the teachings of the nascent Chalcedonian Church as an act of "defection" from Persian control and persecution. They include the tribal chief turned Saracen bishop, Aspebetus (Peter of Parembole) of the early fifth century. His story is told by Cyril of Scythopolis (d. 559) with the pious lore befitting the best lives of saints. The story goes that the desert father Euthemius miraculously healed Terebon, the once disabled son of Aspebetus, and the latter converted, even attending the Council of Ephesus in 431. He is said to have brought the "Saracen barbarians" to the holy man who converted them en masse:

> The holy elder catechized them all and received them into the lower monastery, where he baptized them ... Moreover, these men who had formerly been wolves of Arabia but had joined the rational flock of Christ begged to remain near him.[90]

Otherwise, Arabian tribes frequently belonged to the churches constantly under assault, especially by Greek-speaking church fathers and their emperor. It is little surprise, therefore, that relations between the Arab *foederati* and their Roman lords remained volatile.

Like their Arab predecessors, Ghassan belonged to the West Syrian Church when they joined the *foedus* of 473. This feat was achieved when the Ghassanid chief known as Amorkesos (Imru al-Qays—not to be confused with his namesakes of Lakhm or Kindah!) broke with his Persian patrons. He sent his bishop Petrus, a native of Roman Arabia, to advocate on his behalf at the court of emperor Leo I (d. 474) in Byzantium. This was certainly not the first time an Arab chieftain used their bishop as ambassador, negotiator, and spokesperson to the Romans, or as protector of their people. It was Mavia and Moses who set the precedent for Amorkesos and Petrus a century earlier.

90 Cyril of Scythopolis, *The Lives of the Monks of Palestine*, 20.

The tribe of Ghassan stayed true to the defiant spirit of its Tanukhid forebears. During the Chalcedonian persecution of the Monophysites belonging to the West Syrian Church, the Ghassanids revolted against emperor Justin I (d. 527), refusing to serve him for a decade or longer. Apart from this rupture the Ghassanids enjoyed the status of *foederati* on and off throughout the sixth century, with the exception of the *foedus* in 502 when the remarkably dynamic tribe of Kindah—likely the tribal core of Ma'add—settled Palestine and temporarily took its place.[91]

Remnants of Quda'ah in Medieval Times

The late Umayyad dynasty was dominated by the Marwanids (684–750 CE). They were a clan who developed a strong power base between Syria and Egypt, a feat accomplished through a series of strategic marriages. These were unions between Umayyad princes and Christian *foederati* princesses. The crowning achievement in this regard was the marriage of 'Abd al-'Aziz b. Marwan (d. 86/705), governor of Egypt, and his Kalbid wives.[92] The practice proved successful, and served as the linchpin of tribal dynastic succession. That is before the Abbasids took over and reoriented the realm towards a burgeoning medieval, Persian-Islamic culture.

There is evidence in the writings of medieval Arab historians, moreover, that remnants of the Quda'ah, especially the Tanukhids, Salihids, and Tayyids, remained stubbornly Christian during Abbasid rule. The caliph al-Mahdi (d. 169/785) was evidently exasperated by the persistence of Christianity among the Quda'ah of Abbasid Syria. He is reported to have destroyed some of their churches. Another report claims that a Tanukhid chieftain by the name of Layth b. Mahattah of Qinnasrin (Chalcis) proclaimed to the caliph that his tribe was maternally related to the Abbasids. The association of the devout Muslim

---

91 For discussion on Byzantine and Ghassanid leadership see Ball, *Rome in the East*, 109.

92 See generally Joshua Mabra, *Princely Authority in the Early Marwanid State: The Life of 'Abd al-'Aziz ibn Marwan (d. 86/705)*, Piscataway: Gorgias Press, 2017.

dynasty with the Christian Arabs of old threw al-Mahdi into a rage. He had Layth executed.[93]

Christian Tanukhids endured yet longer through Islamic times. By the thirteenth century CE at least one faction of the Tanukhids remained Christian. The late medieval Syrian historian Ibn Sabat (d. 926/1520) claims, rather strikingly, that they remained "loyal to their alliance with the Crusaders even at the very end of their occupation of Syria."[94]

Mawiyah bt. 'Awf and the Seeds of Pagan Revival, *ca.* 500

Back in pre-Islamic times, the cult of al-'Uzza was making a comeback. Our examination takes us to Mawiyah bt. 'Awf b. Jusham, known as Ma' al-Sama' (or Sikika/Zaqiqa). She was mother of the famously anti-Christian, pagan king of the Lakhmids, al-Mundhir III b. al-Nu'man. She was, moreover, queen regent of al-Hirah. Her name—Mawiyah—was an unmistakably famous designation of power and prestige among the Arabs. It was surely celebrated by the Lakhmids and adopted by their regnal elites. So, what if the Lakhmid queen, Mawiyah bt. 'Awf, shared a first name with queen Mavia of Tanukh from decades earlier? We ought to pay close attention.

If, as introduced earlier in this chapter and as the Arabic sources argue, al-Mundhir was famously known after his mother—al-Mundhir b. Ma' al-Sama'—rather than after his father, this implies a particularly strong connection between mother and son. Could this connection include the queen's raising of a prince to venerate the perennial goddess of Arabia's queens and priestesses, al-'Uzza the "queen of heaven"? Should this hypothesis hold, then unlike their Syro-Arabian neighbors who merged her cult with Mary the mother goddess, the Mesopotamian Arabs of al-Hirah worshipped her in purely pagan and zealously nativist form. Let me summarize:

---

93 Christian Sahner, *Christian Martyrs under Islam: Religious Violence and the Making of the Muslim World*, Princeton: Princeton University Press, 2018, 255–256.
94 *Chronicles of Qalawun and His Son al-Ashraf Khalil*, ed. and trans. David Cook, Abingdon; New York: Routledge, 2020, 27.

(1) al-Mundhir's mother was a powerful queen whose name was Mawiyah.
(2) She was likely named after another powerful queen, Mavia of Tanukh.
(3) They worshipped a powerful goddess, al-'Uzza, in opposition to the prevailing winds of Christianity.

Christian–Pagan Deadlock

Fifty years after the passing of Mavia and Moses, Arabia was beset by competing religious and political fires blazing amid renewed Persian versus Roman hostilities. Female power consolidated the still nascent foundation of the *foederati*, an institution which propagated a growing number of Christian Arab enclaves throughout the fourth–fifth centuries. But female power also contributed to counter-Arabism and anti-Christianity at the dawn of the sixth century, embodied by the pagan revival of al-'Uzza. In other words, the imminent clash between paganism and Christianity would decide the fate of Arabia as a whole.

The *jahiliyyah* was in full swing. And the tug of war between the Abrahamic god and the Arabian goddess would enter its final phase during the sixth–seventh centuries. Traversing this contested terrain would be arguably the last and most revered example of pre-Islamic Arabian queenship and nobility.

6

Khadijah, Muhammad, and Christian–Pagan Confrontation (505–629 CE)

UNLIKE HER PREDECESSORS Mavia or Zenobia, Khadijah is known to us through the Arabic sources of medieval Islamic tradition alone. The researcher is not aided by the slightest rock inscription or scrap of papyrus in divulging the power lady Khadijah embodied and bestowed upon Muhammad the prophet. The convulsions of the *jahiliyyah* saw the demise of the Hellenized city states of Arabian society and dominance of settled nomadic states by the fifth–sixth centuries. The era's volcanoes, bubonic plague, and various schisms caused further volatility and devastation. In short, these convulsions disrupted existing patterns of Arabian commerce.[1] The trade routes between Yemen and greater Syria shifted during this time. The old commercial artery running between ancient Nabataean Hegra and Petra, commonly known as the Darb al-Bakrah, was finally abandoned.[2] In its place a new route running from Mecca to Bosra, commonly known as the Syrian Hajj Road, was adopted by the tribe of Quraysh and its Hijazi kindred.[3]

That being said, the medieval reports of the Arabic sources, when read critically, continue where the Christian and Roman sources leave off, so to speak. The outlines of Khadijah, Muhammad, and sixth-century Arabia are gleaned primarily from the works of Ibn Ishaq, Ibn al-Kalbi, and Ibn Saʿd.

---

1 Smith, *Religion of the Semites*, 71.
2 *The Darb al-Bakrah*, 11.
3 Cf. al-Fassi, "al-Awdaʿ al-siyasiyyah," 471.

The Syriac sources, finally, inform us that "trade route culture" played a vital role in the meeting of east and west, and thereby the shaping of the religious and political culture of Arabian society and its environs, as well as the shaping of the Syriac churches.[4] More importantly, these sources preserve valuable nuggets with respect to female power in the sixth century. This is precisely when Khadijah and Muhammad forged their relationship, and when the Hijaz served as one of the final battlegrounds between Christianity and paganism within Arabian society.

The Pagan Corridor: al-Hirah, 'Aliyat Najd, and Mecca

At the turn of the sixth century, Arabian society was quaking in a state of civil and sectarian warfare. Mired in a growing stalemate between Byzantium and Ctesiphon, Arabia was locked in a standoff between its Christian, Jewish, and pagan adherents. The spread of Judaism in southern and central Arabia in the fourth–fifth centuries was abruptly halted by Ethiopian intervention, following the persecution of Christians in Najran around 523. At this exact moment the spread of Christianity in the north faced a major setback. During the reign of the Lakhmid king al-Mundhir III b. al-Nu'man, the cult of al-'Uzza returned as a bloodthirsty goddess raining vengeance upon the Romans, and Near Eastern Christendom generally, including the Christian soldiers of the Lakhmid army.[5]

To the church historians and heresiologists introduced earlier, the mention of al-'Uzza, whose name meant "the mightiest," conjured the image of a dreadful goddess of war, consuming human and animal sacrifices. This was for good reason. However, the matter is a bit more complicated. For, as introduced in Chapter 3, this goddess is a counterpart to the Canaanite Asherah, whose cult as "queen of heaven" was condemned by biblical authors for its idolatry and human

---

4 Saint-Laurent, *Missionary Stories and the Formation of the Syriac Churches*, 32–34, 112–120.
5 Pseudo-Zacharias Rhetor, *The Chronicle of Pseudo-Zachariah Rhetor: Church and War in Late Antiquity*, ed. Geoffrey Greatrex, Liverpool: Liverpool University Press, 2011, 289–290; Toral-Niehoff, *al-Hira*, 188–199.

sacrifice. During the sixth century, al-'Uzza was back with a vengeance. One of the chief proponents of her revival may have been the Lakhmid queen regent Mawiyah bt. 'Awf, as we have seen. However, it is her son al-Mundhir, the king in al-Hirah, who used al-'Uzza's name to both win wars and terrorize his enemies. The medieval Arabic sources suggest, furthermore, the vitality of the pagan goddess al-'Uzza and her priestesses in the Hijaz. This was long after the Nabataeans and concurrent with Muhammad's emergence in Mecca.

The cult of al-'Uzza had ebbed and flowed throughout late antique Arabia. By the sixth century it subsumed the tribes of:

(1) Lakhm in Mesopotamia
(2) Shayban in the highlands of Najd ('Aliyat Najd)
(3) Quraysh in the Hijazi city of Mecca

These locations also boasted orders of Arabian amazons—priestess-prostitutes. al-'Uzza's cultic centers included the valleys of Nakhlah and Suqam, the water spring of Buss, the forested altar of Ghabghab and garden of Bustan Ibn 'Amir, and a network of verdant landscapes and oases nothing short of paradise located in the blistering deserts between Hijaz and Najd.[6] We may consider the spread of al-'Uzza's revival from al-Hirah southwest through Najd and Hijaz a "pagan corridor," passing through the northern trading hub of Dumah. This route was famously trodden by the kings marching from Babylon or al-Hirah heading towards Yathrib and neighboring cities. The reader might consider the pagan corridor under consideration here analogous to such theoretical constructs as the "Shii Crescent" in the modern Middle East or the "Bible Belt" in the modern United States.

6 Yaqut al-Hamwi, *Mu'jam al-buldan*, ed. Farid al-Jindi, Beirut: Dar al-Kutub al-'Ilmiyyah, 1971, 1:492; Smith, *Religion of the Semites*, 103, 167–169, 339.

All the Goddess's Men—al-Mundhir, 'Abd al-'Uzza, and Muhammad, *ca.* 505–595

Back in sixth-century Arabia, Christianity had reached those very same regions as well.[7] The diffusion and worship of the Abrahamic god in Arabia was, nevertheless, disrupted in midstream, so to speak, by the pagan revival of al-'Uzza. At its origin her cult evolved from the queen of heaven, whose main adherents were women petitioners. The belligerence of the *jahiliyyah* transformed her into the mighty chief goddess of ghastly blood sacrifice. In what follows, I propose that the cult of al-'Uzza surged during the reign of al-'Mundhir III *ca.* 505–554, waning thereafter under increasingly Christian Lakhmid kings. This culminated in 594 with:

(1) The Christian conversion of al-Nu'man III (r. 580–602)
(2) Muhammad's introduction to Christianity or Hanifism through his marriage to Khadijah *ca.* 595

Setting aside the historical evolution of al-'Uzza's cult, should we consider its revival a resurgence of female power in late antique Arabia, then we are confronted by the appropriation of this power by men of war, priesthood, and prophecy. We turn to them now.

In what follows three men from among Arabia's elite demonstrate the enduring or revived legacy of al-'Uzza. They are:

(1) al-Mundhir III b. al-Nu'man (r. 505–554), Lakhmid king in al-Hirah
(2) 'Abd al-'Uzza II b. 'Abd al-Muttalib (d. 2/624), priest of al-'Uzza in Mecca
(3) Muhammad b. 'Abd Allah b. 'Abd al-Muttalib (d. 10/632), his nephew and future prophet in Mecca and Yathrib

---

7 Shahid, *Byzantium and the Arabs in the Fifth Century*, 390–393.

al-Mundhir—Pagan Revival and Christian Persecution

The religious loyalties of the Lakhmid kings throughout late antiquity is a complicated matter. Among their many appearances in this book, they have played a vital role in the stories of their erstwhile Tanukhid kindred following the demise of Zenobia, but prior to the ascent of Mavia. Like their queenly counterparts, the kings of al-Hirah incessantly gravitated towards and away from novel manifestations of the Abrahamic god during the third–fourth centuries. That they adopted Christianity of the "orthodox, heretical or of the Manichaean type" demonstrates the religious volatility among Lakhmid monarchs over this time.[8] By the sixth century, the Lakhmids had fought alongside or in parallel to their Sasanian allies, against their Ghassanid *foederati* nemesis and Byzantium itself.

The Lakhmid king al-Mundhir III b. al-Nuʿman was arguably the mightiest king in Arabia before being slain at the hands of the Ghassanids at the battle of Halimah in 554. In life he was a fervent worshipper of al-ʿUzza, and an ardent anti-Christian enemy. I have suggested that one major influence upon al-Mundhir's revival of al-ʿUzza against his Christian foes may have been his mother, Mawiyah bt. ʿAwf (Maʾ al-Samaʾ). He was a powerful, feared, and loathed commander. He vanquished his foes in multiple "great wars," before falling to the sword himself. His military engagements include:

(1) The Anastasian War (502–506)
(2) A battle against Maʿdi Karib (516)
(3) The Iberian War (526–532)
(4) The battle of Halimah (554)

His exploits included the conquest of Mesopotamia, Bahrayn, and Oman in eastern Arabia along the Persian Gulf, Najd in the central Arabian Peninsula, as well as greater Syria to the west, including the northern fringes of Egypt. The history behind these seismic events, and al-Mundhir's prominence within them, is known to historians and

---

8 Shahid, *Byzantium and the Arabs in the Fourth Century*, 32–34.

is not our immediate concern here. Our concern is how he treated prisoners of war—namely sacrificing them to the goddess al-'Uzza.

al-'Uzza and Blood Offering in Arabia

The ecclesiastical history of the Greek-speaking Syrian church father Zacharias Rhetor of Gaza (d. after 536) and the Syriac addendum of pseudo-Zacharias paint a ghastly picture. Shahid summarizes their insights:

> [al-Mundhir's] raids ranged far and wide along the Oriental limes, but what is relevant for ecclesiastical history is an examination of his raids on the Christian establishment in Oriens, especially his notorious abduction of four hundred nuns or virgins from the congregation of the church of the Apostle Thomas, his massacring them and offering them as a sacrifice to the pagan goddess al-'Uzza ("the most powerful"), the Arabian Aphrodite, in 527. He was to repeat this barbarity later in his career when he captured the son of his Ghassanid adversary, Arethas [al-Harith b. Jabalah; d. 569], in the 540s and sacrificed him to the same goddess.[9]

al-Mundhir's brutality against Christians was deliberate, brazen, and calculated. The reasons for this are threefold.

First, his burning of the four hundred virgins—a number likely exaggerated out of horror—in 527 coincides with soured relations between emperor Justin I (d. 527) and the Ghassanid king Jabalah b. al-Harith (d. 529).[10] In other words, the Ghassanids were weak when al-Mundhir struck them hardest.

Second, the Himyarite persecution of Christians in Najran during the 520s sent shockwaves throughout Near Eastern Christendom. This development only served to embolden al-Mundhir to follow suit.

Third, al-Mundhir's impunity continued unabated. Thus, he sacrificed the life of the Ghassanid prince in the 540s. This is when Himyarite

9 Shahid, *Byzantium and the Arabs in the Sixth Century* 1:2, 722, 732. Square brackets are my own.
10 See in relation Pseudo-Zacharias, *The Chronicle of Pseudo-Zachariah Rhetor*, 327.

and Kindite hegemony collapsed, keeping the Ghassanids weak and leaving the Lakhmids to reign supreme throughout much of Arabia.

Beyond his brutality with prisoners of war, al-Mundhir was reported by the Arabic sources to be a cruel king, a reality no doubt enflamed by good storytellers. But where there is smoke there is fire. It is said not even the court poets, courtiers, or confidants could escape his wrath. He was alleged to have slain or spared man and beast at his whim. This was his tradition during his annual "festival of cruelty" and "festival of splendor."[11]

'Abd al-'Uzza II: Pagan Priest of Mecca

In the Hijaz, 'Abd al-'Uzza b. Qusayy b. Kilab (sixth century) is remembered as one of the forefathers of Quraysh. He is dubbed hereafter 'Abd al-'Uzza I. His namesake, meaning "servant of al-'Uzza," was passed down a century later to Muhammad's uncle, 'Abd al-'Uzza b. 'Abd al-Muttalib (d. 2/624).[12] He is dubbed hereafter 'Abd al-'Uzza II, and the details of his reported enmity with Muhammad are revisited shortly. For now, we can say he is identified by medieval Muslim exegetes and historians with "Abu Lahab," the mysterious figure condemned to hellfire along with his wife in Q 111.

His mother was Lubna bt. Hajar, belonging to the Khuza'ah tribe who the sources claim were caretakers of the Kaabah of Mecca before Quraysh took over this office.[13] If true, she or her kinsfolk could have been the ones to bring al-'Uzza into the Kaabah's pantheon. This prospect may echo the pagan sensibilities of Lakhmid queen regent Mawiyah bt. 'Awf introduced earlier. Intriguing as this possibility may be, there is insufficient evidence for it.

'Abd al-Muttalib and the Oracle

At any rate, the father of 'Abd al-'Uzza II was the fabled Shaybah b. Hashim b. 'Abd Manaf b. Qusayy b. Kilab (d. *ca.* 578), otherwise known

11 Cf. Shawqi Dayf, *al-'Asr al-jahili: min tarikh al-adab al-'arabi*, Cairo: Dar al-Ma'arif, 1960, 45.
12 Cf. Ibn al-Kalbi, *Jamharat al-nasab*, 58.
13 M. J. Kister, *EI²*, "Khuza'a."

to Islamic tradition as 'Abd al-Muttalib. Since he is also the grandfather of Muhammad, the Arabic sources consider him a vital link in pre-Islamic Arabian genealogy. He is portrayed as a second biblical Abraham, marrying six wives from across Hijaz and Najd. They include women from the clans of Quraysh, Khuza'ah, Hawazin, and Namir. He is said to have fathered more than two dozen children, many of whom would become Mecca's ruling class.[14]

'Abd al-Muttalib is said to have made a vow to sacrifice one of his sons to the god Hubal in gratitude for good fortune. Before doing so he is said to have consulted an oracle. She was a mysterious woman by the name of Najjah, Sajjah, or Qatabah. The oracle reportedly served in Wadi al-Qura in the Hijaz, and probably in the vicinity of Khaybar or Hegra. And in the spirit of the biblical Abraham's sacrifice of his son Isaac, 'Abd al-Muttalib is reported to have made an oath to sacrifice one of his sons should they reach ten in number. When this came to pass, the ten boys drew lots and his most beloved son, 'Abd Allah, was fated to fulfill his father's oath. When the people learned of the boy's fateful ransom they intervened, citing how beloved he was to all the Quraysh, and prevented the sacrifice, sacrificing several camels instead.[15] Whoever the oracle may have been, whether historical or legendary, she likely served the chief goddess, al-'Uzza, alongside her consort Hubal. After all, it is not without reason 'Abd al-Muttalib named one of his sons 'Abd al-'Uzza. The name would become relatively common among the Quraysh during the sixth century.[16]

Cults of al-'Uzza in Arabia

Ibn al-Kalbi claims the cult of al-'Uzza was introduced to the Quraysh by a man named Zalim b. As'ad of Ghatafan. He is said to have chosen the lush green oasis of Nakhlah, beneath which gushed a spring called Buss. There he built a cubic shrine or temple known in Arabic as a *ka'bah*, dedicating it to the goddess. According to tradition it rivaled the Kaabah of Mecca. The Arabic sources claim, furthermore, that

14 Ibn Sa'd, *Tabaqat*, 20–28.
15 Ibn Ishaq, *Sirah*, 85–93; Ibn Sa'd, *Tabaqat*, 1:69–74.
16 See Ibn al-Kalbi, *Jamharat al-nasab*, 695.

even male high priests from the tribe of Shayban, especially its Sulaymid bloc, served the goddess al-'Uzza.[17] Epigraphic evidence suggests the antiquity of the Sulaymids goes back to the Nabataean *shalamu* near Hegra. This may, in part, explain the especially deep roots of al-'Uzza's cultic servants among them.

The names of Arabian priestesses from the sources include:

(1) Fatimah bt. Murr al-Khath'amiyyah in Mecca
(2) Zarqa' al-Yamamah in Najd
(3) Turayfah of Yemen
(4) Zabra' of Hadramawt

Male priests include:

(1) Salman from the tribe of Hamdan
(2) Hadas from the tribe of Ghanam
(3) Dubayyah b. Harami of Sulaym, who is the last among them all and to whom we return later[18]

There were surely more whose names and stories went unrecorded. And the details of stories we have may be embellished by medieval storytellers. However, the mention of multiple priests and priestesses therein bespeaks a rich tradition where female power remained part and parcel of pagan Arabia's religious and political culture during the sixth century.

It is said that word of a new pagan shrine reached Zuhayr b. Janab al-Kalbi (d. 564), the indefatigable poet-chieftain of Quda'ah. He is portrayed as larger than life in the sources.[19] The news of new pagan shrines threw the fierce champion into a rage. He is said to have mustered his Kalbid men and Qaynid kin, immediately attacking the

---

17 Ibn al-Kalbi, *Kitab al-asnam*, 20–21; Ibn Ishaq, *Sirah*, 64.
18 al-Fassi, "Kamkam the Nabataean priestess," 6 cites evidence in this regard. See further Ibn al-Kalbi, *Kitab al-asnam*, 22.
19 See *Diwan zuhayr ibn janab al-kalbi*, ed. Muhammad Shafiq, Beirut: Dar Sadir, 1999, 56–57.

pagan Ghatafanids. The story is that they destroyed the temple shrine of al-'Uzza, slaying a prisoner and spilling his blood to desecrate the site. Though it runs counter to the iconoclasm of Zuhayr's battle, this act oddly or deliberately emulates a blood sacrifice to the goddess al-'Uzza. Perhaps this gruesome act was undertaken to liken his wrath to that of his more prominent Lakhmid rival, al-Mundhir III. In any case, this is considered the first destruction of al-'Uzza's shrine. The story of conflict between the pagan Ghatafan and Christian Quda'ah roughly coincides with the death and immediate aftermath of the Lakhmid king al-Mundhir III in 554. I have argued he was the chief architect of pagan revival in the sixth century.

Against this revival came Zuhayr. He is said to have formed an alliance with Christian coreligionists from Ethiopia. Their general turned king Abraha (d. ca. 553) entrusted him as vassal governor over Bakr and Taghlib, rival tribes formerly governed by Lakhm.[20] In other words, the stories of Zalim and Zuhayr, while fanciful, take place in the context where the pagan power of the Lakhmids had been broken. The influence of Christianity had returned to the Quda'ah, with its champions patrolling Arabian communities to eradicate the vestiges of pagan worship.

This hypothesis fits a subsequent claim by Ibn al-Kalbi that in the decades before Islam, the cult of al-'Uzza declined in the Hijaz. This sudden plunge in fortunes coincides with a cluster of reports he cites about the destruction of various idols and cubic shrines around the same time.[21] Based on earlier examination, the death of al-Mundhir marked the demise of al-'Uzza's greatest patron, after which her cult began to weaken throughout Arabia's pagan corridor, including in Mecca. The Lakhmid king's cruelty was also unlikely to leave too many supporters and could have just as easily driven more Arabian tribes toward Christianity.

"Abu Lahab" and the Twilight of al-'Uzza

It is said that one of the last priests or patrons of al-'Uzza in the Hijaz was Abu Uhayhah of Quraysh. Before his death he is reported to have

---

20 al-Kalbi, *Diwan*, 61.
21 Ibn Ishaq, *Sirah*, 65, 107, 113, 152.

transferred his religious office to Abu Lahab, who is considered the same person as 'Abd al-'Uzza II in medieval Islamic tradition. Ibn al-Kalbi reports:

> al-'Uzza continued to be venerated until God sent His Prophet who ridiculed her together with the other idols and forbade her worship. At the same time a revelation concerning her came down in the Qur'an. This proved very hard upon the Quraysh. Then Abu Uhayhah (Sa'id b. al-'As b. Umayyah b. 'Abd Shams b. 'Abd-Manaf) was taken sick by what proved to be his last and fatal sickness. As he lay on his deathbed, Abu Lahab came to visit and found him weeping. Thereupon Abu Lahab asked, "What makes you weep Oh Abu Uhayhah? Is it death which is inevitable?"
>
> Abu Uhayhah replied, "No. But I fear that al-'Uzza will not be worshipped after I depart."
>
> Abu Lahab answered and said, "By God! al-'Uzza was not worshipped during your lifetime for your sake, and her worship will not be discontinued after you depart because of your death."
>
> Abu Uhayhah then said, "Now I know that I have a successor," and was well pleased with Abu Lahab's intense loyalty to al-'Uzza.[22]

This report, while perhaps echoing a distant memory of the final death throes of al-'Uzza's cultic presence in Arabia, is a caricature of reality. More specifically, it is anachronistic, apologetic, and teleological in nature. Like all good stories of its kind, its purpose was to explain Abu Lahab's enmity to Muhammad the prophet, while enforcing the triumph of the Qur'an and forging an Islamic identity for the audience. We cannot recall for certain what the distant memory of this story is. But if behind the figures of Abu Uhayhah or Abu Lahab was a historical figure during the twilight of al-'Uzza's cult, then the whole episode may fit within the plunging fortunes of pagan cults in Arabia during the late sixth century as discussed already. This may have been part of the historical context leading up to Muhammad's prophetic ministry and the appearance of the Qur'an.

22 Ibn al-Kalbi, *Kitab al-asnam*, 23, trans. Nabih Faris, 20 edited. See related discussion in Hawting, *The Idea of Idolatry and the Emergence of Islam*, 27.

While the story may recall a forgotten episode of history, labeling Abu Lahab the "successor" demonstrates the lateness of the report itself. This title is likely used because of the perpetual dispute over political succession between Umayyad, Abbasid, and Shii contenders in later centuries.

The Tafsir and Hadith literature take pains to weave stories to link the historical figure of 'Abd al-'Uzza II with the condemned figures of Abu Lahab and his wife in Q 111. They paint him as the quintessential arch-enemy of Muhammad's prophetic ministry. Abu Lahab is said to have fought Muhammad at the battle of Badr (2/624) and fallen there. His wife is said to have harassed the prophet by throwing spikes in front of his doorstep or where he walked. Against the orthodox tendencies of medieval Muslim authors is their oddly positive description of him and his wife prior to the conflict. His nickname *abu lahab* means in Arabic "he of the flame." The sources claim this nomenclature has nothing to do with his place in hellfire, but rather his "rosy complexion." Belonging to Mecca's elite, both 'Abd al-'Uzza II and his wife, Arwah "Um Jamil" bt. Harb b. Umayyah, were known to the sources for being attractive, wealthy, and generous. The aristocratic couple would have maintained their grace and munificence were it not for their literary portrayal as the staunchest enemies of Muhammad, after his denial of the goddess al-'Uzza.[23]

And so there seems to be more to this story. What about Muhammad's relationship with his uncle during his pagan years, what precisely was Muhammad's relationship to the cult of al-'Uzza, and who or what made him change his religious course?

Muhammad's Worship of al-'Uzza

What follows is neither a full story nor an introduction to the "historical Muhammad," about which there is a wealth of literature and ongoing debate.[24] It is, rather, an exploration of his pagan origins, prior to his own conversion to a variety of Abrahamic faith called Hanifism. This exploration, despite the apologetic impulse of medieval Islamic

---

23 See Bukhari, *Sahih*, 65:472, https://sunnah.com/bukhari/65/472.
24 Cf. Anthony, *Muhammad and the Empires of Faith*, 280–284.

tradition as well as modern controversy, is, I argue, traceable to some extent from the earliest Arabic sources. Our exploration examines three facets of Muhammad:

(1) His genealogy and name
(2) His father's exchange with a priestess
(3) His sacrifice to al-'Uzza

Pagan Genealogy

According to the *Sirah* and long before his prophetic ministry, Muhammad b. 'Abd Allah b. 'Abd al-Muttalib (d. 10/632) belonged to the Hashimid clan under the 'Abd al-Manafid bloc of the Quraysh. His tribe reportedly founded the city of Mecca centuries earlier.[25] His father, 'Abd Allah (d. *ca.* 570), is said to have died mysteriously before his birth. His mother, Aminah bt. Wahb b. 'Abd Manaf (d. *ca.* 577), is said to have died when her son was six years old.

Muhammad was further uprooted when he moved into a pre-modern foster care system based on kinship or tribal alliance. His foster family lived outside Mecca, and was composed of his wet nurse, Halimah bt. Abi Dhu'ayb (Halimah al-Sa'diyyah); her husband, al-Harith b. 'Abd al-'Uzza of Hawazin; and their two children. He spent some years with Halimah. Then he is said to have lived with his paternal grandfather 'Abd al-Muttalib. Finally, he moved in with his paternal uncle 'Imran or 'Abd Manaf b. 'Abd al-Muttalib (d. 619), otherwise known to Islamic tradition as Abu Talib.[26]

While the details of his life are saturated in hagiographical lore, there can be little doubt Muhammad's youth was difficult. He was a destitute orphan shuffled incessantly from one home to another. Life imposed upon him curiosity, anxiety, and introspection about the cruel world into which he was plunged, and his predicament within it.

25 See further Sayyid al-Qimani, *al-Hizb al-hashimi wa ta'sis al-dawlah al-islamiyyah*, Cairo: Maktabat Madbuli al-Saghir, 2008.
26 Ibn Ishaq, *Sirah*, 100, 116, 120.

A Pagan Name with Monotheistic Titles?

To the researcher his name and lineage stand out. Generations of scholars have pondered whether the name *muhammad ibn 'abdallah*— "the praised one, son of the servant of Allah"—is itself a hagiographic title for Islam's founder. The earliest Arabic sources' exploration of pre-Islamic men by the name of Muhammad is meagre and apocryphal at best, and inexorably tied to the miracle of prophecy.[27] The name Muhammad, though rarely attested if at all, may have echoes in the theophoric names of Greco-Palmyrene or Safaitic inscriptions, or a proper name in the Syriac *Book of the Himyarites*.[28] Another proposal suggests it was a title for Christ, derived from Syriac *mahmed*.[29] This seems unlikely. The name and similar derivations of the root *HMD* is, however, most likely South Arabian in form. Among its attestations is a Jewish epithet for God, occurring in an inscription from Najran dated 523 CE.[30] Thus, the name Muhammad is likely a Jewish or Christian honorific title for the prophet cited in Q 3:144; 33:40; 47:2; 48:29; 61:6, but whose birth name is unknown.

The sources claim the prophet enumerated several names for himself. In the sources he states, "I am the praised (*muhammad*), the most praised (*ahmad*), the gatherer (*al-hashir*), the fulfiller (*al-muqaffi*), the prophet of mercy, repentance and tribulation."[31] To this are added other clearly Christian honorifics, the "trustworthy, faithful, reliable" (cf. Genesis 37:36; 1 Kings 22:9; Isaiah 33:16; Matthew 19:12; Acts 16:1; Sirach 30:20) and "comforter, consoler, resurrector" (John 15:24–27).[32] None of these are likely birth names, but they are *absolutely*

---

27 Ibn Sa'd, *Tabaqat*, 1:142–143.

28 Gabriel Reynolds, *The Qur'an and Its Biblical Subtext*, London; New York: Routledge, 2010, 190–192.

29 Karl-Heinz Ohlig, "Vom muhammad Jesus zum Propheten der Araber: Die Historisierung eines christologischen Prädikats," *Der frühe Islam eine historisch-kritische Rekonstruktion anhand zeitgenössischer Quellen*, ed. Karl-Heinz Ohlig, Berlin: Verlag Hans Schiller, 2007, 330.

30 Christian Robin, "Himyar et Israël," *CRS* 148, 2004, 876.

31 Ibn Sa'd, *Tabaqat*, 1:84–85.

32 'Abd al-Malik b. Hisham, *al-Sirah al-nabawiyyah*, 4 vols., ed. 'Umar A. Tadmuri, Beirut: Dar al-Kitab al-'Arabi, 1990, 1:262; J. Payne-Smith, *A Compendious Syriac Dictionary*, Oxford: Clarendon Press, 1979, 335.

divine epithets demonstrating his fulfillment of Christian prophecy through the Qur'an.

Could Muhammad have originally had a pagan name? It seems possible. This hypothesis is advanced by modern researchers and reinforced by medieval Arab genealogists. The prophet's lineage is replete with theophoric names in service of the pagan deities:

(1) al-'Uzza
(2) al-Muttalib
(3) al-Dar
(4) Manaf
(5) Shams and others[33]

His father's name, 'Abd Allah, seems similarly out of place. This is because of the absence of that theophoric name among the pre-Islamic Quraysh and the paucity of Allah's cult in pre-Islamic times, a matter explored in Chapter 3. One of Khadijah's ex-husbands is descended from 'Abd Allah, though he came from the neighboring tribe of Makhzum outside Mecca.[34] The name *abdallas* is otherwise attested in contemporaneous sixth-century Greek papyri from Nessana, Palestine. Prior to that the name *'abdallah/i* occurs in some ancient North Arabian and Nabataean inscriptions.[35] It is possible that Muhammad's father's given name was 'Abd Allah, but only if we concede that he alone enjoyed such a theologically correct name within pre-Islamic Mecca.

Once again, it is from within the sources that we find evidence of an alternate name for Muhammad. One report suggests his name was originally Qutham b. 'Abd Allat.[36] Could this truly have been what he was called? And could his father have been named "servant of Allat" despite her being eclipsed by the goddess al-'Uzza?[37] Anything is possible, but outside this paltry mention, we have no evidence for the

---

33 Cf. Ibn al-Kalbi, *Jamharat al-nasab*, 694–698.
34 Ibn Sa'd, *Tabaqat*, 10:16.
35 Ahmad Al-Jallad, "Graeco-Arabica I: The southern Levant," *Arabic in Context*, ed. Ahmad Al-Jallad, Leiden: Brill, 2017, 163–164.
36 Al-Azmeh, *The Emergence of Islam in Late Antiquity*, 377.
37 Ibn al-Kalbi, *Jamharat al-nasab*, 590; *Kitab al-asnam*, 17.

veracity of this or any other name for Muhammad. We have no prudent choice but to remain agnostic.

'Abd Allah and the Priestess

The sources suggest, furthermore, that 'Abd Allah participated with a pagan priestess in the sexual rite identified by later jurists as "polyandrous group marriage." This was known in Arabic as *nikah al-raht* or *sifah*. Sources report the woman was Qutaylah or Ruqayyah bt. Nawfal. She was reportedly the sister of a Christian cleric called Waraqah b. Nawfal (d. 610) of the 'Abd al-'Uzzid bloc of Quraysh.[38] The contradiction of a pagan priestess whose brother was a Christian cleric deserves our careful attention later.

Returning to the identity of the priestess, Ibn Sa'd and others report her as Fatimah bt. Murr of the Khath'am tribe, already introduced, and the more likely candidate.

'Abd Allah b. 'Abd al-Muttalib passed by a woman of Khath'am called Fatimah bt. Murr who was the most beautiful, attractive and purest of people. She had read the scriptures and the youths of Quraysh would consult her. But she saw the light of prophecy in the face of 'Abd Allah, so she said, "and who are you young man?" So he told her. She replied, "would you lay with me then I gift you one hundred camels?" So he looked upon her and said:

As for the forbidden, I shall die without it.
The permissible is not permissible unless you seek it.
So how can you command what you desire?

Then he left for his wife Aminah bt. Wahb, and lay with her, and he mentioned the Kahath'amid woman, her beauty and what she offered him. Then he approached her [Fatimah] but he did not see her approach him now as she did before. So he said, "will you offer

38 Ibn Ishaq, *Sirah*, 93–97; Shihab al-Din al-Tifashi, *Nuzhat al-albab fima la yujad fi kitab*, ed. Jamal Jum'ah, London: Riyad al-Rayyis, 1992, 16–17.

me what you did earlier?" She said, "that was once, but not today," which became a proverb. She said, "what did you do after leaving me?" He said, "I lay with my wife Aminah bt. Wahb." She said, "I swear by Allah and I am no possessor of doubt, but I saw the light of prophecy in your face and I wanted it to be mine, but Allah chose to place you where he did."[39]

An alternate narration claims 'Abd Allah replied to Fatimah's sexual advance by explicitly consenting on one condition. He concedes to her, stating, "yes, but only once I have cast a stone." This act, I argue, endorses the distinctly Islamic ritual of "stone throwing" against the pagan goddesses, demon, or devil during the Hajj pilgrimage. Anyway, he performs the act of pelting a stone—conquering the devil—and then lies with his wife, Aminah, instead of the priestess. The narration continues with commensurate poetry and praise for 'Abd Allah. Only once he has conquered his desire for the priestess does he return to his wife, who conveniently conceives the long-awaited baby who will one day become Arabia's greatest prophet.[40]

This story is yet another episode of hagiographic triumphalism. This time it extolls the purity of Muhammad's conception and biological parents, while demonstrating the aversion of his 'nearly pagan' conception through the priestess. So just how much of this fictional drama could have been historically true? Well, confrontation between Muhammad's male lineage and the female power of pagan priestesses is striking and deserves our attention.

The visit by Qurashi youth, including 'Abd Allah, to the local priestess is a *topos*. She was "beautiful, attractive, and purest of people" and the "possessor of no doubt." Meaning she was an oracle. This parallels the story of 'Abd al-Muttalib visiting the oracle of Hegra or Khaybar in Wadi al-Qura one generation earlier. It seems the young men of Quraysh, and probably Hijaz more broadly, sought sexual indulgence with the priestess/oracle in order to conceive a child.

39 Ibn Sa'd, *Tabaqat*, 1:76, translated by the author.
40 Ibid., 1:77–79.

There are Hadith reports expressing Muhammad's concern about his own noble lineage and whether he was the product of such a polyandrous union. In the words of Hela Ouardi:

> Muhammad himself was concerned about his origins. A hadith shows him insisting on the nobility and purity of his ancestry. It details that his parents conceived him as part of a "regular" marriage, and not an extramarital affair. The prophet does not use the word *zina* (adultery), but rather *sifah*. This is a term which refers precisely to a group sexual practice accepted in pre-Islamic society, but which Islam would later prohibit. Would these words by the prophet be a response to accusations which present him as an illegitimate child?[41]

Be that as it may, it is the woman in this case who is the possessor of power. She enjoys the prestige of nobility, purity, and divine office. She copulates with Quraysh's finest men and chooses whomsoever she desires. The practice of polyandrous group marriage and subsequent matrilineality, condemned by later jurists, has echoes in ancient Hegra going back to the first-century Nabataean priestess Kamkam bt. Wa'ilah bt. Haram introduced in Chapter 3. It may, furthermore, be connected to sixth-century priestesses of al-'Uzza and Hubal. In sum, beneath the pious retelling of this episode is the polyandry of late antique Hijaz—and the need to erase its stain from the person of Muhammad the prophet—and the matrilineality of its female nobility.

Sacrifice to al-'Uzza

To what extent did the pagan rites of his father and grandfather have an influence on Muhammad? Ibn al-Kalbi reports that he worshipped al-'Uzza before his prophetic mission:

> We have been told that the apostle of God once mentioned al-'Uzza saying, "I have offered a white sheep to al-'Uzza, while I was a

41 Hela Ouardi, *Les Derniers Jours de Muhammad*, Paris: Albin Michel, 2016, 190.

follower of the religion of my people." The Quraysh were wont to circumambulate the Kaabah and say:

> By Allat and al-'Uzza, and Manat, the third idol besides.
> Verily they are the most exalted females, whose intercession is to be sought.

These were also called "the daughters of Allah," and were supposed to intercede before God. When the Apostle of God was sent, God revealed unto him [concerning them] the following:

> Have you seen Allat and al-'Uzza, and Manat the third idol besides? What? Shall ye have male progeny and God female? This indeed were an unfair partition! These are mere names: ye and your fathers named them thus: God hath not sent down any warranty in their regard [Q 53:1–23].[42]

This is one among a series of such reports found in the Hadith and *Sirah*. It illustrates Muhammad's worship of al-'Uzza during his pagan days, prior to his prophetic ministry.[43] Another report narrates an episode between Muhammad and his slave turned adopted son Zayd b. Harithah (d. 7/629) and an old man living outside Mecca as an outcast. His name was Zayd b. 'Amr b. Nufayl (d. 605).

> I was told that the apostle of God while speaking of Zayd b. 'Amr b. Nufayl said, "He was the first to blame me for worshipping idols and forbade me to do so. I had come from Ta'if with Zayd b. Harithah when I passed by Zayd b. 'Amr on the high ground above Mecca, for Quraysh had made a public example of him for abandoning their religion, so that he went forth from among them and (stayed) in the high ground of Mecca. I went and sat with him. I had with me a bag of meat from our sacrifices to our idols which Zayd b. Harithah was carrying, and I offered it to him. I was a young

---

42 Ibn al-Kalbi, *Kitab al-asnam*, 19, trans. Nabih Faris, 16–17, edited.
43 M. J. Kister, "A bag of meat: A study of an early Hadith," *BSOAS* 33.2, 1970, 267–275.

lad at the time. I said 'Eat some of this food, O my uncle.' He replied 'Nephew, it is a part of those sacrifices of yours which you offer to your idols, isn't it?' When I answered that it was he said 'If you were to ask the daughters of 'Abd al-Muttalib they would tell you that I never eat of these sacrifices and I want nothing to do with them.' Then he blamed me and those who worship idols and sacrifice to them saying, 'They are futile: they can do neither good nor harm,' or words to that effect." The apostle added "After that with that knowledge I never stroked an idol of theirs nor did I sacrifice to them until God honoured me with His apostleship."[44]

It is said that Zayd b. 'Amr frequented Syria, becoming shaped by its now widespread Jewish and Christian communities. His frequent travels and abandoning of Arabian paganism ruined his relationship with his wife and relatives. He was reportedly ousted from Mecca by his uncle al-Khattab b. Nufayl, who happened to be the father of the second caliph, 'Umar b. al-Khattab (d. 3/644). The outcast eked out an existence outside the city until his inexplicable murder in Lakhmid Mesopotamia.[45] According to tradition, Zayd was a leading member of the Hanifs, a fragmented Arabian community of pre-Islamic monotheists. The details of Mecca's archetypical Hanif in the sixth century may be fiction. But its kernel bespeaks parallels with the near-*contemporaneous* conversion of Mesopotamian Arabs to Christianity reported by Ahudemmeh. In other words, Zayd's legendary conversion comes shortly after the conversion of Syrian Arabs during the fifth century, according to Theodoret of Cyrrhus and Sozomen of Gaza.

Yet other traditions integrate the partnership of so-called Hanifs returning to the faith of the biblical Abraham, citing Zayd b. 'Amr and Waraqah b. Nawfal, in contradistinction to the stubborn paganism of Mecca's governor Abu Sufyan b. Harb (d. 31/653) and his circle of political elites. While there is no denying the many pious embellishments to reports of Muhammad's worship of al-'Uzza, the fact that such shocking episodes in his life are reported at all is striking. Its historical outlines are accepted by renowned medieval Muslim

---

44 Kister, "A bag of meat," 267, edited. See also Ibn Ishaq, *Sirah*, 163–166.
45 Ibn Ishaq, *Sirah*, 164.

scholars, including Bukhari, Ibn Hanbal, and Ibn Kathir, as well as modern researchers who have examined the reports meticulously, including M. J. Kister and A. Guillaume.[46]

But Muhammad's introduction to monotheism could have been at the hands of neither Zayd nor Waraqah. Their influence over Muhammad came late in life. Muhammad found God the day he met Khadijah.

Mother of the Believers, Princess of Quraysh

According to the Arabic sources, Khadijah bt. Khuwaylid b. Asad (*ca.* 555–619) belonged to the Asadid clan of the 'Abd al-'Uzzids of the Quraysh in Mecca. Like their 'Abd al-Manafid/Hashimid kin, this tribal bloc was an integral "co-founder" of Quraysh a century or so earlier. Among her honorifics were "Khadijah the great," "princess of Quraysh" and "pure lady." These titles reflect her supremacy, nobility, and piety in the classical Muslim imagination. Some associate Khadijah with priesthood given her highborn status and great influence prior to Islam, although the evidence for such a claim is meagre.[47] The sources extol her as "mother of the believers," adding:

> Four women are best in all the world: Maryam daughter of Amram, Asyah wife of Pharaoh, Khadijah bt. Khuwaylid and Fatimah bt. Muhammad.[48]

Khadijah's mother, Fatimah bt. Za'idah, is little known but had deep roots in Meccan genealogy. Muhammad's first wife looms larger than any other woman in his life and indeed in early Islamic history, equaled only by their daughter Fatimah bt. Muhammad. Khadijah's entry, while surprisingly short, appears chronologically first in classical biographical works. She is vaunted for being among the wealthiest

---

46 Kister, "A bag of meat," 268–269.

47 Cf. in relation 'Abd al-Karim, *Fatrat al-takwin*, 35–38.

48 Ibn Ishaq, *Sirah*, 272; Shariati, *Fatemeh fatemeh ast*, trans. Bakhtiar, *Ali Shariati's Fatima is Fatima*, 171. See further Marek Halter, *La Trilogie: Les Femmes de l'Islam (Khadija, Fatima et Aisha)*, Paris: Groupe Robert Laffont, 2015.

elites of Mecca—male or female—reportedly boasting more than a thousand camels. And she is celebrated for being the first official Muslim on record.

In what follows, I endeavor to focus on Khadijah as the final paragon of female power in late antique Arabia, rather than telling her whole story, which the sources catalog in more detail.[49] There are two parts to our examination:

(1) Her role as Mecca's wealthiest noblewoman—echoing, though to a much lesser extent, that of empress Zenobia of Palmyra
(2) Her role as prophet-maker—resembling, this time to a greater extent, that of queen Mavia of Tanukh

Men, Marriage, and the Marketplace

We learn from the Arabic sources that Khadijah descended from nobility. She declined a traditionally arranged marriage to her first cousin Waraqah b. Nawfal. Reading between the lines of hagiographic piety and lore, the young lass appears strong-willed, free-spirited, and ambitious in her search for a man. She chose as her first husband a nobleman from outside Mecca, whose name was Hind b. al-Nabbash of Tamim (Abu Halah). Her second husband, 'Atiq b. 'Abid of Makhzum, was an outsider as well. It is unclear what fate befell these men. It may be that, like her father, Khuwaylid, they perished in the Sacrilegious War *ca.* 580–590. Reports about the names of Khadijah's children from these first two marriages are equally muddled. She may have had two sons from her first marriage carrying characteristically female names, Hind and Halah. She reportedly had a daughter, Hind(ah), from the second.[50] Again, the reports seem oddly unreliable and the reader would be well advised to take them with a grain of salt. Whatever the case, that Khadijah had marriages prior to Muhammad, and that she ostensibly chose men from out of town certainly seems most likely.

49 Ibn Sa'd, *Tabaqat*, 10:15–16.
50 Ibid., 10:15–17; Ibn al-Kalbi, *Jamharat al-nasab*, 269. See discussion in M. J. Kister, "The sons of Khadija," *JSAI* 16, 1993, 61.

The Arabic sources claim, perhaps with recourse to hyperbole, that Khadijah possessed the largest trade caravans to Bosra, Syria, equaling that of all Quraysh. Some reports add that she inherited business capital from her late husbands.[51] But her grit and determination were clearly the main source of success for her commercial enterprise. We hear of no other Qurashi businesswomen like her. But not even a tycoon of her caliber traveled on trade voyages. Why? No reason is given for this anomaly. One reason may be, however, that the annual marketplace festivals were no longer safe for women to traverse by the sixth century. This is especially after the attempted gang rape known as the "sacrilege of the woman" during the Sacrilegious War, which is addressed in Chapter 7.

Tayma and an Annual Festival for Women?

It seems Meccan women had developed or maintained their own annual festival in the Hijazi city of Tayma. It took place in the month of Rajab (possibly Tishrin I). Khadijah is said to have attended the boisterous women-only gathering, which proved too wild for the orthodox sensibilities of medieval Muslim storytellers. They interrupt the story by inserting a clearly misplaced pious prophecy about Muhammad's coming. It is said that at one of the annual festivals, while attendees publicly worshipped an idol, a strange man appeared out of nowhere. He disrupted their celebration and proclaimed the coming of a new prophet who would marry one of the eligible females. In the spirit of any good hagiography, the pagan women scoff at the news, except for Khadijah. She is portrayed as patiently awaiting her third husband.

Back to the idol in the story, could it have been the chief goddess al-'Uzza, or her male consort Hubal? We are not told. The idol is not identified, but Khadijah here and elsewhere is exonerated by the story-tellers from the stain of idolatry.[52]

Khadijah actively sought out clever young men and hired them as employees. In this respect, her boldness, initiative, and acquaintance

---

51 Kister, "The sons of Khadija," 66.
52 Ibn Sa'd, *Tabaqat*, 10:16.

with young men is reminiscent of the Hijazi priestesses documented earlier, as well as Mavia and Zenobia. At any rate, her wealth and successful commercial ventures attracted hard-working, enterprising men from all over the city. One young man—Muhammad—was hungry for opportunity and had already frequented Syria for trade under his uncle Abu Talib, who could no longer guarantee his nephew a living wage. Good for him. It is said Khadijah paid double.

Mecca's Christian House—'Abd al-'Uzza I

The Arabic sources suggest the tribal bloc of Quraysh to which Khadijah belonged—'Abd al-'Uzza I—had converted to Christianity. Modern scholars have debated the extent of Khadijah's Christian background, and the matter remains unresolved.[53] A recently discovered Arabic inscription near Ta'if preserves the name of a Christian by the name of 'Abd al-'Uzza.[54] This is not the same individual as the head of Mecca's Christian house. But at the very least, this find serves as evidence for the abrupt conversion of staunchly pagan circles to Christianity in that vicinity.

Nevertheless, the justification for Khadijah's Christian background primarily rests upon claims made in the hagiographies of Ibn Hisham (d. 218/833) and 'Ali b. Burhan al-Din (d. 593/1197), the topographical reports of Mecca by Azraqi (d. 250/837), and the history of Ya'qubi (d. 284/898). The following examination lays out the evidence in this vein.

Khadijah's Kin: Conversion in Syria and Mesopotamia

First come reports asserting that Khadijah never worshipped idols and was otherwise counted among pre-Islamic Mecca's Hanifs.[55] While the

53 Cf. 'Abd al-Karim, *Fatrat al-takwin fi hayat al-sadiq al-amin*, 9–10; al-Hariri, *Qiss wa nabi*, 33–34; Tayyib al-Tizini, *Muqaddimat awwaliyyah fi al-islam al-muhammadi al-bakir nash'atan wa ta'sisan*, Damascus: Dar Dimashq li al-Tiba'ah wa al-Sahafah wa al-Nashr, 1994, 260, 300–302.
54 See forthcoming article by Ahmad Al-Jallad and Hythem Sidky.
55 Ibn Sa'd, *Tabaqat*, 15–16.

exaggeration of her virtues to fit the narrative of Muhammad's hagiography may be dismissed, the researcher should seriously consider her monotheistic upbringing. This is not least because it stands in stark contrast to that of Muhammad's pagan upbringing discussed earlier. The two came from such different families.

Second, Khadijah's parents and elders may have been Christian. Some suggest her father, Asad, may have been the first one to convert, introducing Christianity into the family.[56]

Third comes a series of startling reports situating Mecca's prominent Christians (including Hanifs) amid the religious schism and geopolitical struggle of late-sixth-century Arabia. They were four:

(1) 'Ubayd Allah b. Jahsh, who is said to have migrated permanently to Ethiopia and converted there
(2) 'Uthman b. al-Huwayrith, who is said to have permanently migrated to Roman lands, where he converted, finding favor with the emperor in Constantinople and seeking the title of "patriarch" before settling in Syria, where he was mysteriously killed by poisoning
(3) Zayd b. 'Amr, already introduced as a Hanif, who lived out his last days between Syria and Lakhmid Mesopotamia, where he was also mysteriously killed
(4) Waraqah b. Nawfal, introduced already, who is said to have translated the gospel from Aramaic into Arabic for the people of Mecca, and who the sources identify as *both* Christian and Hanif[57]

The latter three—'Uthman, Zayd, and Waraqah—were all Khadijah's kin. What can explain the concentration of so many highborn Christian leaders among the 'Abd al-'Uzzid bloc of Quraysh? And why do all the reports insist they "converted" in far-off Christian lands? What church, if any, did they belong to? The sources do not tell us.

This brings us to the fourth and final point. The years *ca.* 550–600 witnessed a surge in Christian military and missionary activity

56 Ghada Osman, "Pre-Islamic Arab converts to Christianity in Mecca and Medina: An investigation into the Arabic sources," *MW* 95, 2005, 67–80.
57 al-Hariri, *Qiss wa nabi*, 16–19.

throughout Arabia, notably following the pagan revival discussed already. Cities and towns of the Hijaz, including Mecca, became embroiled in the religious and political disorder wrought by Byzantium and Axum. King Abraha's conquest of Arabia in the name of the "Messiah" from the south left an indelible imprint on the medieval Arab memory as Mecca's "year of the elephant." Their memory, though rife with inconsistencies, sought to date Arabian events from the time of Abraha. This practice resembled that of the Syrians who dated events back to Alexander of Macedon centuries earlier. The Ethiopians linked up with the Quda'ah from the north, briefly at least. Their chieftain Zuhayr b. Janab al-Kalbi embarked from Syria on a campaign of smashing idols and desecrating pagan shrines as far as the Hijaz.

The West Syrians were converting the Arabs under Ahudemmeh of Beth Arbaye (*ca.* 559–575), who "establish[ed] in every tribe a priest and a deacon" before they went off, as introduced in Chapter 1. The East Syrians made similar gains along the Persian Gulf coast of Arabia. Beth Qatraye (Qatar) would develop into a major center of Syriac Christian learning, boasting numerous Christian Arab luminaries.[58]

The West Syrian Church was, furthermore, being fractured and reforged during this time as well. And the religious and political leaders of Arabia, Syria, and Egypt played an instrumental role in its sectarian evolution *ca.* 565–576. Under Paul the Black (d. *ca.* 584) patriarch of Antioch, the flock first suffered the "tritheist controversy," followed by the "Alexandrine schism." Paul tried and failed to install a bishop of his choosing in Alexandria, rousing an uproar in Egypt. He then fled to emperor Justin II (d. 578) in Constantinople, leaving the bishop of Edessa, Jacob bar Addai (d. 578), to reconsolidate what would be famously called after him, the "Jacobite Church." Critical to this church saga is the leadership of the Ghassanids.

The Ghassanid phylarchs al-Harith b. Jabalah (d. 569) and his son al-Mundhir III b. al-Harith (d. 581) played an integral role in reconciling Paul with Jacob, keeping the West Syrian Church intact.[59] In the

---

58 See *The Syriac Writers of Qatar in the Seventh Century*, eds. Mario Kozah et al., Piscataway: Gorgias Press, 2014.

59 See Robert Hoyland, "Late Roman Provincia Arabia, Monophysite monks and Arab tribes: A problem of centre and periphery," *SC* 3, 2010, 117–139.

years before 600, almost all Arabian tribes had been shaken by Christianity, whether by military force or missionary conversion.[60] This would have included those in the Hijaz.

Christian Landmarks in the Hijaz

In its wake the surge of Christian activity left several landmarks which dotted the valleys and mountains between Mecca and Yathrib. They included:

(1) Mary's church
(2) The Christian station
(3) The Christian cemetery
(4) The icon of the Virgin Mary within the Ka'bah's pantheon in Mecca[61]

Could the descendants of 'Abd al-'Uzza I have turned their back on the pagan goddess of their forefather, joined one of the Syrian churches, and brought Christianity to Mecca? It seems plausible. The civilizing of pagan Arab notables by Christian priests is, after all, a common theme within Syriac as well as Islamic hagiography.[62]

One final observation takes us back to Qutaylah bt. Nawfal, sister of Waraqah the priest, who some reports claim was the pagan priestess to proposition Muhammad's father, 'Abd Allah, to perform sexual rites. Only a minority of sources name her at all. Furthermore, the reports seem suspicious, as though their aim was to disparage both Waraqah and the 'Abd al-'Uzzid lineage. But why?

---

60 Cf. generally Richard Bell, *The Origin of Islam in its Christian Environment: The Gunning Lectures 1925, Edinburgh University*, London: F. Cass, 1926; John Trimingham, *Christianity among the Arabs in Pre-Islamic Times*, London; New York: Longman, 1979.
61 Muhammad b. 'Abd Allah al-Azraqi, *Akhbar makkah wa ma ja'fiha min al-athar*, ed. 'Abd al-Malik b. Duhaysh, Mecca: Maktabat al-Asadi, 2003, 248, 962.
62 Saint-Laurent, *Missionary Stories and the Formation of the Syriac Churches*, 120–121.

Mecca's Pagan House—'Abd Manaf

Since Muhammad belongs to the 'Abd Manafid bloc of Quraysh, the Arabic sources of medieval Islamic tradition speak both mythically and copiously about him and his descendants. This is besides the fact that the sources claim Qusayy preferred his eldest son, 'Abd al-Dar, over his younger siblings, 'Abd Manaf and 'Abd al-'Uzza I. And so he bequeathed his eldest son the upkeep of the Kaabah.[63] As the preceding discussion demonstrates about Muhammad and his elders—'Abd Allah, 'Abd al-Muttalib, and 'Abd al-'Uzza II—the 'Abd Manafids were staunch worshippers of the Arabian goddess al-'Uzza, and practitioners of pagan sexual rites. All manner of medieval Muslim orthodox piety and propaganda was superimposed over this uncomfortable, and likely historical, reality. This was necessary in order to rehabilitate the holy prophet's clearly pagan family and upbringing.

Muhammad's Uncles: Pagan Elites vs. the 'Alids and Zubayrids

All Muhammad's paternal uncles, including those wrangling with Khadijah at their wedding, were pagan. Among them Hamzah was the only one reported to have joined the early Muslim movement in Mecca. His untimely death in 3/625 at the battle of Uhud was a huge loss to the movement. Abu Talib, who served as Muhammad's guardian into adulthood, never converted. The Meccan nobility opposed Muhammad's religious movement till the very last moment, when he conquered Mecca in 630 and they no longer had a choice!

They included the city's governor Sakhr b. Harb b. Umayyah (d. 31/653), known to Islamic tradition as Abu Sufyan; as well as al-'Abbas, a distant half uncle of Muhammad. Their descendants would found the powerful Umayyad and Abbasid caliphates, which came to rule much of the known world.

After Muhammad's death in 632, the passing of power to his erstwhile antagonists would evoke the outrage and insurrection of both Muhammad's and Khadijah's closest relations, namely 'Ali b. Abi Talib (d. 27/661) and al-Zubayr b. al-'Awwam (d. 36/656). Much attention

---

63 Peters, *Muhammad and the Origins of Islam*, 20–29.

has been paid to the early Islamic civil wars and crisis of succession. But what if the 'Alid and Zubayrid revolts against the Umayyads also manifested pre-existing Christian–Hanafite animus towards paganism? To this end, the Arabic sources, replete with bias, repeatedly underscore the Umayyads' impiety and lack of Islamic values.[64]

Bahira the Monk and Suppressing Muhammad's Pagan Origin

None of the 'Abd Manafids were Christian. None were Hanifs, with one suspicious exception, namely Muhammad's grandfather 'Abd al-Muttalib. His clearly pagan credentials were embellished and redacted so he appeared both a pagan and a Hanif. With not a single *legitimate* Christian–Hanafite bone in the proverbial body of the 'Abd Manafids, the hagiographers conjured a surrogate Christian guardian to validate Muhammad's prophetic ministry.

Thus was created the Bahira legend. It claims that on a journey to Bosra with his uncle Abu Talib, the young boy Muhammad was identified by a Syrian monk. His name was Bahira, a name which in Syriac means "chosen/pure one." The monk discovers the "seal of prophecy" on the boy's back. Unlike Waraqah's relationship to Muhammad, investigated shortly, the Bahira legend appears to have been crafted in later times. It circulated widely in Arabic and Syriac, and was debated vigorously between medieval Muslims and Christians.[65]

The authors of medieval Islamic tradition worked hard to rehabilitate the religious image of 'Abd Manaf and his descendants on account of Muhammad's prophetic ministry and political rule. In doing so they de-emphasized 'Abd al-'Uzza I and his Christian–Hanafite descendants, including Khadijah.

---

64 See Hodgson, *The Venture of Islam*, 1:110–125, 221.
65 Cf. Ibn Ishaq, *Sirah*, 1:122–24, 171; Ibn Hisham, *Sirah*, 1:213; Ibn Sa'd, *Tabaqat*, 2:309; 5:306. See further Krisztina Szilágyi, "Muhammad and the monk: The making of the Christian Bahira legend," *JSAI* 34, 2008.

Marrying Muhammad

Having argued for the prominence of Christianity among Khadijah's family, and of paganism in that of Muhammad, we turn now to their union. Syrian canon law suggests inter-religious marriage was forbidden, unless the pagan party converted.[66] By marrying Khadijah, Muhammad indeed entered into the fold of Abrahamic monotheism. He then conquered Arabia in its name. But how did this union come to pass?

The Baroness and Her Apprentice

The sources say nothing about precisely how Khadijah met Muhammad or their daily exchanges, let alone the ensuing romance which could only have sparked during moments of intimacy beyond the boundaries of pious hagiographical storytelling. In any case, Muhammad's grit and determination matched that of his wealthy mistress. She soon entrusted him with no less than her lead caravan to Bosra, sending with him one of her male slaves by the name of Maysarah. The trade mission is said to have been a huge success, making double the expected profit. When Maysarah informed Khadijah of her growing fortunes, she was impressed and enamored.[67] And as a shrewd businesswoman and free-spirited noblewoman, she would stop at nothing to have her man. Among the myriad reports, however, the main story is that Khadijah approached Muhammad directly, stating:

> "Oh son of my uncle I like you because of our relationship and your high reputation among your people, your trustworthiness and good character and truthfulness." Then she proposed marriage (lit. "offered herself to him"). Now Khadijah at that time was the best born woman in Quraysh, of the greatest dignity and, too, the

66 Cf. Lev Weitz, *Between Christ and Caliph: Law, Marriage, and Christian Community in Early Islam*, Philadelphia: University of Pennsylvania Press, 2018, 53–58.
67 Ibn Ishaq, *Sirah*, 128–129.

The Angel Gabriel visits Muhammad in Khadijah's house,
Seyer-i-Nebi, ca. 1595

richest. All her people were eager to get possession of her wealth if
it were possible.[68]

Khadijah's active courting of Muhammad and her direct proposal have
garnered the support of modern Islamic feminists, but otherwise
reflect the prerogative of late antique Arabian female nobility. They
surrounded themselves with men in their service, imposing their will
and plucking for themselves the clever stallions of their predilection.
In it are echoes of al-Zabba', Mawiyah bt. 'Afzar, Fatimah bt. Murr, and
Qutaylah bt. Nawfal. The story continues with the engagement and
marriage of the couple. Throughout this process the sources portray
Muhammad as poor, passive, and well-nigh absent. Khadijah, on the
other hand, is calling all the shots. She rushes the wedding, and

---

68 Ibid., 19, trans. Guillaume, *The Life of Muhammad*, 82, edited.

wrangles directly with the men of her and Muhammad's family, using sheer wealth as leverage throughout.

Khadijah Officiates Her Own Ceremony

It seems Khadijah *gave herself away* to Muhammad. She had no need for a male guardian. Later Shii tradition, notably the *Kitab al-Kafi* by the jurist al-Kulayni (d. 329/941), suggests Khadijah's family objected to her marrying Muhammad given he was penniless and unable to pay a dowry. She fired back at her uncle and all the men crowding her chambers:

> Oh uncle, I know my interest better than you! I have married myself to you (*zawwajtuk nasfi*) oh Muhammad, and the dowry is upon me from my wealth. Now go tell your uncle (Abu Talib) to slaughter a camel to feed the party, and enter upon your wife.[69]

In the preceding report Khadijah is said to have performed her own marriage ceremony, over and against Mecca's male elites assembled against her. It is unlikely the marriage took place precisely as al-Kulayni records, but he rightfully recognizes the unsurpassed independence Khadijah enjoyed as a noblewoman of Mecca, not unlike Mavia or Zenobia before her. This report contributed, in part, to more lenient marriage laws within Shii tradition.[70]

Earlier sources which some may consider Sunni, however, found this appalling. In this respect, the prospect that the mother of the believers and first Muslim was a fully autonomous woman who married freely and that she took God's prophet under her wing, was simply unacceptable to certain medieval Muslim authors. They endeavored to curb the female power of old, and to assert their new masculine orthodoxy in its place. These authors whimsically and

---

69 Muhammad b. Ya'qub al-Kulayni, *al-Kafi*, 8 vols., Beirut: Manshurat al-Fajr, 2007, 5:239.

70 Ibid., 5:232. Cf. further debate in Nayel Badareen, "Shi'i marriage law in the pre-modern period: Who decides for women?" *ILS* 23.4, 2016, 368–391, but esp. 369.

incoherently assigned Khadijah several male guardians, even resurrecting her father from the dead as we shall see.

Waraqah Officiates a Christian Ceremony

Another report found in the late hagiographic collection of 'Ali b. Burhan al-Din claims that Waraqah presided over the wedding, as expected by a Christian priest. In this scenario Waraqah and Abu Talib exchange formalities and praise.

> Waraqah replied, "praise be to God who made us as you stated, and who favored us over those you enumerated. For we are the masters over the Arabs and their leaders; as are you as well. The Arabs do not deny your favor. So bear witness over me oh people of Quraysh that I have married Khadijah bt. Khuwaylid to Muhammad b. 'Abd Allah."
>
> Then Abu Talib was greatly overjoyed, and said, "praise be God who sent away our anxiety and repelled our despair."[71]

There is no telling for sure, given the plethora of reports, whether the marriage ceremony was Christian or pagan in nature. But clearly this seminal occasion was hotly contested territory for medieval Muslim storytellers and writers, and it remains a possibility that Khadijah simply married herself without a male guardian. We will return to the implications of a potentially Christian marriage performed by Waraqah shortly. Meanwhile, there is yet one more report asserting that neither Khadijah's uncle nor cousin gave her away, but rather her father, assuming the latter was still alive.

Khadijah Pays the Dowry

One report claims that one of Khadijah's close friends or servants by the name of Nafisah described her mistress as a "stern, harsh and noble

---

71 'Ali b. Burhan al-Din, *al-Sirah al-halabiyyah: insan al-'uyun fi sirat al-amin al-ma'mun*, ed. Abd Allah al-Khalili, 3 vols., Beirut: Dar al-Kutub al-'Ilmiyyah, 2005, 1:202, translated by the author.

woman, generous and kind with whomever God willed." The report implies that Muhammad was reluctant about marriage, especially to such a wealthy and domineering woman.[72] So he had cold feet. The implication is that his reluctance, indecisiveness, or downright refusal tested Khadijah's patience. She was after all an aggressive business-woman and a veteran of marriage. When she set her sights on some-thing or someone, she moved swiftly and without hesitation.[73] Khadijah reportedly sent Nafisah to intervene.

> I (Nafisah) said, "Oh Muhammad, what is preventing you from marriage?"
> He said, "I have nothing with which to get married."
> So I said, "But what if it was paid for, and you were invited to beauty, wealth, nobility and splendor, will you not accept?"
> He said, "Who is she?"
> I said, "Khadijah."
> He said, "How is that possible?"
> She said, "Leave it to me."
> He said, "Then I will do it."
> So she left and told her (Khadijah). Then she sent word to him requesting he come at so and so time. And she sent word to her uncle 'Amr b. Asad to marry her off. Then the prophet attended with his uncles and one of them married him off.
> Then 'Amr b. Asad said, "This deal is irreversible," and he married her off to the messenger of God when he was twenty-five years old, and when Khadijah was that day forty years old, being fifteen years before the (year of) the elephant.[74]

And so Khadijah was the one to pay the dowry to marry her third husband, a striking detail unlikely to be contrived and deserving of the reader's attention.

There are, nonetheless, conflicting reports about the details of this encounter. Khadijah's age is disputed, with some reports putting her as

---

72 Ibn Sa'd, *Tabaqat*, 1:109.
73 'Abd al-Karim, *Fatrat al-takwin*, 38.
74 Ibid., 109–110, translated by the author.

young as twenty-eight years of age, and a matter taken up by modern Islamic debates on marriage.[75] Which uncle gave away Muhammad is uncertain, although Hamzah or Abu Talib are likely. Finally, the sources debate who gave away Khadijah.

Wine, Women, and Wily Stories

The reported encounter between Khadijah and her erstwhile father, first recorded by Ibn Sa'd, deserves careful examination. For the scheme embedded in this alternate marriage scenario, while perhaps unremarkable to the unassuming reader, is of great significance to our appraisal of Khadijah's story and the demonstration of her power in its late antique Arabian context.

> … Khadijah said to her sister [Halah?], "Set off for Muhammad and tell him about me …" Then her sister returned and replied to her as God willed, and the two of them plotted to marry her [Khadijah] off to the messenger of God … So Khadijah's father was given wine to drink until he was overcome. Then he invited Muhammad to marry him off … She draped him in a cloak. But when he awoke, he said, "What is this cloak?" They said, "Your son-in-law Muhammad clothed you in it." So he was angered and took up arms, and Banu Hashim took up arms saying, "We had no desire of you." But they reconciled after that.[76]

Similar reports state explicitly that Khadijah got her father drunk on wine, slaughtered a cow, doused her father in perfume, and then draped him in a red cloak.[77]

The "Wiles" of Dushfari, Mawiyah, and Lot's Daughters

The experienced researcher will immediately find parallels between this scandalous encounter and similar stories concerning the "wiles of

75 For example, Ali, *The Lives of Muhammad*, 114–119, 274.
76 Ibid., 110, translated by the author.
77 Ibid.

women" found in ancient and medieval Near Eastern literature.[78] For pre-modern readers the parallel of Khadijah and her sister inebriating their father and causing mischief echoes the cheap *topos* of wine seduction at the hands of misbehaving women, already introduced in preceding chapters. Thus, the princess Dushfari bt. Sanatruq II was said to have seduced Shahpur I, betrayed her people, and won favor with the Sasanian king of kings; the literary figure of Mawiyah bt. 'Afzar attempts to seduce Hatim al-Ta'i with wine; and in the Hebrew Bible the daughters of Lot intoxicate their father in order to commit incest with him (Genesis 19:30–38).[79]

The stories, shocking as they appear, are pure fantasy. So why did Ibn Sa'd and others besmirch the otherwise glowing image of such fine women? To ask this question from a different angle, what did all these women have in common? In a word, *power*. Within the Arabic sources especially, the unnamed Dushfari, the semi-legendary Mawiyah bt. 'Afzar, and the matriarch Khadijah were literally the most venerated women of their Hatran, Tanukhid, and Qurashi communities. This was a problem. The primacy of medieval orthodox Islam all but demanded the weakening of female nobility, evidently by smearing their reputation with the cheap *topos* of wine seduction. Their literary disgrace blunted the edge of pre-Islamic Arabian female power and helped construct the artificial, decadent edifice known as the *jahiliyyah*.[80] There is more.

Recalling Inanna, Anticipating Shahrazad

Behind Khadijah as wine seductress is none other than the ancient Mesopotamian goddess Inanna. She meets her father, Enki the god of wisdom. The two have a boisterous exchange over beer where Inanna deliberately plies Enki with drink, and then snatches by force the virtues

78 For example, Zinon Papakonstantinou, "Wine and wine drinking in the Homeric world," *AC* 78, 2009, 1–24; Ulrich Marzolph et al., *The Arabian Nights Encyclopedia*, Santa Barbara, CA: ABC-CLIO, 2004, 1:739.

79 See further 'Abd al-Rahman, *Tarikh al-'arab qabl al-islam*, 91; Streete, *The Strange Woman*, 25–32.

80 Cf. El Cheikh, *Women, Islam, and Abbasid Identity*, 8–15.

of civilization from him. Enki willingly surrenders his powers to Inanna and then calls her his "equal." She then became the queen of heaven and earth.[81] In the story of Inanna and Enki, strong drink is the instrument by which to seize female power. Lastly, in either scenario of Khadijah's betrothal to Muhammad, her actions are facilitated through a sidekick. This too is another ancient narrative trope ultimately traceable to Inanna's confidante Ninshubur, and inherited in the person of Dunyazad who is sister of Shahrazad in the *Arabian Nights.*[82] In sum, Khadijah's unnamed sister reproduces Inanna's sister Ereshkigal, while her confidante Nafisah fulfills the function of Ninshubur.

For Ibn Saʿd and his predecessors, strong drink, while clearly in violation of orthodox Islamic norms, was recalled as a handy age-old instrument for good storytelling. It conveyed how Khadijah secured Muhammad as a husband. In their pious refashioning of Innana's story, and the cheapening of the story's *topoi*, the Muslim redactors nevertheless demonstrate that Khadijah was remembered as part of the elite class of late antique Arabian queens and goddesses.

Making Muhammad: Khadijah and Waraqah at Work

There is every indication that Khadijah and Muhammad had a long, monogamous, and happy marriage, lasting at least twenty-four years (*ca.* 595–619). Khadijah bore him several children. Their sons are said to have died young. But their daughters became luminaries of medieval Islamic devotion.[83] Khadijah transferred ownership of her slave Zayd b. Harithah, introduced earlier, to her new husband, who adopted the slightly younger boy as his son.[84] This was Muhammad's *longest relationship* with any woman. And for a quarter century Khadijah satiated her husband with the wealth, security, and stability he so lacked as a struggling orphan.

81 Wolkstein and Kramer, *Inanna*, 12–18.
82 Stephanie Jones, "Emboldening Dinarzad: The Thousand and One Nights in contemporary fiction," *New Perspectives on Arabian Nights*, ed. Geert Jan van Gelder, London: Routledge, 2014, 125–131.
83 Ali, *The Lives of Muhammad*, 123–124.
84 Cf. David Powers, *Zayd*, Philadelphia: University of Pennsylvania Press, 2014.

Mother Figure

Some have interpreted Muhammad's espousal of Khadijah as his long-ing for the love of a mother figure.[85] This is precisely the image reported in the sources describing how Khadijah authenticated and tempered Muhammad's otherwise wild ecstatic experiences. She is reported to have said:

> "Oh son of my uncle [i.e. Muhammad], can you inform me when that companion who appears to you comes next?"
>
> He said, "Yes."
>
> She said, "So when he comes then inform me about it."
>
> So Gabriel, peace be upon him, appeared to him as he does. So the messenger of God said to Khadijah, "Oh Khadijah, behold Gabriel has come to me."
>
> She said, "Arise oh son of my uncle then sit on my left thigh."
>
> So the messenger of God arose and sat on her. Then she said, "Do you see him?"
>
> He said, "Yes."
>
> Then she said, "Now move and sit on my right thigh."
>
> So the messenger of God moved and sat on her right thigh. Then she said, "Do you see him?"
>
> He said, "Yes."
>
> Then she said, "Now move and sit on my lap."
>
> So the messenger of God moved and sat on her lap. Then she said, "Do you see him?"
>
> He said, "Yes."
>
> Then she showed her face, removing her veil while the messen-ger sat on her lap. Then she said, "Do you see him?"
>
> He said, "No."
>
> She said, "Oh son of my uncle, stand firm and hold fast to the good news. He is indeed an angel. For this is not a demon."[86]

---

85 Stowasser, *Women in the Qur'an*, 126; Ali, *The Lives of Muhammad*, 238; 'Abd al-Karim, *Fatrat al-takwin*, 77–94.

86 Ibn Hisham, *Sirah*, 1:271, translated by the author.

The message behind this story is that Khadijah was reassured of Muhammad's vision because the angel fled out of a sense of piety or shame, to avoid seeing an unveiled woman. Taking for granted the orthodox assumptions about women's dress, this story is striking for a couple of reasons.

First, the story appears to be a set of instructions by a mother to her child. Did Muhammad treat Khadijah as his long-lost mother, and did she treat him as her child? Second, this story is situated within a biblical context as it retells the prophecy against Jerusalem found in Ezekiel 4:4–7. This implies Muhammad came with a similar prophecy against Mecca. Whether such an episode happened or not, it implies that Khadijah was not merely a mother figure but more importantly— physically—a vessel for Muhammad's revelation.

If Muhammad found in Khadijah the warmth and certitude of the mother he never had as an orphan, he evidently found her family, the 'Abd al-'Uzzids, equally as supportive of his prophetic mission. Most significant in this regard is the potential father figure who guided him, Waraqah. There is much controversy surrounding Waraqah's relationship to Muhammad.

Islamic tradition considers Waraqah one of several Christian or Jewish authorities whose stories merely validate Muhammad's prophecy. Christian apologists, on the other hand, consider Waraqah the mastermind of a heretical Christian conspiracy, indoctrinating Muhammad. Neither position is tenable as both are the product of medieval Christian–Muslim polemic. The truth, if found, lies somewhere in between. We must focus on the sources and shed any religious bias.

Missionary Mentor?

Does Waraqah's role as a scribe and wedding officiator mean he was deacon or bishop of a Jewish-Christian church in Mecca as suggested by Abu Musa al-Hariri (Joseph Azzi) and others?[87] We are encouraged by the Syriac characterizations of Arab conversion, but it remains

---

87 al-Hariri, *Qiss wa nabi*, 29–30. See further Joseph Dorra-Haddad, *al-Qur'an da'wah nasraniyyah*, Beirut: Durus Qur'aniyyah, 1970.

unclear. In this case the reports of his missionary work are murky. Moreover, the reports about the marriage at which he officiated are contradictory. We simply do not have sufficient evidence.

Even the Arabic word *waraqah* signifies "paper," identifying him as a scribe rather than serving as a good name.[88] Furthermore, as introduced in the first chapter of this book, we have no hard evidence of a pre-Islamic Arabic Bible or apocryphal Jewish-Christian writings. Waraqah may have been a priest, scribe, or cleric of some sort. Beyond these barest details, however, we can say little more about his qualifications or identity.

Still, it is indisputable that Waraqah was a historical figure, that he served as a mentor to Muhammad for about fifteen years (*ca.* 595–610), so much so that his companionship was somehow associated with divine revelation. Yet Khadijah was the link between them both. This complex and striking relationship is revealed in the strictest Hadith authorities claim. The story first emerges in Ibn Ishaq's hagiography of Muhammad. But it reappears a century later in five reports found in the *Sahih* collections of Bukhari (d. 256/870) and Muslim (d. 261/875). In these reports, Muhammad is on one of his night vigils in the cave of Hira' outside Mecca, similar in manner to Syrian ascetic monks.[89] He is visited by the angel Gabriel, who reveals Q 96:1–5 to him. Muhammad is awestruck and horrified by the experience of revelation and flees to the only comfort he ever knew in this world—Khadijah.

Then Allah's Messenger returned with that experience; and the muscles between his neck and shoulders were trembling till he came upon Khadijah (his wife) and said, "Cover me!"

They covered him, and when the state of fear was over, he said to Khadijah, "O Khadijah! What is wrong with me? I was afraid that something bad might happen to me." Then he told her the story.

Khadijah said, "Nay! But receive the good tidings! By Allah, Allah will never disgrace you, for by Allah, you keep good

88 Cf. C. F. Robinson, *EI²*, "Waraka b. Nawfal."
89 Cf. Tor Andrae, *Der Ursprung der Islams und das Christentum*, Uppsala: Almqvist & Wiksells, 1926, trans. Jules Roche, *Les origines de l'Islam et le Christianisme*, Paris: Adrien-Maisonneuve, 1955, 126.

relations with your kith and kin, speak the truth, help the poor and the destitute, entertain your guests generously and assist those who are stricken with calamities." Khadijah then took him to Waraqah bin Naufal, the son of Khadijah's paternal uncle. Waraqah had been converted to Christianity in the pre-Islamic period and used to write Arabic and write of the Gospel in Arabic as much as Allah wished him to write. He was an old man and had lost his eyesight.

Khadijah said (to Waraqah), "O my cousin! Listen to what your nephew is going to say."

Waraqah said, "O my nephew! What have you seen?" The Prophet then described whatever he had seen.

Waraqah said, "This is the same Angel (Gabriel) who was sent to Moses. I wish I were young." He added some other statement.

Allah's Messenger asked, "Will these people drive me out?"

Waraqah said, "Yes, for nobody brought the like of what you have brought, but was treated with hostility. If I were to remain alive till your day (when you start preaching), then I would support you strongly." But a short while later Waraqah died and the Divine Inspiration was paused for a while so that Allah's Messenger was very much grieved.[90]

In other reports Waraqah hails Muhammad's revelation as the return of the "Law of Moses," exclaiming "holy" three times.[91] The event of qur'anic revelation is told using the finest literary instruments, echoing Isaiah 6:3; 29:11–12, and building upon Syriac hagiographical themes and techniques examined elsewhere.[92] There is no surprise given the Christian background of his mentor that the prophetic messenger cited in the Medinan Surahs illustrate "Muhammad as an episcopal figure."[93]

It is Khadijah, however, who believes Muhammad from the very beginning. She used to visit Muhammad during his ascetic retreats at

---

90 Bukhari, *Sahih*, 65:475, translation edited, https://sunnah.com/bukhari/65/475.
91 Ibn Ishaq, *Sirah*, 1:169.
92 Neuenkirchen, "Visions et Ascensions," 309–311, 315.
93 Nicolai Sinai, "Muhammad as an episcopal figure," *A* 65, 2018, 1–30.

the cave, bringing him warm soup.[94] It is she who takes him in, comforts him, and offers "good tidings" in the manner of the Synoptic Gospels. By taking him to Waraqah, she gave Muhammad voice. And she ensured his voice reached its intended audience. It was through Khadijah and her 'Abd al-'Uzzid kindred that Muhammad left the ancestral cult of al-'Uzza and was ushered into the world of Christian–Hanafite monotheism taking over Arabia at the time. It may be argued that without her many interventions Muhammad would not have been afforded the opportunity to become a prophet of Arabia.

Protecting Muhammad: Abu Talib or Khadijah?

With Waraqah dead, however, tradition reports that Muhammad suffered depression, anxiety, and suicidal thoughts.[95] Once again, only Khadijah was there to lift him up. Her mission now was to protect the messenger of God to the Arabs. It was no easy task, and again the sources are skewed in favor of Muhammad's immediate kindred, the 'Abd Manafids. That is to say, they shun the powerful protectress that Khadijah was in favor of propping up the image of the now decrepit and near destitute Abu Talib. In any case, the sources call 619 the "year of sorrow," because both Abu Talib and Khadijah died that year, reportedly three days apart.

> Khadijah bt. Khuwaylid and Abu Talib died in one year, and then a series of crises fell upon the messenger of God by the death of Khadijah and Abu Talib. For Khadijah was a counselor of truth over Islam. He used to dwell in her.[96]

The report above recorded by Ibn Ishaq may be our oldest recollection of Khadijah's passing, and it is she who is accorded the title "counselor of truth over Islam" as though it were an official post. This honor is not granted Abu Talib, who was neither a Muslim nor ostensibly capable of such a magnificent title. Despite their affection for him as the prophet's

94 'Abd al-Karim, *Fatrat al-takwin*, 325.
95 See Bukhari, *Sahih*, 91:1, https://sunnah.com/bukhari:6982.
96 Ibn Ishaq, *Sirah*, 271.

uncle, the hagiographers had no choice but to concede Abu Talib's fate in hellfire.

Khadijah is said to have died on the 10th of Ramadan, a date I argue is symbolic rather than historical as it converges with the sacred month within which the Qur'an was revealed. We also have no mention of how she died, an odd omission for Islam's greatest woman.

Erasing Khadijah and Amplifying Abu Talib

The sources go to pains rehabilitating the image of Abu Talib. He was compelled to raise Muhammad by oath, but was otherwise unsupportive of his nephew's religious mission, even deriding it in resentment.[97] Abu Talib had grown old. He had many children to rear and was struggling financially. His so-called protection of Muhammad from the wrath of his pagan uncles and Meccan notables was symbolic. That is to say, he *merely* followed tribal laws of protection. Khadijah, on the other hand, *actively* protected, comforted, and guided Muhammad, as evidenced in the reports about his prophecy already cited.

At any rate it is said Abu Talib fell ill in his old age. At his deathbed, Muhammad was joined by his pagan uncles. He is said to have refused pronouncing the Muslim testimony of faith. And yet he is also said to have advised his people to follow Muhammad.[98] How could such a far-fetched series of events even be possible?

The sources, including the *Sirah* of Ibn Ishaq, add insult to injury by inserting a fabricated soliloquy ascribed to this *man* at his deathbed followed by lines of ornate poetry. This was no doubt the work of articulate male hagiographers. No such deathbed fabrication is afforded to the *woman* who actually protected Muhammad, day in and day out. On the matter of Khadijah's protection of Muhammad the sources are deafeningly silent, preferring to regurgitate the tribal customs of Mecca's patriarchs and to shroud their paganism in hagiographical fiction.

---

97 Ibn Hisham, *Sirah*, 1:123.
98 Ibn Ishaq, *Sirah*, 268–269.

The Agony of Losing Khadijah

Muhammad never recovered from the loss of Khadijah. His demeanor grew dark and heavy, likely relapsing to his years of trauma as an orphan. With the death of his closest loved ones—Khadijah, Waraqah, and Abu Talib—he struggled for three years to regain his footing, and to rise to the challenge of leading a new nation. From 622 to 628 he is said to have remarried to Sawdah bt. Zamʿah (d. 23/632 or 54/674), his oldest wife ever, followed by ʿAʾishah bt. Abi Bakr (d. 58/678) who was the youngest, most jealous, and assertive of his wives.

Muhammad wrestled with the process of grief and soul searching after Khadijah. He was broken-hearted after the loss of his life partner. He is said to have taken up to thirteen wives from across Arabia's tribal and religious nations, enacting several more alliances through unconsummated marriages. He became a conqueror seemingly overnight, fighting almost thirty battles and subjugating the entire Arabian Peninsula.[99]

Some Western scholars have described the transformation in his conduct as "mov[ing] from ethical exemplar to bloodthirsty warrior," with others adding that he was motivated by "political reasons," carried by "deepening religious experiences, or suffering from epilepsy and mental decay."[100] In this context, his subsequent conquests and numerous marriages, while advancing the spread of Islam, are seen as constituting a desperate attempt to fill a void left behind by tragic loss. After enjoying unprecedented power Muhammad fell ill and died.

Before his body claimed the solace of burial, his closest confidants abandoned him and began squabbling over power.[101] Though his life was fraught with controversy, there is no report of Muhammad ever striking a woman. He is reported to have demonstrated immeasurable patience with his wives, perhaps to the point of timidity before some of his companions.[102]

99 Cf. Ibn Saʿd, *Tabaqat*, 10:136–138.
100 Ali, *The Lives of Muhammad*, 131–132.
101 Ouardi, *Les Derniers Jours de Muhammad*, 7.
102 Ibn Saʿd, *Tabaqat*, 10:193–194.

Khadijah's Legacy

As this chapter demonstrates, female power and male power had switched sides, with the former espousing Christianity and the latter espousing the pagan cult of al-'Uzza. Muhammad was mostly likely a typical pagan before meeting Khadijah. Her cousin, clan, and cohort of companions most likely introduced Muhammad to Abrahamic monotheism, if not inculcated its values within him. Nevertheless, by Khadijah's time, the scale and depth of female power in late antique Arabia had slowly but surely dwindled before the rising tide of conquest in the name of Christianity, Hanifism, and finally Islam.

Forgotten Friend

That being said, Khadijah looms large within the Shii and Sunni traditions. She was first wife to Muhammad, and in some cases offering him the support of a mother. She was the first Muslim and founding mother of the believers. Khadijah was quite simply the *best friend* Muhammad ever had. She was closer to him than Abu Bakr or 'Umar, who left Muhammad's side at the end in order to participate in the transition of political power after his passing.[103] What we know about her from the sources is limited to the authors' hagiographical focus on Muhammad as messenger of God, not on her as the lady of Quraysh. We know little more about her own personal characteristics beyond the stories of her bold audacity in hiring, marrying, and raising Muhammad. This is in spite of the sources' bias against the tribal bloc of 'Abd al-'Uzza I, in favor of 'Abd Manaf, as I have argued.

 The entire corpus of sayings attributed to Muhammad, known as the Hadith, is predicated upon the time period of his prophetic mission (610–632). It privileges the latter decades of his life, when his wife 'A'ishah had barely reached maturity, while claiming or pretending virtually nothing from Khadijah, who was instrumental in building Muhammad's career and reputation over the course of twenty-four years (595–619). There is good reason to conclude that Muhammad loved Khadijah most dearly and mentioned her often as it is reported.

103 Ali, *The Lives of Muhammad*, 150.

No one disputes that 'A'ishah envied her husband's first wife in death, and that her jealousy drove her to insult Khadijah as an "old hag" before Muhammad's very person.[104]

Fatimah al-Zahra'

So who was there left to bear the now exceedingly dim torch of female power? In short, I argue Khadijah is perhaps the most radiant noblewoman within both a tradition and legacy exemplifying the autonomy enjoyed by Arabian noblewomen. Moreover, I argue that the daughter of Khadijah and Muhammad—Fatimah al-Zahra'—is the locus of pagan, Christian, and Islamic symbols of female power. Fatimah was, of course, wife of 'Ali b. Abi Talib (d. 661), Muhammad's cousin whom Khadijah raised for some time in their home, and who as a result became the second Muslim. The scene of Muhammad, Khadijah, and 'Ali performing the first ever public prayer, while likely apocryphal, is a powerful image evoking the divine Father, Mother, and Son found in Syro-Arabian pagan and Christian circles.[105] Fatimah and 'Ali are revered as the ideal Muslim couple. They are extolled with divine epithets within the Shii sources especially. It is intriguing to consider that the Shii ethos of resistance against Sunni injustice contains within it the last vestiges of female power in late antique Arabia.

The Final Destruction of al-'Uzza, 594–629

Our chapter closes where it began, with the Arabian goddess al-'Uzza whose time had come to an end. Zooming out of the story between Khadijah and Muhammad, we consider the final destruction of al-'Uzza's cultic centers in Arabia during the late sixth–early seventh centuries. Our final analysis in this regard takes us back to the Christian court of al-Hirah under al-Nu'man III, and the newly Islamic court of Yathrib (Medina) under Muhammad the prophet.

---

104 Muslim, *Sahih*, 44:112, https://sunnah.com/muslim/44/112.
105 Cf. Ibn Ishaq, *Sirah*, 182; Ibn Sa'd, *Tabaqat*, 10:19.

The Golden Idol

The Ghassanids slew al-Mundhir in battle in 554, ending his "reign of terror." The reign of al-'Uzza continued for decades more. Arabian paganism, not least the cult of al-'Uzza, remained the official religious affiliation of successive Lakhmid kings throughout the latter half of the sixth century. 'Amr III b. al-Mundhir (d. 570) may have been pagan with private Christian leanings, while his brothers and successors Qabus (d. 573) and al-Mundhir IV were more staunchly pagan. The reluctance to accept Christianity by sixth-century Lakhmids was probably out of fear of repercussion by their Sasanian lords, who mistrusted the religion as a competing, clandestine Roman allegiance.[106] Only with the conversion of al-Nu'man III b. al-Mundhir (r. 580–602) did East Syrian Christianity find firm footing, and was the famed golden idol of al-'Uzza dismantled for good.

Several church fathers and historians bemoan the worship of al-'Uzza-Aphrodite by the Arabs of late antiquity. They include Nilus of Sinai (d. 430), Isaac of Antioch (d. 460), Jacob of Serugh (d. 521), and Procopius (d. *ca.* 570). One can appreciate, therefore, that once her most vicious and bloodthirsty champions, the Lakhmid kings of al-Hirah made infamous by al-Mundhir III, permanently abandoned al-'Uzza to finally embrace Christianity, subsequent chroniclers were relieved and overjoyed.

There are several Syriac accounts of the baptism of al-Nu'man III in 594. The main sources in this regard are the account attributed to Evagrius Scholasticus (d. 594) found in the medieval compilation known as the *Chronicle of Seert*, and the *Life of Sabrisho'* told by Peter the Solitary (d. after 604).[107]

106 Philip Wood, *The Chronicle of Seert: Christian Historical Imagination in Late Antique Iraq*, Oxford: Oxford University Press, 2013, 20; Fisher, "From Mavia to al-Mundhir," 216–218.

107 *Chronicle of Seert*, trans. Addai Scher, PO 13, 1919, 468–69; Peter the Solitary, "Life of Sabrisho'," *Histoire de Mar-Jabalaha de trois autres patriarches d'un prêtre et de deux laïques Nestoriens*, ed. Paul Bedjan, Leipzig: Otto Harrassowitz, 1895, 322–327, with thanks to Philip Wood.

Just as Paul adhered to Judaism and Aba [the *catholicos*] to Magianism, this man [al-Nuʿman, r. *ca.* 583–602/4] was addicted to paganism. He adored the star named Zohra and offered sacrifices to idols. This demon possessed him, and he vainly asked the priests of the idols for help. He met Simeon bin Jabir, bishop of Hira; Sabrishoʿ, bishop of Lashom, who would become *catholicos*; and the monk Ishoʿzkha and asked for help. God cured him and the demon left him.[108]

It is reported that al-Nuʿman toppled or melted down a golden statue of al-ʿUzza in the form of Aphrodite, called by her Arabic name *zuhrah*, and surrendered it to the church in repentance.[109]

He commanded immediately that all those seeking after the error of evil falsity be put to the sword by his troops. So suddenly like bats in the night, by the brilliance of the sun, by the power of truth in the prayer of Mar Sabrishoʿ he was illuminated, and by the zeal of Mar Simeon he shone forth, so they fled and hid in their caves of idolatry. And the crown of victory over his enemies and rebels was bound by his servants. And they baptized the king, his wives, children, and all the people of his household. And there was great news throughout the church about the baptism of Nuʿman, king of the Arabs and all his helpers. Then king Nuʿman commanded, "break the goddess-statue of idol worship al-ʿUzza (*'azay*)!" So it was said there was a jug of oil for Aphrodite as he was weeping over the shame of the Greeks. And all its gold and pearls he paid to the treasury of the church that he built.[110]

The gold associated with al-ʿUzza may be a *topos* reminiscent of the biblical golden calf (Exodus 32:4), but one can scarcely doubt the existence of a royal idol to the goddess al-ʿUzza in the court of al-Hira. Such an opulent cult breaks with ancient Arabian iconography representing goddesses as stone betyls or tree groves. It demonstrates, furthermore,

---

108 Fisher et al., "Arabs and Christianity," 359.
109 Ibid. See further al-Mallah, *al-Wasit fi tarikh al-ʿarab qabl al-islam*, 239.
110 Peter the Solitary, "Life of Sabrishoʿ," 327, translated by the author.

the continued Hellenic influence over the court of al-Hirah, as illustrated in the account above.[111] Moreover, these reports make clear the Lakhmid cult of al-'Uzza venerated the brutality and rich spoils of kings making war, rather than the ancient mother goddess or queen of heaven, whose life-giving properties have been discussed at length.

The envelopment of Arabia by Christian phylarchs, viceroys, and tribal chieftains exasperated the Persian king of kings. He installed a new Himyarite king, Sayf b. Dhi Yazan (d. 578), to reconquer Arabia from Ethiopian hands. This was achieved at the battle of Hadramaut *ca.* 570, after which the might of Persian influence descended once again upon Yemen.[112] Likewise, the Lakhmid turn to East Syrian Christianity incensed their Persian patrons. And in 602, on the eve of his conquest of Roman lands, king Khusrow II had al-Nu'man III killed.

The Black Goddess

Two decades after the passing of the Lakhmid king, Muhammad was undertaking a new national conquest of Arabia, this time not in the name of Christianity, but Islam. In pre-Islamic times Arabian religion was held together, so to speak, by cultic practice rather than theological belief. This could persist no longer if Arabian society would birth the "middle nation" uniting Christians and Jews under the newest Abrahamic banner.[113]

This new world did not take kindly to goddesses. Among the cities of the Hijaz, Muhammad is said to have conquered Mecca, Yathrib, and Ta'if. Some say he did this deliberately in order to unify remnant worshippers of the Arabian "daughters of Allah." These were namely al-'Uzza, Manat, and Allat.[114] Islamic tradition teaches that Muhammad

111 Shahid, *Byzantium and the Arabs in the Sixth Century*, 2:2:314.
112 al-Fassi, "*al-Awda' al-siyasiyyah*," 453.
113 Cf. in relation Martin Tamcke, "The relationship between theological teaching and religious practice by the East-Syrian Christians in Qatar (sixth–seventh centuries)," *Religious Culture in Late Antique Arabia: Selected Studies on the Late Antique Religious Mind*, Piscataway: Gorgias Press, 2017, 89–102.
114 Al-Azmeh, *The Emergence of Islam in Late Antiquity*, 325. Cf. further al-Mallah, *al-Wasit fi tarikh al-'arab qabl al-islam*, 321.

dispatched armies under his elite generals to destroy each of them at their respective shrines. After its desecration by the Christian icono-clast of Qudaʿah, Zuhayr b. Janab al-Kalbi, the final and total annihila-tion of al-ʿUzzaʾs shrine at Nakhlah came at the hands of Khalid b. al-Walid. ʿAli b. Abi Talib is said to have smashed the idol of Manat in a town called Qadid, near the Red Sea coast. And al-Mughirah b. Shuʿbah is reported to have reclaimed Allatʾs shrine in Taʾif, trans-forming it into a mosque.[115]

But it is the destruction of al-ʿUzza which is taken to be emblematic of the rupture between paganism and Islam. Ibn al-Kalbi states:

> We were told ... al-ʿUzza was a she-devil which used to frequent three trees in the valley of Nakhlah. When the prophet captured Mecca, he dispatched Khalid b. al-Walid saying, "Go to the valley of Nakhlah; there you will find three trees. Cut down the first one." Khalid went and cut it down. On his return to report, the Prophet asked him saying, "Have you seen anything there?"
> Khalid replied and said, "No."
> The prophet ordered him to return and cut down the second tree. He went and cut it down. On his return to report the Prophet asked him a second time, "Have you seen anything there?"
> Khalid answered, "No."
> Thereupon the prophet ordered him to go back and cut down the third tree. When Khalid arrived on the scene he found an Abyssinian woman with disheveled hair and her hands placed on her shoulder[s], gnashing and grating her teeth. Behind her stood Dubayyah al-Sulami who was then the custodian of al-ʿUzza.
> When Dubayyah saw Khalid approaching, he said:
> "O thou al-ʿUzza! Remove thy veil and tuck up thy sleeves;
> Summon up thy strength and deal Khalid an unmistakable blow.
> For unless thou killest him this very day,
> Thou shalt be doomed to ignominy and shame."
> Thereupon Khalid replied:
> "O al-ʿUzza! May thou be blasphemed, not exalted!

---

115 Ibn al-Kalbi, *Kitab al-asnam*, 17.

Verily I see that God hath abased thee."

Turning to the woman, he dealt her a blow which severed her head in twain, and lo, she crumbled into ashes. He then cut down the tree and killed Dubayyah the custodian, after which he returned to the Prophet and reported to him his exploit. Thereupon the prophet said, "That was al-ʿUzza. But she is no more. The Arabs shall have none after her. Verily she shall never be worshipped again."[116]

The ancient shrine of al-ʿUzza at Nakhlah was entirely different than its opulent golden counterpart in al-Hirah. For it was contained within the palm tree grove of Nakhlah, staying true to the ancient worship of the mother goddess and queen of heaven. The site belonged to the same tradition of the Nabataean Sulaymids, Canaanite Asherah groves outside Jerusalem, and Inanna's Huluppu Tree in ancient Sumeria. Although this account is clearly not without its fantastic elements, the claim that Muhammad ordered Khalid to strike down three trees, or that he ordered his commanders to demolish three shrines, echoes the worship of the Arabian "daughters of Allah." Nakhlah may have been the most ancient shrine among the three sacred sites, perhaps at some point housing idols to Allat, al-ʿUzza, and Manat.

Like Evagrius and other Syriac accounts of al-ʿUzza at al-Hira, Ibn al-Kalbi's account claims that al-ʿUzza at Nakhlah was a demon or devil. Before Khalid dealt her the final blow she is said to have manifested as an "Abyssinian woman with disheveled hair ... gnashing and grating her teeth." The point behind this misogynistic and racist characterization is to depict the final hour of pagan female power in the most humiliating light—wild, black, and evil.[117]

The careful researcher, however, should explore the historical kernel behind it. Her "disheveled hair" is likely a demonization of coiled, African hair, likening the woman to a tree in a grove. This hypothesis finds backing in other reports suggesting that at the center of the grove were fennel or acacia trees, whose sprouting leaves resemble hair, or

116 Ibn al-Kalbi, *Kitab al-asnam*, 25–26, trans. Nabih Faris, 21–22, edited.
117 Cf. Al-Azmeh, *The Emergence of Islam in Late Antiquity*, 338.

Safaitic inscriptions to this effect.[118] More broadly, there is an abundance of scholarship on the Afroasiatic origins of Abrahamic religions and classical civilization.[119] There is, likewise, research on the connection between "sexual insult and female militancy" with respect to African women.[120]

So, could al-'Uzza's human representative have been an Ethiopian priestess, consorting with the Arab priest Dubayyah al-Sulami? If so, it means that the manifestation of Arabia's very last goddess—al-'Uzza of Nakhlah—was *black*.

118 See al-Mallah, *al-Wasit fi tarikh al-'arab qabl al-islam*, 403; Smith, *Religion of the Semites*, 185; Macdonald, "Goddesses, dancing girls or cheerleaders?" 280.
119 Cf. generally Martin Bernal, *Black Athena: The Afroasiatic Roots of Classical Civilization*, 2 vols., New Brunswick: Rutgers University Press, 1987; Julian Baldick, *Black God: Afroasiatic Roots of the Jewish, Christian and Muslim Religions*, London: Bloomsbury Academic, 1997.
120 Shirley Ardener, "Sexual Insult and Female Militancy," *M* 8.3, 1973, 422–440.

PART III

Men of the *Jahiliyyah*

7

Pagans, Pontiffs, and Political Power

WITH MUHAMMAD'S CONQUEST of Arabia, Abrahamic monotheism was here to stay. But the seeds of male power were planted
centuries earlier. The female nobility, including lofty sovereigns and
humble chieftains, were systematically supplanted by their male rivals.
Various strong men built lasting structures that violently crushed
female power. Our attention turns to three institutions which pervaded
the so-called *jahiliyyah*, namely:

(1) Empire
(2) Church
(3) War

Indigenous pagan cults, which supported the worship of goddesses
and respected female sovereignty, were exterminated. In their wake
stood a single deity molded by the distinctly masculine forces of imperialism, sectarianism, and violence.

Empire

The Roman conquest of the Mediterranean Basin and large parts of the
Near East in the first–third centuries CE would transform the religious
and political culture in much of Arabian society. The capital of "Roman
Arabia" moved away from Petra to Bosra. Romans redirected international trade headed to the Indian Ocean away from the west Arabian
coast, to the African Red Sea coast, both reviving and developing the

Ptolemaic maritime route.[1] Roman hegemony was rivaled only by the Parthian and later Sassanian Empire which exerted tremendous influence on Arabian society through Mesopotamia and the Persian Gulf.

Roman Conquest of Semitic Peoples

Rome destroyed rival empires and kingdoms that stood in its way. Local queens and kings were gradually replaced by male governors or phylarchs. They ruled on behalf of Rome or Persia. Nevertheless, the empire left wealthy ruling families and petty fiefdoms in its service largely intact, while respecting their religious customs. This is the story of powerful Semitic houses of Syro-Arabian origin, notably those of Phoenician, Syrian, and Arab background. Roman emperors during 193–235 and 244–249 emerged from the Libyan city of Leptis Magna, and the Syro-Arabian cities of Emesa and Trachonitis.

The Roman Empire was beset from within and without by enemies. It buckled under the pressure of "barbarian" incursions. The empire relented to the demands of newly incorporated peoples, affording them the opportunity to participate in political life. Thus, Arabian male nobility turned their ambitions towards ruling Rome directly. Unlike the case within Arabian society, only men could rise to the rank of emperor. Their women continued exercising power nevertheless, but from behind the scenes. Their limited exercise of power was remarkable nonetheless.

The empire inevitably became dominated by military men from the periphery. They were nicknamed by later historians "barrack emperors."[2] And they sought to secure the empire through brute force, seizing power for themselves in the process. The ensuing crisis of the third century saw an ethnically diverse cadre of barrack emperors whose rule was short, volatile, and typically ended in their violent death. Their ranks included military generals from formerly conquered "barbarian" regions, namely: the Near East, North Africa, and the Balkans. The empire's growing diversity and instability prepared the

---

1 al-Fassi, "al-Awda' al-siyasiyyah," 471–472.
2 Ramsay MacMullen, "Roman imperial building in the provinces," *HSCP* 64, 1959, 221.

conditions necessary for a "counter-emperor" from Palmyra, Zenobia, whose reign did not last.

The Severan and Palmyrene dynasties—rulers of Semitic origin—enjoyed immense power in the third century. Rome's Semitic emperors not only helped shape the fate of the empire on a grand scale, they influenced Arabia specifically. In both cases, these powerful rulers reinvigorated male power, and planted the seed for the betrayal and downfall of female power in the Arabian sphere. One final note in this regard is, while the influence of Arabian society upon the Roman Empire is hardly deniable, the extent of this influence is hotly debated.[3]

Semitic Emperors and the Severan Dynasty, 193–235

The Severan dynasty (193–235) inherited an overextended empire, which was slowly but surely entering its twilight. At the tail end of its zenith, the empire began its gradual decline following this period. Rome was overstretched and neighboring "barbarian" populations began to exert more power and influence. The growing diversity of Roman citizens, and therefore its emperors, was inevitable. Septimius Severus, a Punic soldier who rose out of Leptis Magna in Libya, is remembered as a great emperor. He chose Julia Domna of Emesa as his empress and the matriarch of his line, whose tragic fate we have seen.

Severus oversaw grand construction projects and enlarged the eastern frontier of his realm by conquering lands from the Parthians. He also expanded the *Limes Arabicus* to include Aqaba and the northern fringes of the Hijaz.[4] Roman garrisons and mounted units patrolled the Arabian cities of Bosra, Dumah, Rawwafa, and Hegra, just two

---

3 Irfan Shahid's multivolume study on *Byzantium and the Arabs* between the fourth and seventh centuries CE largely accepts the literary sources on Roman–Arab exchange at face value. Whereas Millar, *The Roman Near East*, 4, 423 disputes the unity of nomadic and pastoral groups typically identified as "Arab," and is generally skeptical about their influence upon neighboring cultures, and the empire itself. Ball, *Rome in the East*, 32, 96 treads a middle path, arguing that Arab communities built cohesion and solidarity as Roman *foederati* and possessed centuries of military expertise culminating in the seventh-century Arab conquests.

4 Glenn Bowersock, "Limes Arabicus," *HSCP* 80, 1976, 219–229.

hundred miles north of Yathrib, from where Muhammad would rule centuries later.[5] His expansion of military expenditure and pursuits led to the further integration of ethnic populations on the frontier, and the acceleration of economic inflation.

His son emperor Caracalla (d. 217), whose lineage was Punic and Syrian, is remembered as a cruel tyrant by the Roman sources. His poor reputation is partly the result of his brutality and unpopular decisions. Besides exacting retribution against his foes, he increased military expenditure, exacerbating economic inflation. However, we cannot dismiss the hostility of Roman authors and later orientalist historians towards his Semitic origins—they had an evident interest in exaggerating the terror of his reign.[6]

Semitic Men and the Constitutio Antoniniana *of 212*

Caracalla's great achievement, aside from the famous complex of baths which carry his name in Rome, is the *Constitutio Antoniniana* of 212. This was an edict allowing all free men in the empire to become citizens. The reason for the historic edict is generally believed to be the emperor's need for a wider base of taxation, which can hardly be disputed given the gradual depletion of Rome's coffers.[7] There may have been another reason as well.

The Semitic origin of his lineage was viewed with some disdain by his Italic near contemporaries.[8] To this end consider the words of the satirical poet Juvenal in the second century CE:

> Syrian Orontes has long since flowed into the Tiber, and brought with it its language, morals, and the crooked harps with the

---

5 Bowersock, *Roman Arabia*, 103–115; Crone, *The Qur'anic Pagans and Related Matters*, 72.

6 Gibbon, *The Decline and Fall of the Roman Empire*, 86–102 typifies this bias. See criticism in Al-Ani, *Araber als Teil der hellenistisch-römischen und christlichen Welt*, 39–45, 102–107.

7 Gibbon, *The Decline and Fall of the Roman Empire*, 101.

8 Millar, *The Roman Near East*, 141; Adam Kemezis, *Greek Narratives of the Roman Empire under the Severans: Cassius Dio, Philostratus and Herodian*, Cambridge: Cambridge University Press, 2014, 31–33.

flute-player, and its national tambourines, and girls made to stand for hire at the Circus. Go thither, you who fancy a barbarian harlot with embroidered turban![9]

Rome was increasingly populated by Asian, African, and Balkan claimants to the throne from around the Mediterranean Basin. In this context Caracalla's economic and social policies cannot be ignored. While developing new ways to feed the Roman military behemoth, he established an edict promoting greater citizenship and diversity. It is not mere happenstance that Semitic pretenders to the imperial throne would arise even after the Severan dynasty had passed.

So the edict served to induct Syro-Arabian men into Roman life. But it excluded women by default. At any rate, if Caracalla's policies slowly but surely empowered Arabian male nobility, then his cousin Elagabalus had an equal impact on the Arabian religious landscape.

Several developments during this time influenced the cultural fabric of Arabia itself. They include the following:

(1) Roman citizenship was expanded to include barbarian peoples, including Syro-Arabians.
(2) The worship of Syro-Arabian deities spread into the Roman Mediterranean.
(3) Abstention from pork, the practice of circumcision, and Christianity were adopted by the Roman ruling class.[10]

The Severan dynasty also promoted the cult of Elagabal, to which we turn next.

---

9 Juvenal, *The Satires of Juvenal, Persius, Sulpicia and Lucilius*, trans. Lewis Evans, London: Bell & Daldy, 1869, 15 (Satire 3, "On the City of Rome"). My thanks go to Kristina Neumann for her insights.
10 Millar, *The Roman Near East*, 21, 108, 221, 307.

Bayt Allah: The Kaabah of Rome

Elagabalus (d. 222) was not merely emperor. He was a circumcised patron of the Emesan sun god of his maternal ancestry, the Sampsiceramids. He and his cousin and successor, Alexander, served as priests of Elagabal and considered themselves endowed with his divine authority.[11] Elagabalus in particular was a leader "before his time." His assimilation of eastern gods and religious customs into western Roman practice built bridges between both worlds. His syncretism became part of the fabric of Christianity, and the cult of Elagabal which he served influenced the monotheistic beliefs of later emperors, several of whom were of Balkan extraction. In this regard, emperor Aurelian credited his conquest of Palmyra in 274 to his worship of Elagabal, integrated into the Roman pantheon as Sol Invictus or the "unconquered sun."[12] Sol Invictus was at the heart of Constantine's vision connected to the battle of the Milvian Bridge in 312. The solar god is further integrated, either by the emperor or his contemporary Eusebius of Caesarea, into the symbol of the Christian Cross.[13]

As examined already, the role of high priest and priestess in ancient Arabia blurred the line between king and queen, on the one hand, and god and goddess, on the other. It is little surprise, therefore, that Elagabalus may have considered himself an emperor-god, and that among his troubled marriages was an alleged union with, or rape of, a Vestal Virgin.[14] Again the bias of the Roman sources makes the truth of such claims impossible to know with certainty. Some have supported the idea that he was bisexual or transgender.[15] While this hypothesis may be disputed on the grounds of prejudiced authors, it was certainly

11 John McHugh, *Emperor Alexander Severus: Rome's Age of Insurrection, AD 222–235*, Barnsley, UK: Pen & Sword Military, 2017, 48; Clare Rowan, *Under Divine Auspices: Divine Ideology and the Visualisation of Imperial Power in the Severan Period*, Cambridge: Cambridge University Press, 2012, 168.

12 Andrade, *Zenobia*, 204.

13 See Ball, *Rome in the East*, 412–413, 462–466.

14 Rowan, *Under Divine Auspices*, 214.

15 Roland Betancourt, *Byzantine Intersectionality: Sexuality, Gender, and Race in the Middle Ages*, Princeton: Princeton University Press, 2020, 106–108.

Elagabalus (left); stone in temple (right)

not unheard of for Roman elites to practice alternate forms of sexuality. But Elagabalus' behavior was not a fluke.

The god Elagabal was depicted on coins as a black stone guarded by an eagle or pulled by horse-drawn chariot. He melded Arabian and Roman cultural iconography.[16] The sacred stone itself harkens back to the very founder of the Sampsiceramid Arabs. Sampsiceramus I lived in the first century BCE. He was the son of "Azizus of the Arabs," forefather and priest king of the Emesan house. The idol representing him was a meteorite believed to have been imbued with divine powers, and housed within a temple.

The temple was understood to be the "house of god" or betyl. This term originated from Canaanite *beth el*. Its unmistakable cognate in Arabic is *bayt allah*. From its humble origins among the ancient Canaanites, this cult was adopted by the Hebrews (cf. 2 Kings 23:4; Amos 7:13) and Nabataeans alike. Sacred stones housed in cubic shrines or temples became the prototype for sanctuaries throughout Arabia.[17] Each cubic shrine was called a Kaabah.

Priests or priestesses would make animal sacrifices before the sacred stone. Late antique epigraphy and literary sources demonstrate the pervasiveness of Kaabah shrines beyond that of Mecca. They include

16 See gold Roman Aures coin featuring emperor Elagabalus (recto), and "stone of Emesa" (verso) https://upload.wikimedia.org/wikipedia/commons/f/f2/Elagabalus_Aureus_Sol_Invictus.png.

17 Cf. Ibn Ishaq, *Sirah*, 142–43.

sanctuaries to various deities in Petra, Hegra, Ta'if, and other Arabian locales. The Kaabah of Tabalah, Yemen was a phallic white quartz shrine to the god Dhu al-Khalasah. Muhammad promptly had it destroyed, crushing the armies of Bajilah and Khath'am who had come out to meet him in battle.[18] The goddess Manat was said to have been worshipped in the form of a carved stone betyl by the tribes of Hudhayl, Ghassan, and Azd in the town of Qadid, and by the Aws and Khazraj tribes in Yathrib.[19]

The always rich and sometimes violent cultural background of these Kaabahs is best appreciated when compared to their iconic counterparts. That is to say, they were worshipped, loved, and adorned as idols. Worshippers dedicated ornaments and fine garments known in Arabic as *kiswah*. We know from the medieval Arabic sources that the Kaabah in Mecca was, as it remains today, adorned with a fine, embroidered *kiswah*.[20]

And so the cult of Elagabal clearly belonged to the long tradition of Syro-Arabian cubic shrines. Despite its promotion of the "unconquered sun" this ancient cult had an uneasy relationship with the Roman pantheon. It would come into conflict with the new cult of Christ, emerging from Antioch and Jerusalem. The Severans were, moreover, no friends to Christians, Jews, or Samaritans. It was said they persecuted them.[21] With the death of emperor Alexander in 235, political crisis raged on for decades. And by the early fourth century the sun had set on Elagabal himself.

Daughters of Allah: Remnants of Female Power

With the shattering of independent Arabian states—most notably Nabataea—Arabian noblewomen lost the political power they once took for granted. This is because the destruction of central authority led to the deterioration of law and order. It weakened women in

18 Ibn al-Kalbi, *Kitab al-asnam*, 34–37.
19 al-Mallah, *al-Wasit fi tarikh al-'arab qabl al-islam*, 338.
20 Robin, "Les 'Filles de Dieu' de Saba' à La Mecque," 159.
21 Geoffrey Croix, *Christian Persecution, Martyrdom, and Orthodoxy*, Oxford: Oxford University Press, 2006, 119 debates this point.

society, whose recourse was increasingly the protection of male kindred. This expanded the mandate of tribal structures instead.[22] An exceedingly fragmented Arabian society sought to recollect and re-consolidate its identity in religious terms.

Vestiges of female power remained in the temples, sanctuaries, and shrines erected throughout Arabia. Though women had been stripped of their political power, the collective memory of the goddess-queen was a potent reminder that pagan queens once ruled here. The epigraphic and archeological record demonstrates that "betyls" found in the ancient cities of Petra and Hegra were endowed with the qualities of female goddesses.[23]

With time the aniconic stone betyls representing goddesses were reforged in Greco-Roman fashion, as anthropomorphic statues in Palmyra and Hatra. They were recast as statues in the form of Arabian queens.[24] The reassertion or revival of these pagan cults not only served to preserve female power. I argue it was also a reaction to the rise of Roman hegemony, on the one hand, and the Christian Trinity, on the other. The merger of Roman–Christian power was manifested in the universal patriarch—the Father. Against Him stood the newly organized female trinity, pejoratively known to medieval Islamic tradition as the cult of the "daughters of Allah," namely Allat, al-'Uzza, and Manat. But they were doomed.

The Church

Male power came to threaten and gradually dominate female power. Most notable in this regard was the rise of a new class of powerful holy men, who were both influenced by and challenged the authority of the church. I have argued in the foregoing pages that the queens of late antique Arabia could no longer operate with the autonomy of their

22 Cf. in relation al-Fassi, *Women in pre-Islamic Arabia*, 72–73; El Cheikh, *Women, Islam, and Abbasid Identity*, 118.
23 Cf. Henry Lammens, *L'Islam: Croyances et Institutions*, Beirut: Imp. Catholique, 1943, 24.
24 Macdonald, "Goddesses, dancing girls or cheerleaders," 289–291 concedes Levantine or Hellenic influence but rejects outright all attempts to define the newly anthropomorphic entities.

forebears without recourse to holy men. It was only a matter of time till bishops, missionaries, and monks cast their spell on the Roman emperor as well.

Philip the Arab: First Christian Emperor?

Emperor Philip the Arab (d. 249) was a Syrian of Arab origin. His Semitic pedigree was, however, less prominent than that of his Severan predecessors.[25] There were other differences as well. He came from Hawran in the province of Arabia. His religious commitments, unlike the pagan sensibilities of his forerunners from Emesa, may have been Christian. Philip is reported to have worshipped at the Easter Vigil in Antioch, which is why some historians consider him the first Christian emperor. The extent to which this religious ritual made him in fact Christian is, however, hotly disputed.[26] Philip is said to have expanded the nearby Arabian city of Bosra to the status of metropolis. And its marketplace fed no less than the kings of Ghassan. It also housed the legendary Christian monk Bahira, who is said to have "discovered" Muhammad's prophecy on one of his visits to Syria as a youth.[27]

In any case, the Christian god began his slow but inevitable rise to the court of Rome in the mid third century, long before the edicts of Constantine (d. 337) or the proclamations of Theodosius I (d. 395). Christianity fundamentally transformed the late antique Near East. With it changed the religious and political culture of Arabian society. Christianity would become a truly "Arabian religion" in the fourth century CE. Much of the credit in this regard should be given to queen Mavia of Tanukh, explored already.

Roman culture and Christian religion formally endorsed the rise of male power in the religious sphere of Arabian society. The developments slowly but surely etched away the authority and sovereignty once exercised by Arabian queens and symbolized by goddesses. The twilight of female power and divinity became inevitable.

---

25 Millar, *The Roman Near East*, 530; Ball, *Rome in the East*, 418.
26 Ball, *Rome in the East*, 412–413 cites the controversy but clearly concedes that Philip was "Rome's first Christian." Bowersock, *Roman Arabia*, 127 accepts this as fact.
27 Crone, *The Qur'anic Pagans and Related Matters*, 39.

Through the masculine cults of Elagabal and then Christ, the political and religious power of males rose to new heights in Arabian society. The unlikely male gods were propped up by Christian Arabs who worshipped a god named *Allah* in Arabic, or *Alaha* in Syriac.[28]

But what of the pagan cults of Allat, al-ʿUzza, and Manat worshipped in seemingly every corner of Arabia and neighboring societies? They were smashed to bits!

Smashing Idols and Femicide, ca. 388–415

Legend has it that the Syro-Arabian Abgar V of Edessa (d. 40) was the first king to accept Christ and convert his realm of Osrhoene accordingly. He is said to have outlawed the worship of Atargatis (Allat). This detail preserved in Syriac literary sources is anachronistic, and probably took place closer to the fourth century.[29] This is when Arabian society began large-scale conversion to the Abrahamic traditions—Christianity and Judaism. Varieties of "Jewish-Christianity" or Hanifism were detectable thereafter as well.[30]

Christianity exerted great power upon the tribes serving as *foederati* of the rebranded "Byzantine Empire." The new imperial capital, Constantinople (Byzantium), was envisioned as the birthplace and new center of imperial Christendom. It merged the political might of Caesar with the Gentile piety of the biblical patriarch Abraham (Galatians 3; Q 3:67). It also perpetuated the "Greek [idea] of conquest and dominance over nature."[31]

The proto-Byzantine Church was molded into an altogether masculine hierarchy of power. It was heir to the Roman–Semitic cultural synthesis under the Severan dynasty a century earlier. The newer manifestation of this synthesis promoted male power and actively worked to supplant female power.

---

28 Cf. in relation Hawting, *The Idea of Idolatry and the Emergence of Islam*, 124–125.
29 Ball, *Rome in the East*, 100.
30 Shahid, *Byzantium and the Arabs in the fourth century*, 225; El-Badawi, *The Qurʾan and the Aramaic Gospel Traditions*, 64–66; Zellentin, *The Qurʾans Legal Culture*, 197.
31 Frymer-Kensky, *In the Wake of the Goddesses*, 216.

Perhaps no single act of violence exemplifies this shift in power better than the desecration of pagan temples in Palmyra by the Romans between 384 and 388. The statue of Allat, depicted as Athena brandishing her lance and shield, was smashed by Christian zealots. It was finally destroyed in 2017 by so-called "Islamic State" terrorists.[32]

The simultaneous contempt for female power *and* "pagan heresy" swept through the rapidly Christianizing Near East and North Africa. The *Life of Poryphyry: Bishop of Gaza*, who died *ca.* 420, by Mark the Deacon celebrates the destruction of Aphrodite's temple in Gaza *ca.* 400. This was paralleled by the renunciation of her cult by the Arabs of northern Syria converted by Simeon the Stylite, as narrated by Theodoret. Be that as it may, the story goes that Poryphyry accuses—slanders—a Manichaean woman named Julia of Antioch. He claims that she had "bewitched" crowds with her "godless" doctrine and "gifts of money." In due course, the story goes that Poryphyry smites her with his own spell, killing her instantly.[33]

Then there is the famous case of the philosopher and "pagan martyr," Hypatia of Alexandria (d. 415). Though not an Arab, she was a pagan woman lynched by a Christian mob during Lent. According to the church historian Socrates Scholasticus (d. 439), she was stripped naked, gored, and bludgeoned to death. Then her body was mutilated and torched.[34] One can only attempt to fathom the frenzy of terror, bloodlust, and treachery shown by the zealous gang of men who violated and butchered one of the most stunning intellects of late antiquity.

To this may be added the destruction of later centuries. These include the systematic razing of pagan shrines by the Christians of Quda'ah and early Muslims of Quraysh already explored.

32 Intagliata, *Palmyra after Zenobia*, 46–47.
33 Mark the Deacon, *The Life of Poryphry: Bishop of Gaza*, ed. G. F. Hill, Oxford: Clarendon Press, 1913, 94–99.
34 Cf. discussion in Edward Watts, *Hypatia: The Life and Legend of an Ancient Philosopher*, Oxford: Oxford University Press, 2017, 119–139.

Organized Men, Expelled Women

Holy men were urban clerics vying for power in various metropoles, or saintly hermits who renounced worldly affairs and practiced asceticism in the desert.[35] Their relationship to women as well as paganism is encapsulated in the words of Peter Brown, who says of the archetypical holy man:

> He was a ruthless professional; and as is often the case, his rise was a victory of men over women, who had been the previous guardians of the diffuse occult traditions of their neighborhood.[36]

The statement rings true with the emendation, at least within Arabian society, that female occult traditions were often near universal in appeal and practice. Be that as it may, in greater Syria, where some of the earliest Arabian communities thrived, foremost among them were the bishops, monks, and prophets of the eastern churches. The holy men of the church were organized into a hierarchical body of clergy at the top of which sat various patriarchs or church fathers. The Syrian church fathers had an especially strong impact on the Christians of Arabia. Furthermore, new bodies of governance known as "church canons" were modeled after Roman law and authored by men for men, generally to the exclusion of women.[37]

Syrian Churches and Arab Conversion, Fifth–Sixth Centuries

The East and West Syrian churches spread throughout Arabia. This was especially the case in the fifth–sixth centuries. They built upon the legacy of Syriac-speaking poet-theologians and desert ascetics. Christian Arabs remained committed to their new faith despite the

---

35 See Peter Brown, "The Rise and Function of the Holy Man in Late Antiquity," *JRS* 61, 1971, 80–101; *Society and the Holy in Late Antiquity*, Berkeley: University of California Press, 1989; *Power and Persuasion in Late Antiquity: Towards a Christian Empire*, Madison: University of Wisconsin Press, 1992.
36 Cf. in relation Brown, *Society and the Holy in Late Antiquity*, 150–151.
37 Fowden, *Before and after Muhammad*, 57, 167–169.

apparent absence of an "Arabic Bible."[38] The liturgical language of Arabic-speaking Christians remained Aramaic, especially the dialect of Syriac.

The semi-legendary Syriac Christian origin story, known as the *Doctrine of Addai*, claims the "Arab" Abgarid dynasty of Edessa was the first ever to convert to Christianity. As an instrumental actor in the context of late antique Near Eastern politics and religion, the tribal loyalties of Arabian communities were divided not only in service of Ctesiphon and Byzantium, but also to a particular Christian sect. The religious dimension of late antique Arabian tribal and civil war is undervalued by specialists. The role of religion is demonstrated perfectly in the endless wars between the pagan, later East Syrian, Lakhmid kingdom, on the one hand, and the West Syrian Ghassanid kingdom, on the other.

The Syriac-speaking church of the East was dominant in Persian Mesopotamia and the east Arabian coast all along the Persian Gulf. Their numerous dioceses included:

- al-Hirah, the Lakhmid capital at the head of the Persian Gulf
- Beth Arbaye or "land of the Arabs" (Adiabene and upper Mesopotamia)
- Beth Qatraye (Qatar)
- Beth Mazunaye (Oman)
- Smaller dioceses in Mashmahig, Dairin (Bahrain), Hagar, Hatta, Soqotra, and Sanaa

Dairin was home to several synods during the seventh century, including that of 676. During the Abbasid or early medieval period (750–1258), the East Syrian Church penetrated deep within the societies of Central, East, and South Asia, becoming the largest church in the medieval world.[39]

---

38 See Sidney Griffith, *The Bible in Arabic: The Scriptures of the "People of the Book" in the Language of Islam*, Princeton: Princeton University Press, 2015, 7–53 *contra.* Shahid, *Byzantium and the Arabs in the Fourth Century*, 435–442.

39 Cf. Holger Gzella, *A Cultural History of Aramaic: From the Beginnings to the Advent of Islam*, Leiden; Boston: Brill, 2015, 390.

The Syriac-speaking church of the West dominated greater Syria and northwest Arabia. Arabs were part of their congregations in:

- Najran in South Arabia
- Bosra, which served as the Ghassanid capital
- Rusafa
- Edessa
- Aleppo
- Antioch

Some Christian Arabs belonged to the Chalcedonian Church in Palestine and Sinai, whose liturgical language was a sister dialect known as Christian Palestinian Aramaic. The Chalcedonian Arabs of Petra worshipped in Greek well into the sixth century.[40]

Syriac Christian hagiography and ecclesiastical history contain many stories of church missions proselytizing to the Arabs, Saracens, and Ishmaelites. Syrians writing in Greek, namely Sozomen of Gaza and Theodoret of Cyrus, document the conversion of Arabian communities away from the ancestral worship of Aphrodite (Allat), towards Abrahamic monotheism and Ishmaelite genealogy, and ultimately Christianity.[41]

Simeon the Stylite (d. 459) is known for converting the Arab throngs to Christianity near Aleppo and throughout northern Syria. Theodoret claims they renounced Aphrodite and their old dietary customs.[42] Soon after Arethas of Najran, otherwise known as al-Harith b. Ka'b (d. 523), was counted among the martyrs of Najran during the persecution of the church in South Arabia by the Jewish Himyarite king Dhu Nuwas (d. 525).[43] Simeon of Beth Arsham (d. 540) famously

40 Ibid., 242–248, 316–326; Zbigniew Fiema et al., "*Provincia Arabia*: Nabataea, the emergence of Arabic as written language, and Graeco-Arabica," *Arabs and Empires before Islam*, ed. Greg Fisher, Oxford: Oxford University Press, 2015, 392–393.

41 Millar, "Hagar, Ishmael, Josephus, and the origins of Islam," 23–45 implies beginnings as early as Josephus in the first century CE.

42 Millar, "Ethnic identity in the Roman Near East," 402.

43 Sergius, *The Book of the Himyarites*, lix.

proselytized to the Arabs of Persian Mesopotamia where he was not always welcome.[44]

Later missions to the Arabs included Ahudemmeh of Beth Arbaye's (d. 575); the proselytization of Simeon bin Jabir (sixth century) and Sabrisho' I of Beth Lashom (d. 604) at the Lakhmid court of al-Hirah; the theology of Isaac of Nineveh/Beth Qatraye (d. *ca.* 700) and George, Bishop of the Arabs (d. 725); and others.[45] Ahudemmeh gives us a snapshot of how widespread and rapid the spread of Christianity was among the Arabs of the north:

> The holy Ahudemmeh set himself with great patience to visit all the camps of the Arabs, instructing and teaching them in many sermons ... He has priests come from many regions ... in order to establish in every tribe a priest and a deacon. He founded churches and names them after tribal chiefs so that they would support them ... Thus he inclined the hearts of the Arabs to the love of God and particularly to giving to the needy ... Their alms extended to all men and all places, but especially to the holy monasteries ... Nor do their confine their piety to making gifts to churches, monks, poor, and strangers, but they love fasting and ascetic life more than any other Christians.[46]

George became bishop of Aqula (Kufah) over the tribes of Tayyi', 'Uqayl, and Tanukh in 686, covering most of North Arabia and Syria. It is little surprise that among the champions of pre-Islamic poetry are numerous Christians. They include Imru al-Qays b. Hujr al-Kindi (d. 544), Hatim al-Ta'i (d. 578), al-Nabighah al-Dhubyani (d. *ca.* 604), Zuhayr b. Abi Sulma (d. *ca.* 609), al-A'sha (d. 625), and others.[47]

44 Saint-Laurent, *Missionary Stories and the Formation of the Syriac Churches*, 87.
45 Cf. in relation Hoyland, *Arabia and the Arabs*, 146–147. See further Vööbus, *History of Asceticism*, 222.
46 Hoyland, *Arabia and the Arabs*, 148; Saint-Laurent, *Missionary Stories and the Formation of the Syriac Churches*, 110–128.
47 See generally Louis Cheikho, *Le Christianisme et la littérature chrétienne en Arabie avant l'Islam*, vols. 1–3, Beirut: Imprimerie catholique, 1912–23.

One way or another, Arabian society—including the *entire* peninsula—was so thoroughly penetrated by Christianity on the eve of Islam as to make stubborn pagan outposts the exception rather than the rule.[48] Much of this was directly thanks to the active proselytizing of Syriac-speaking church fathers in Arabia.[49] The one exception to this rule, as I've argued, is the sixth-century pagan revival of al-'Uzza along the "pagan corridor" running through al-Hirah, 'Aliyat Najd, and Mecca.

War and the *Jahiliyyah*

Historically speaking, the *jahiliyyah* is precisely when Judaism and Christianity penetrated Arabia, spreading to every corner of the peninsula.[50] The old ways of paganism were slowly but surely being eradicated.

After the third century CE the storied Arabian metropolises of Syria and Mesopotamia suffered decline or collapse. This gave way to tribal structures utilized primarily as "war machines" by the Persians or Romans, the likes of which are recalled by later Islamic tradition.[51] Epigraphic evidence demonstrates that Arab auxiliaries were locked in combat between Roman and Persian wars, and willing to rebel if and when necessary.[52] In this respect, the patron deity of Tayma, Salm, was invoked regularly for military fortune and success on the battlefield.[53]

Christianity exercised dominion over the whole peninsula and beyond. According to Christian Robin—"seventy years prior to Islam

---

48 Cf. in relation al-Mallah, *al-Wasit fi tarikh al-'arab qabl al-islam*, 410. See further Hawting, *The Idea of Idolatry and the Emergence of Islam*, 15–16.

49 Hoyland, *Arabia and the Arabs*, 30, 51, 79–82.

50 Christian Robin, "L'évêché nestorien de Mashmahig dans l'archipel d'al-Bahrayn (Ve–IXe siècle)," *BBVO* 2, 1983, 171–196; "Chrétiens de l'Arabie heureuse et de l'Arabie déserte: de la victoire à l'échec," *DASO* 309, 2005–2006, 24–30.

51 Crone, *The Qur'anic Pagans and Related Matters*, 50.

52 Ahmad Al-Jallad, *An Outline of the Grammar of the Safaitic Inscriptions*, Leiden; Boston: Brill, 2015, 190.

53 F. V. Winnett, *Ancient Records from North Arabia*, Toronto: University of Toronto Press, 1970, 96.

all of Arabia was ruled by a single Christian king"—Abraha![54] We return to the Ethiopian king of Arabia shortly.

Abrahamic religions expanded where Arabian paganism contracted, mostly that is. I contend that the rise of Christianity caused a resurgence of paganism. In short, the prestige and enfranchisement that Byzantine Christianity granted the Ghassanids provoked a powerful response by the Sassanian-backed Lakhmids. There must have been some reason why the Arabic sources took crude pagan idolatry as the antithesis of Islam, rather than say Christianity. This was, in part, the pagan revival of the sixth century. The complex historical picture historians draw of the *jahiliyyah* contradicts the simplistic, apologetic, and teleological presentation of the medieval Arabic sources.

These imperfect sources are right about one thing, however. The *jahiliyyah* was a time of heightened warfare and increased plunder for nomadic communities. They formed new permanent settlements, turning to a livelihood entrenched in trade and warfare.

Christian, Jewish, and Pagan Conflict, Fifth–Sixth Centuries

War fed the Arabian economies of Syria and Mesopotamia, bringing an otherwise unexpected time of plunder and plenty in the fifth–sixth centuries.[55] The collective trauma recalled by later generations of Arab authors could just as likely be attributed to Jewish versus Christian sectarianism, competing nationalist loyalties to Ma'add or Quda'ah, or endless Persian–Roman proxy warfare throughout the lands.[56]

This period of revolution and turmoil in Arabia is manifested in the epigraphic record. Old scripts went extinct. New scripts began to emerge. More precisely, Old North Arabian inscriptions disappeared from the Hijaz by the latter part of the fifth century. Old South Arabian inscriptions disappear from the monuments of Yemen after 575, owing

---

54 Christian Robin, "Soixante-dix ans avant l'Islam: l'Arabie toute entière dominée par un roi chrétien," *CRS* 156.1, 2012, 525–553.
55 Crone, *The Qur'anic Pagans and Related Matters*, 49; al-Fassi, "al-Awda' al-siyasi-yyah," 452.
56 Cf. also Sergius, *The Book of the Himyarites*, lxi–lxii.

to the Persian and Ethiopian incursions there.[57] It is unclear to what extent these disruptions were impacted by the global climate crisis caused by volcanic eruptions *ca.* 535–542, and the Plague of Justinian *ca.* 541–549 as reported by Procopius of Caesaria (d. *ca.* 570). However, we may assume these factors contributed to convulsions within Arabian society at this time.[58] Persecution preoccupied the psyche of Christians, whose tradition of martyrdom first developed in response to pagan emperors of Rome. Their trauma was awakened once again in 523 by the famous story of the martyrs of Najran, addressed shortly.

Religious conflict, including church controversy and a resurgence in paganism, contributed to animosity between the Ghassanids and Lakhmids.[59] The religious and political culture of Arabian society experienced seismic changes during the late fifth and early sixth centuries. The Council of Chalcedon in 451, like *all* so-called "ecumenical" gatherings of the clergy, only served to fragment the early churches and sow discord. The council served to craft a distinctly "Chalcedonian" Christology and establish an imperial Byzantine Church. The aftermath of this council distanced both the church of the Roman emperor and the Monophysite Church of the Syrian, Egyptian, and Arabian countryside.

The Roman and Persian empires were locked in a century's worth of sporadic war between 524 and 629, ravaging the political stability of Arabian states caught in the middle. During this time, the most powerful Arab states were emboldened to batter their Christian adversaries and neighbors. These were especially the Jewish Himyarites under Dhu Nuwas and the pagan Lakhmids under al-Mundhir III.

Himyar fell in 525; and its kindred vassal Kindah, which held together the central lands of the Arabian Peninsula, fell shortly thereafter in 540, plunging the Arabian tribes of the north into civil war.

57 See Al-Jallad, "Pre-Islamic Arabic," 38; Bowersock, *The Crucible of Islam*, 33–34. Cf. further Juan Cole, *Muhammad: Prophet of Peace Amid the Clash of Empires*, New York: Public Affairs, 2018.

58 Ann Gibbons, "Why 536 was 'the worst year to be alive,'" *Science*, 15 November 2018.

59 Webb, *Imagining the Arabs*, 79–80.

Prior to this the Himyarites enjoyed prosperity in South Arabia and exerted great power over North Arabia.[60]

Martyrs of Najran and the Lapsed Christians of Arabia, ca. 523–525

History teaches that war and religious persecution created not only brave "witnesses to the faith," or martyrs. It created many more fearful apostates, who under pain of death renounced their allegiance to Christ in exchange for their very lives. Several early Roman emperors committed atrocities against early Christian communities. The intermittent torture and extermination of early Christians created an entire generation of "lapsed Christians" by the late third century. They were called in Latin the *Lapsi*. The two extremes posed by those who lapsed versus those who martyred themselves further fractured the early churches. This, in turn, had a profound effect on Christian theology as a whole.[61] How could it not?

And how could the same conditions in Najran under the Himyarite king Dhu Nuwas not have created a new class of "Arabian *Lapsi*" among survivors? The *Book of the Himyarites*, whose authorship is disputed but otherwise attributed to one Sergius of Resafa, attests to "Christians in name," "Judaizing Christians," and wars and alliances between Christians and Jews.[62] The hostilities between South Arabian Jews and Christians was part and parcel of war in sixth-century Arabia. They were fueled by the imperial rivalry between the Persians and Romans, and the ongoing military struggle between Himyar and Axum. The latter's invasion of South Arabia was seen by Near Eastern Christendom as Ethiopia's divine rescue. It came as retribution for the sake of their co-religionists, suffering under Jewish oppression.[63] After the war, the remaining Jews were subjected to a new wave of Christian missionizing under the pseudo-legendary leadership of

---

60 See further Christian Robin, "Faut-il réinventer la Jahiliyya?" *OM* 3, 2009, 5–14.

61 Wolfram Kinzig, *Christenverfolgung in der Antike*, Munich: Verlag C. H. Beck, 2019, 117–122.

62 Sergius, *The Book of the Himyarites*, lxx.

63 Cf. ibid., xxxiii, lxii; Hoyland, *Arabia and the Arabs*, 147–148.

Gregentios (d. 5 5 2). It is said he reintroduced the Byzantine Church to Yemen.[64]

The Himyarite persecution may have produced dozens of martyrs. But it produced potentially thousands of lapsed Christians and unconverted Jews during the sixth century. This context fits perfectly the qur'anic "people of the Bible," referring to Christians and Jews. Most of the Christians were viewed as friendly but misguided, while its Jews remained defiant against conversion (Q 5:14, 82).[65] One final note in this regard is that the Muslim exegetes and historians considered Q 18 inspired by the Decian persecution centuries earlier, while Q 85 echoed events from the Himyarite persecution almost two centuries later.[66] It is simply impossible to divorce Arabian tribal warfare from Near Eastern sectarian conflict.[67]

The tribal and sectarian turmoil of the *jahiliyyah* is precisely what gave birth to the Arabic script. Put simply, Christian Arabs developed the Arabic script out of the Nabataean-Aramaic script of their forerunners. They did this in opposition to Jewish Himyarite expansion. The first book ever written in the Arabic script—the Qur'an—is also our only literary witness of this time period. It describes the features of the *jahiliyyah* when demonstrating:

(1) The hopelessness of believers in battle (Q 3:152–154)
(2) The lawlessness of Jewish–Christian conflict (Q 5:47–50)
(3) The public display of beauty by aristocratic women (Q 33:33)
(4) The wrath of enemies in battle (Q 48:26)[68]

From this glance it is readily evident how the later generations of Muslim exegetes wove fanciful legends out of the Qur'an's distress about warfare, powerful women, and lapsed Christians.

64 Bowersock, *The Crucible of Islam*, 24.
65 Cf. Sergius, *The Book of the Himyarites*, lxxvii.
66 Ibn Ishaq, *Sirah*, 36–40.
67 Cf. in relation Sergius, *The Book of the Himyarites*, xxiv.
68 See further Webb, "al-Jahiliyya," 74–77, 80–83.

Civil War and the Age of Ignorance, Mid Sixth Century

Himyar fell in 525 and Kindah followed *ca.* 540. By the mid sixth century, the cohesion of Arabian society had collapsed. What was formerly a "structured, differentiated, and often hierarchical system of politico-legal-economic positions" lapsed into ancient patterns of tribalism, or the "unstructured or rudimentarily structured and relatively undifferentiated *commitatus.*" Over the course of a century or so, *ca.* 560–660 according to Aram Shahin, the fractured tribes of Arabia clawed their way back into history, ultimately "[submitting] together to the general authority of the ritual elders." This he dubs *communitas.*[69]

The ensuing civil war between Arabian tribes of Jewish, Christian, and pagan backgrounds, scrambling toward alliance with Byzantium or Ctesiphon, suggests identity, once undermined, became unstable and fluid. This may be one of many reasons why the medieval Arabic sources associate this age with ignorance.[70]

A Hadith compiled by al-Nasa'i (d. 303/915) claims that Quraysh had "only recently adopted *jahiliyyah*" as though it were a formal conversion.[71] But conversion to what? This is not clear. However, should the report recall the slightest inkling of truth, then religious loyalties were abruptly shifting or convulsed in Quraysh leading up to Muhammad's mission.

Alternately, the conception of an "ignorant" pre-history may itself be fed by late antique Chalcedonian Church writings, or meditations on the relationship between ignorance and repentance within scripture (cf. Acts 17:30; Q 4:17).[72] It may also be fed by the *topoi* of heathen ignorance found in West and East Syrian Church writings. These include stereotypical representations of Arab pagan barbarism prior to their conversion to Christianity. In this vein, one explanation why pagan Arab nomads were labeled ignorant heathens may come from

69 Shahin, "Struggling for communitas," 800–801.
70 Cf. Ibrahim, *Ayyam al-'arab fi al-jahiliyyah*, viii–xi.
71 Ibid., 73.
72 Webb, "al-Jahiliyya," 72; Hawting, *The Idea of Idolatry and the Emergence of Islam*, 99.

Ahudemmeh of Beth Arbaye (d. 575), who while converting them en masse states:

> There were many peoples between the Tigris and Euphrates in the land of Mesopotamia who live in tents and were barbarous and warlike. Numerous were their superstitions and they were the most <u>ignorant</u> of all the peoples of the earth until the moment when the light of Christ came to them.[73]

The researcher should be cautious of taking the theme of pre-Islamic "ignorance" too seriously for another reason as well. Medieval Arab authors writing in opulent Abbasid palaces and libraries were too far removed from the trauma of the distant Arabian *jahiliyyah* to properly recall its features. Motivated by Abbasid propaganda and patronage, they often framed the period of the *jahiliyyah* as Arabia's clumsy lapse into idolatry and hedonism. Earlier documentary and literary evidence demonstrates that the situation was far more complex, and, as yet, not entirely understood.

Civil War and Marketplace Violation, ca. 580–590

Constant war ruined public life for women of all classes. The Arabic sources allude to their limited autonomy, as women merchants lost access to the power center of Arabian society—the marketplace—except through male proxy.

According to the sources, the famous annual Arabian market fairs were a magnet for young men and women to meet and find a partner. This space served as a fair for free folk and not just for the transaction of buying and selling slaves.[74] The marketplace was where nobility enjoyed lavish merriment and pleasure. It was where they perpetually rebuilt lasting social bonds, serving to strengthen the very backbone of the religious and political culture in late antique Arabia. It is little surprise that powerful men would covet this space for themselves.

---

73 Hoyland, *Arabia and the Arabs*, 148. See further Saint-Laurent, *Missionary Stories and the Formation of the Syriac Churches*, 121.
74 al-Fassi, "*Aswaq al-'arab*," 565.

A story from pre-Islamic Arabian battle folklore gives some historical precedent for the violation of women by men at the marketplace.
The annual marketplace of 'Ukaz—one of the major centers of Arabian
economic, legal, and religious life from the sixth century until *ca.* 746
CE[75]—had become inhospitable to women.

The "Sacrilegious War" violated the sanctuary of the marketplace
and its sacred months by engulfing the Hijaz region in conflict *ca.*
580–590. Among its many battles, the third was known as the "sacrilege of the woman," where a group of youths from Kinanah sexually
assaulted a young woman of Hawazin while she was buying goods at
the marketplace. The story goes that the perpetrator caught sight of a
young woman bending over to buy goods. He propositioned the
woman to remove her clothes. She refused, whereupon he forcibly
stripped her naked in public. She cried out for the aid of her tribes-
men, and widespread violence broke out.[76]

The annual marketplace festival was designed, so to speak, to be the
safe space wherein tribal arbitration and peace negotiations were rati-
fied. It was safe for men to traverse[77]—evidently not for women. It
would take a decade of warfare to restore law and order to the marketplace. But it seems the women may not have returned. Meaning, we do
not know how long it took for women to return, or to what extent they
re-emerged within the annual marketplace festival. Insofar as women
were absent from Arabia's most prominent arena of public life, we can
conclude that this was an inescapable consequence of the hostilities.

There is reason to believe the "sacrilege of the woman" saw the
demise of autonomous, commercial public life for Arabian female
nobility. Arabia became rife with civil war during the latter sixth
century. Women had every reason to circumvent the annual marketplaces, or to send male representatives in their stead. This appears to
be the final phase of female nobility delegating their power to male

---

75 Ibid., 566 dates its origin to 586 CE, i.e. ten years after the (dubious) "year of the
elephant." The market is likely much older.

76 al-Bajawi, *Ayyam al-'arab fi al-jahiliyyah*, 324.

77 Ahmed Moussalli, "An Islamic model for political conflict resolution: *Tahkim*
(Arbitration)," *Peace and Conflict Resolution in Islam: Precept and Practice*, eds. Abdul
Aziz Said et al., Washington, D.C.: University Press of America, 2009, 147–148; al-Fassi,
"*Aswaq al-'arab*," 565.

agents acting on their behalf. The greatest beneficiaries of the trust bestowed upon them by Arabian noblewomen during the breakdown of society or widespread civil strife were bishops, monks, and prophets. They were almost exclusively men. Soon their ranks would give rise to forms of Abrahamic monotheism attested in Arabian inscriptions, as well as Arabic, Syriac, and Greek literary sources.[78]

Inventing a Father for Arabia, Seventh Century

The ravages of warfare created scars in the fabric of Arab identity. The seemingly endless civil wars and conquests culminated in the rise of an Arab caliphate in the seventh century. Once the dust settled, so to speak, old grievances resurfaced within the sources in the form of genealogical disputes. Reawakening ancient grievances ensured that the male power of the *jahiliyyah* lived on in later Islamic times.

A new class of Arab male elites asked, "Who was the first Arab, and which Arabian tribe could claim the honor of descent from his lineage?" The question was deeply political and took traditional scholars deep into the rivalry between North and South Arabia, and the very origins of the Arabic language itself. We embark on our final examination.

We consider our only Arabic literary witness, the Qur'an. The text corroborates the existence of fractured Arabian communities. According to the text, northern communities were transient, continually replaced, and survived by new generations (cf. Q 30:9, 43; 35:44; 40:21, 82; 47:10, 38). Southern communities, however, were ruined and dispersed (Q 34:15–19).[79] It also alludes to trade between greater Syria and Yemen (Q 34:18; 37:137). The text proudly celebrates itself as the first scripture in the "clear Arabic tongue" (Q 16:103; 26:195). It distinguishes its urban community from *a'rab* (Q 49:14), or nomadic allies attested in late antique South and North Arabian inscriptions.

---

78 Cf. Robert Hoyland, *Seeing Islam as Others Saw it: A Survey and Evaluation of Christian, Jewish and Zoroastrian Writings on Early Islam*, Princeton: Darwin Press, 1997.

79 See further 'Abd al-Rahman al-Ansari, *"al-Qaba'il al-ba'idah kama arrakhaha al-qur'an al-karim,"* AM 66, 2004, 64–69.

The text also equates the deterioration of the Ma'rib dam with the permanent collapse of South Arabian civilization (Q 34:16). Although the ancient kingdom of Saba' is mentioned explicitly, the final destruction of the Ma'rib dam likely occurred between 450 and 543 CE,[80] during or shortly following the time of the Himyarite kingdom.

These precious attestations demonstrate that separate ethnic, tribal, or political communities populated the Arabian Peninsula. The northern Arabs of the Qur'an were distinct from Sabaean-Himyarite dominated communities in the south, whose glory days had since passed.

'Adnan vs. Qahtan

Later Arabic sources purport the forefather of Syrian and North Arabian tribes to have been a figure known as 'Adnan. He was followed by his grandsons Mudar or Qays. And his later descendants are said to include all the biblical patriarchs—of whom Ishmael was dubbed "father of the Arabs"—the Quraysh tribe, and the prophet Muhammad himself. The purported forefather of tribes originating from Yemen was called Yaman, also known as Ya'rub b. Qahtan/Tayman b. Yuqtan (cf. Genesis 10:25–29). Their descendants include the powerful South Arabian kingdom of Himyar, and a number of powerful Arabian tribes in Syria and northern Arabia as well. These included the kingdoms of Kindah, Lakhm, and Ghassan.[81] There is meagre epigraphic evidence linking an extinct "kingdom of Qahtan" to Kindah, which as discussed below is an exceptional tribe given its central position between northern and southern Arabs.[82]

This paltry evidence, however, is not genealogical in nature. The genealogical controversy emerges from the medieval Arabic sources and is known as the rivalry between 'Adnan and Qahtan. So, the emergence of Islamic sectarianism and new tribal disputes in the eighth–ninth centuries was projected back onto pre-Islamic times. And the

---

80 al-Fassi, "al-Awda' al-siyasiyyah," 458.
81 Hoyland, Arabia and the Arabs, 50.
82 al-Ansari, Qaryat al-faw, 20.

primacy of the south was essentially concocted by medieval authors settling scores with the northern Umayyad dynasty.[83]

Imagined Patriarchs of the Arabic Language

To be clear, all this is all *highly* peculiar. Some medieval authors claimed Qahtani tribes of the south to be the original stock of Arabic speakers in the north. And 'Adnani tribes of the north were only later "Arabized" by their southern brethren. This narrative, dubbed here "southern primacy," is impossible for several reasons.

First and foremost, the Qur'an indirectly distinguishes between north and south as referenced earlier. By the seventh century CE, South Arabian communities were all but collapsed, if not conquered by their Persian or Ethiopian overlords, with northern communities of urban and nomadic Arabic speakers on the rise.[84]

Second, late antique South Arabia spoke dialects of Old South Arabian—most notably Sabaic and Himyaritic—distinct from Arabic, which shares a linguistic ancestor with Old North Arabian (ONA). There is ample scholarship establishing the northern origins of the Arabic language, and refuting the absurd argument of southern primacy.[85]

Third, the languages of (proto/paleo) Arabic and Himyaritic were competitors in late antiquity. After the fall of Nabataea in the north around 106 CE, the alliance of south central Arabian tribes emerging from Yemen—Himyar and Kindah—reforged the pan-Arabian kingdom of Ma'add, which came to dominate the entire peninsula *ca.* 325–540 CE (but leaving aside parts of Syria dominated by Quda'ah and the Roman *foederati*).[86]

During this time, monumental Nabataean Aramaic became extinct and Arabic speakers began writing their language for the first time in

83 Taha Husayn, *Fi al-adab al-jahili*, Cairo: Matba'at Faruq, 1933, 257.
84 Bowersock, *The Crucible of Islam*, 66.
85 Gruendler, *The Development of the Arabic Scripts*, 123–30. See further Webb, *Imagining the Arabs*, 34–35; al-Fassi, "*al-Awda' al-siyasiyyah*," 461. See further Al-Jallad, "Pre-Islamic Arabic," 46–47.
86 See Robin, "Les religions pratiquées," 218.

a new script.[87] In doing so, however, they broke with tradition. For they did not utilize the conventions of Old North Arabian writing, which employed the Musnad or Zabur script. This script was crafted by the far-off Sabaean and Himyarite kingdoms. Rather than utilize the Musnad alphabet, Arabic speakers utilized the Aramaic alphabet of their local Nabataean predecessors. Scholars agree this move was both a "political act and deliberate choice."[88]

Fourth, there was a sectarian dimension to the defiance of Arabic speakers towards Himyarite dominance. The Himyarite kingdom in part adopted Judaism until its demise, while using the Musnad script in its monumental and epigraphic texts.[89] The existence of such writings in the Musnad "script of Yaman" is mentioned in the sixth-century poetry of Imru al-Qays.[90] Should these poems preserve some verses from the time of the last king of Kindah intact, then it means he abandoned the Jewish religion of his forefathers and embraced Christianity.[91]

On the other hand, our earliest Arabic inscriptions, dating to the same time, are mostly of Christian origin, as previously introduced. This suggests a relationship between the spread of the Arabic script and the Christian religion in Arabia during this time. The Jewish king of Himyar, Masruq/Dhu Nuwas, was defeated at the hands of the Christian Axumites of Ethiopia, who included a series of regents culminating in Abraha. This episode was seen by hagiographers as the victory of Christianity over Judaism in the Arabian Peninsula. Abraha declared himself the new king of Himyar and began the conquest of

---

87 Macdonald, "Arabs, Arabias, and Arabic before Late Antiquity," 311.

88 Hoyland, *Arabia and the Arabs*, 242; Al-Azmeh, *The Emergence of Islam in Late Antiquity*, 158. Ahmad Al-Jallad, "On the genetic background of the Rbbl bn Hf'm grave inscription at Qaryat al-Faw," *BSOAS* 77.3, 2014, 1–21 disputes the Arabic nature of 'Ijl b. Haf'am Inscription (first century BCE) in the Musnad script, *contra* al-Ansari, *Qaryat al-faw*, 24.

89 Christian Robin, "Quel judaïsme en Arabie?" *Le judaïsme de l'Arabie antique: Actes du colloque de Jérusalem*, ed. Christian Julien Robin, Turnhout: Brepols, 2015, 36.

90 'Ali, *Tarikh al-'arab qabl al-islam*, 40.

91 Cf. in relation Christian Robin, "Arabia and Ethiopia," *The Oxford Handbook of Late Antiquity*, ed. Scott Johnson, Oxford: Oxford University Press, 2012, 298–300; Robin, "Les religions de Kinda," 235.

the peninsula in the name of Christianity. He shifted the power balance of the region.

Even as Christianity engulfed the Arabian Peninsula by the sixth century, northern inscriptions remained in the Arabic script while the Musnad script was used in the south. This suggests that sixth-century Arabic-speaking communities were predominantly Christian, and were furthermore as defiant of the Musnad script as they were of the Jewish religion.

Fifth, Kindah succeeded in ruling most of northern Arabia on behalf of its southern kindred, Himyar, because of its uniquely "central Arabian" identity.[92] As a tribe believed to be of southern origin, but whose native or acquired language was Arabic, Kindah played a fascinating role in the evolution of Arabian society. It was capable of dominating both east–west Arabian trade routes by first establishing a southern capital in Qaryat al-Faw, and later a northern capital in Dumah. These and other locales attest to the influence of Kindah in the Ayyam, reaching as far as al-Hirah in the east and Bosra in the west. This made Kindah the most powerful, independent Arabic-speaking kingdom of the late fifth and early sixth centuries CE.[93] During this period of independence and political stability, Arabic-speaking communities spread throughout the peninsula.[94]

Kindah fended off Byzantium and Persia for a century before its abrupt collapse in 540 CE. The collapse of Kindi-Himyarite hegemony fractured the unity of Arabian society in the sixth century, plunging it into civil war. The collapse of southern political dominance, furthermore, coincided with the qur'anic story of Sabaean extinction, and it gave rise to pre-Islamic Arabian nostalgia in the form of battle folklore, legendary hanged poems of their heroes, and "grieving over ruins" whose memory lives on in the medieval Arabic sources.[95]

---

92 Macdonald, "Arabs, Arabias, and Arabic before Late Antiquity," 310 cites the 'Ijl b. Haf'am Inscription and explores the extent to which Arabic was written in the Musnad script in Qaryat al-Faw. See further Abd al-Rahman al-Ansari, "*Adwa' jadidah 'ala dawlat kindah min khilal athar wa nuqush qaryat al-faw,*" AA 11–12, 1977, 864–875.

93 Cf. in relation Robin, "Les rois de Kinda," 61–134.

94 Cf. Nehmé, "Aramaic or Arabic?" 77–78.

95 See Shahin, "Struggling for communitas," 191–197, 571–574, as sometimes attested in the poetic verses of Safaitic inscriptions.

Sixth and finally, the rivalry between north and south is said to have ignited after the battle of Marj Rahit in 64/684 between the Umayyad Caliphate and the Zubayrid counter-caliphate. It was early medieval authors descended from southern tribes who articulated the myth of Arabia's southern origins, at least in the manner we know today. Some have suggested they were resentful of northern tribes for monopolizing power during and after the Arab conquest of the Middle East (632–750 CE).[96] Foremost among the northern tribes was the newly formed Muslim alliance coming out of the Hijaz. It included Quraysh, Thaqif, and the still Christian alliance of Syria known as Quda'ah, especially the tribe of Kalb.

96 Shahid, *Byzantium and the Arabs in the Fifth Century*, 340.

Conclusion

THIS BOOK HAS told the story of female power in late antique Arabian society. Its proponents were queens and royal nobility with origins in ancient, pagan North Arabia and neighboring Near Eastern societies. Their power was forever memorialized in the cultic veneration of goddesses—notably Allat, al-'Uzza, and Manat—who thrived in Nabataean, Hatran, and Palmyrene communities, and were inherited by successor states including the Quraysh of Mecca. With the spread of Greco-Roman colonization, Abrahamic religious missions, and mercantile urbanization, the power wielded by Arabian noblewomen diminished over time. During this age of transition, I argued that Arabian noblewomen increasingly delegated their autonomy and authority to a rising class of holy men, and prophets in particular.

To this end the stories of empress Zenobia and Paul of Samosata, queen Mavia and Moses of Sinai, and lady Khadijah and Muhammad of Mecca demonstrate a process of power sharing which shaped the religious and political culture of the region, including that of the early church. Nevertheless, faced with the growing might of organized imperialism and hierarchical male clergy, female power was doomed. But it left behind traces of a magnificent heritage. The eastern churches and the nascent Islamic caliphate slowly but surely dominated successive generations of Arabian noblewomen. The ravages of politics, sectarianism, and warfare ultimately curtailed their power to rule or maintain independent public life.

New Findings

The numerous stories explored concerning late antique Arabian female power contribute a number of primary insights for the scholar and public alike. The first and most immediate of these is that gender is at the heart of understanding pre-Islamic Arabia. Paganism was portrayed by Islamic tradition as crude idolatry and rampant whoredom, which I have argued was deliberately tied to femininity. Christian and Muslim piety on the other hand was directly and unequivocally tied to masculinity. Arabian society benefited from the existence of woman-led communities, institutions, and households before Islam. Limited forms of matrilineality and localized matriarchal structures likely existed in parallel to patriarchal structures.

It appears that Arabia's most elite noblewomen and queens were pro-Christian, without themselves practicing Christianity in any manner discernable through the sources. There is no evidence that Zenobia, Mavia, or Khadijah were themselves practicing Christians, despite their adamant support for church-inspired holy men. This may have been because the gendered hierarchy of the church readily impeded the leadership of women. The received traditions about these women, and their many Arabian predecessors, portray them unequivocally as widows, divorcees, and autonomous women in command of the finest men. As heads of state, the empress, queen, or chieftain shaped Arabia's relationship with both the Roman and Persian empires. As makers of these holy men, nonetheless, they shaped Christianity and Islam as well.

With the decline of paganism in the Oriens, female power became increasingly expressed through both military might and church disputation. By supporting Paul of Samosata, empress Zenobia gave backing to beliefs and customs associated with Semitic churches, including the loosely connected consortium of Syro-Arabian congregations dubbed the Nativist church. These were deemed heretical by the Byzantine (later Chalcedonian) Church. But their beliefs and customs survived outside the grip of the Greek-speaking clergy and emperor. And elements of their teachings resurfaced in the milieu of the Qur'an and proto-Islam.

By installing Moses of Sinai as bishop, queen Mavia moved ever closer towards establishing an Arab national church, whose liturgical language was likely Syriac. The historical details of this context are, of course, a mystery. Still, Mavia's founding achievements qualified her as a matriarch with no peer. However, the Arabic sources made no room for women as matriarchs of Arabia. Yet the genealogical legends of Arabia's forefathers recall their Christian and Syriac ancestry from the north, thanks to the religious enterprise of Mavia and Moses. Their partnership contributed to the theory that the ancient cultural, religious, and linguistic homeland of the Arab people is greater Syria and North Arabia, as growing epigraphic evidence shows, and not South Arabia as told by the legends of medieval Islamic tradition.

Lady Khadijah played an equally vital role in making Muhammad the archetypal prophet of Arabia. Islamic tradition deliberately downplays the influence of Khadijah's Christian family upon Muhammad, while trying its best to pardon the paganism of his childhood guardian and uncle, Abu Talib. It is likely that Muhammad lost his political immunity in Mecca when his noble wife's trading enterprise collapsed under the Meccan economic boycott, after which she fell ill and died.

In contrast to criticism of women's intellect and morality found within medieval traditions, stories of Zenobia, Mavia, and Khadijah demonstrate that Arabian noblewomen were exceptionally intelligent and highly disciplined leaders. Their stories attest to the efficacy of leadership by women, especially in times of crisis.[1]

Lessons for Today

Every political and religious system covered here appears antagonistic towards female power. The influence of Roman imperialism and Abrahamic religions upon late antique Arabian society seems only to have compounded existing patterns of misogyny. Traditional biblical, Christian, and Islamic hostility towards indigenous forms of female power were often camouflaged in the smashing of temple idols, the formulation of new laws, or the crushing of dissenters in combat.

Even today, the deadly manifestations of secular or religious violence disproportionately harm women. Modern right-wing, populist, and fundamentalist ideologies all have one thing in common—toxic manifestations of masculinity. Both neoconservatism and jihadism, among

---

1 See M. K. Ryan et al., "Think crisis—think female: The glass cliff and contextual variation in the think manager—think male stereotype," *JAP* 96.3, 2011, 470–484.

countless militant ideologies violently disrupting modern life, actively oppose women's rights.

Large-scale wars create equally widespread repression. The status of pre-modern Arabian women was, moreover, beholden to the outcomes of provincial sectarian violence, or great wars between the Romans and Persians. I have argued that the Sacrilegious War irreparably damaged the autonomy and public life of women in Arabia over a millennium ago. It might be helpful, therefore, to consider the profound and long-lasting impact warfare has had in curtailing the rights of women in once thriving Arab or Muslim societies in modern times. One cannot separate the struggle for women's rights in Iraq and Afghanistan today, for example, from the long-term devastation wrought by American and Soviet warfare. Media pundits routinely discuss the strategic, economic, or geopolitical reasons for going to war, but are yet to address the problem of "military masculinity," which is a common force in all global conflicts today.[2]

If we are to live in the world without repeating the atrocities of the past, it seems evident that women's leadership is key to success. In the words of Iraqi-American activist Zainab Salbi, "like life, peace begins with women. We are the first to forge lines of alliance and collaboration across conflict zones."[3]

Closing

In closing, female power was an instrumental force in the shaping of late antique Arabia. Its actors and institutions crafted the politics, religion, and culture of the Near East more broadly. While power was first delegated by queens to prophets, it was later wrested by force by successive generations of men speaking in the name of God. This is why it is impossible to study the origins of the eastern churches, Islam, and the ripple effects they had on our world thereafter, without first considering this extraordinary shift in power.

2 R. B. Ferguson, "Masculinity and war," CA 62.23, 2021, S120.
3 Maria Holt, Violence against Women in Peace and War: Cases from the Middle East, Lanham: Lexington Books, 2021, 51.

Bibliography

Sources

Abu Mikhnaf. *Nusus min tarikh abi mikhnaf,* first edition, ed. Kamil S. al-Jabburi. Beirut: Dar al-Mahajjah al-Bayda'; Dar al-Rasul al-Akram, 1999.

Aphrahat. "Demonstrations." *Patrologia Syriaca* 1 (1894): 265–70.

al-Azraqi, Muhammad b. 'Abd Allah. *Akhbar makkah wa ma ja' fiha min al-athar,* ed. 'Abd al-Malik b. Duhaysh. Mecca: Maktabat al-Asadi, 2003.

al-Bukhari. *Sahih.* Sunnah.com.

Chronicles of Qalawun and His Son al-Ashraf Khalil, ed. and trans. David Cook. Abingdon; New York: Routledge, 2020.

Chronicle of Seert, trans. Addai Scher. *Patrologia Orientalis* 13 (1919): 468–69.

Cyril of Scythopolis. *The Lives of the Monks of Palestine,* trans. R. M. Price. Collegeville: Cistercian Publications, 1991.

Diodorus Siculus. *Library of History,* trans. C. H. Oldfather. Cambridge: Harvard University Press, 1933.

Diwan hatim al-ta'i, ed. Ahmad Rashad. Beirut: Dar al-Kutub al-'Ilmiyyah, 2002.

Diwan zuhayr ibn janab al-kalbi, ed. Muhammad Shafiq. Beirut: Dar Sadir, 1999.

Ephrem the Syrian. *S. Ephraim's Prose Refutations of Mani, Marcion, and Bardaisan,* ed. Charles Mitchell. Farnborough: Gregg International Publishers, 1969.

Eusebius of Caesaria. *The Fathers of the Church, Eusebius Panphili, Ecclesiastical History, Books 6–10,* trans. Roy Deferrari. Washington, D.C.: The Catholic University of America Press, 1955.

Herodotus. *Histories,* trans. George Rawlinson. Ware, Hertfordshire: Wordsworth, 1996.

Ibn Ahmad, al-Khalil. *Kitab al-'ayn: Murataban 'ala huruf al-mu'jam,* ed. 'Abd al-Hamid Hindawi. Beirut: Dar al-Kutub al-'Ilmiyah, 2003.

Ibn Anas, Malik. *al-Muwatta: The First Formulation of Islamic Law,* trans. Aisha Bewley. London; New York: Routledge, 2016.

Ibn Burhan al-Din, 'Ali. *al-Sirah al-halabiyyah: insan al-'uyun fi sirat al-amin al-ma'mun,* ed. Abd Allah al-Khalili. Beirut: Dar al-Kutub al-'Ilmiyyah, 2005, 1:202, translated by the author.

Ibn Ishaq, Muhammad. *al-Sirah al-nabawiyyah*, ed. Ahmad F. al-Mazidi. Beirut: Dar al-Kutub al-'Ilmiyah, 2004, trans. A. Guillaume, *The Life of Muhammad: A Translation of Ibn Ishaq's Sirat Rasul Allah*. Oxford; New York, Oxford University Press, 1955.

Ibn al-Kalbi, Hisham. *The Book of Idols: Being a Translation from the Arabic of the Kitab al-Asnam*, trans. Nabih Faris. Princeton: Princeton University Press, 1952.

_____. *Gamharat an-nasab: das genealogische Werk des Hisam Ibn Muḥammad al-Kalbi*, ed. Werner Caskel. Leiden: Brill, 1966.

_____. *Jamharat al-nasab*, ed. Naji Hasan. Beirut: Maktabat al-Nahdah al-'Arabiyyah, 1986.

_____. *Kitab al-asnam*, ed. Ahmad Zaki Basha. Cairo: Dar al-Kutub al-Misriyyah, 1924.

_____. *Nasab ma'add wal-yaman al-kabir*, ed. Naji Hasan. Beirut: Maktabat al-Nahdah al-'Arabiyyah, 1988.

Ibn Hisham, 'Abd al-Malik. *al-Sirah al-nabawiyyah*, ed. 'Umar A. Tadmuri. Beirut: Dar al-Kitab al-'Arabi, 1990.

Ibn Rashid, Ma'mar. *The Expeditions: An Early Biography of Muhammad*, ed. Sean Anthony. New York; London: New York University Press, 2017.

Ibn Sa'd, Muhammad. *Kitab al-tabaqat al-kabir*, ed. 'Ali 'Umar. Cairo: Maktabat al-Khanji, 2001.

Ibn Tayfur. *Balaghat al-nisa'*, ed. Ahmad al-Alfi. Cairo: Madrasat Walidat 'Abbas al-Awwal, 1908.

al-Hamwi, Yaqut. *Mu'jam al-buldan*, ed. Farid al-Jindi. Beirut: Dar al-Kutub al-'Ilmiyyah, 1971.

al-Isfahani, Abu al-Faraj. *Kitab al-aghani*, ed. Muhammad Ibrahim. Cairo: al-Hay'ah al-Misriyyah al-'Ammah lil-Kitab, 1993.

Jacob of Serugh. "Homélies contre les Juifs." *Patrologio Orientalis* 38 (1976): 44–181.

Jerome. *On Illustrious Men*, trans. Ernest Richardson. Buffalo: Dalcassian Publishing, 2017.

Juvenal. *The Satires of Juvenal, Persius, Sulpicia and Lucilius*, trans. Lewis Evans. London: Bell & Daldy, 1869.

al-Kulayni, Muhammad b. Ya'qub. *al-Kafi*. Beirut: Manshurat al-Fajr, 2007, 5:239.

The Kebra Nagast: The Glory of Kings, ed. E. A. W. Budge. Rockville, MD: Silk Pagoda, 2007.

Mark the Deacon. *The Life of Poryphry: Bishop of Gaza*, ed. G. F. Hill. Oxford: Clarendon Press, 1913.

Muslim. *Sahih*. Sunnah.com.

Peter the Solitary. "Life of Sabrisho'." *Histoire de Mar-Jabalaha de trois autres patriarches d'un prêtre et de deux laïques Nestoriens*, ed. Paul Bedjan. Leipzig: Otto Harrassowitz, 1895.

Pseudo-Zacharias Rhetor. *The Chronicle of Pseudo-Zachariah Rhetor: Church and War in Late Antiquity*, ed. Geoffrey Greatrex. Liverpool: Liverpool University Press, 2011.

al-Qurashi, Abu Zayd. *Jamharat ash'ar al-'arab fi al-jahiliyyah wa al-islam*, ed. Muhammad al-Hashimi, Riyadh: al-Mamlakah al-'Arabiyyah al-Sa'udiyyah, 1981.

Rufinus of Aquileia. *The Church History of Rufinus of Aquileia: Books 10 and 11*, trans. Philip Amidon. New York; Oxford: Oxford University Press, 1997.

Sergius of Rusafa. *The Book of the Himyarites: Fragments of a Hitherto Unknown Syriac Work*, ed. Axel Moberg. London; Oxford; Paris; Leipzig: Lund, C. W. K. Gleerup, 1924.

Sozomen of Gaza. *The Eccelesiastical History of Sozomen, Comprising a History of the Church from A. D. 323 to A. D. 425*, trans. Chester Hartranft. London: Bohn, 1855.

_____. *Historia ecclesiastica*, ed. Edward Walford. London: S. Bagster, 1846.

Strabo. *The Geography of Strabo: An English Translation with Introduction and Notes*, trans. Duane Roller. Cambridge: Cambridge University Press, 2014.

The Syriac Writers of Qatar in the Seventh Century, eds. Mario Kozah, Abdulrahim Abu-Husayn, and Saif Shaheen Al-Murikhi. Piscataway: Gorgias Press, 2014.

al-Tabari, Muhammad b. Jarir. *Tafsir al-tabari: jami' al-bayan 'an ta'wil ay al-qur'an*. Cairo: Hajr, 2001.

_____. *Tarikh al-tabari: tarikh al-rusul wal-muluk wa man kan fi zaman kul minhum*, ed. Sidqi al-'Attar. Beirut: Dar al-Fikr, 2017.

al-Tifashi, Shihab al-Din. *Nuzhat al-albab fima la yujad fi kitab*, ed. Jamal Jum'ah. London: Riyad al-Rayyis, 1992.

al-Waqidi, Muhammad. *The Life of Muhammad: al-Waqidi's Kitab al-Maghazi*, trans. Rizwi Faizer. London; New York: Routledge, 2011.

Scholarship

Abbot, Nabia. "Pre-Islamic Arab queens." *The American Journal of Semitic Languages and Literatures*, 58.1 (1941): 1–22.

'Abd al-Karim, Khalil. *Fatrat al-takwin fi hayat al-sadiq al-amin*. Cairo: Mirit li al-Nashr wa al-Ma'lumat, 2001.

'Abd al-Rahman, Nawaf. *Tarikh al-'arab qabl al-islam*. Amman: Dar al-Janadria, 2015.

Abu al-Hasan, Husayn. *Qira'ah li-kitabat lihyaniyyah min jabal 'akmah bi mintaqat al-'ula*. Riyadh: Maktabat al-Malik fahd al-wataniyyah, 1997.

Ahmed, Leila. *Women and Gender in Islam: Historical Roots of a Modern Debate*. New Haven: Yale University Press, 1992.

Akoum, Dalida. "La représentation de la femme dans la littérature arabe préislamique et dans ses sources." PhD diss. Université Bordeaux Montaigne, 1996.

Akyol, Mustafa. *The Islamic Jesus: How the King of the Jews Became a Prophet of the Muslims*. New York: St. Martin's Press, 2017.

Al-Azmeh, Aziz. *The Arabs and Islam in Late Antiquity: A Critique of Approaches to Arabic Sources*. Berlin: Gerlach Press, 2014.

_____. *The Emergence of Islam in Late Antiquity: Allah and His People*. Cambridge: Cambridge University Press, 2014.

_____. "Pagan Arabs, Arabia, and monotheism." *Marginalia: LA Review of Books*, 1 March 2019.

Al-Jallad, Ahmad. "'Arab, 'A'rab, and Arabic in Ancient North Arabia: The first attestation of (')'rb as a group name in Safaitic." *Arabian Archaeology and Epigraphy* 31.2 (2020): 422–435.

_____. *An Outline of the Grammar of the Safaitic Inscriptions*. Leiden; Boston: Brill, 2015.

_____. "Graeco-Arabica I: The southern Levant," *Arabic in Context*, ed. Ahmad Al-Jallad. Leiden: Brill, 2017.

_____. "On the genetic background of the Rbbl bn Hf'm grave inscription at Qaryat al-Faw." *Bulletin of the School of Oriental and African Studies* 77.3 (2014): 1–21.

_____. "Pre-Islamic Arabic," *Arabic and Contact-Induced Change*, eds. Christopher Lucas and Stefano Manfredi. Berlin: Language Science Press, 2020.

'Ali, Jawad. *al-Mufassal fi tarikh al-'arab qabl al-islam*. London: Dar al-Saqi, 2001.

Ali, Kecia. *Marriage and Slavery in Early Islam*. Cambridge: Harvard University Press, 2010.

Alzoubi, Mahdi and Eyad al Masri and Fardous al Ajlouny. "Woman in the Nabataean society." *Mediterranean Archaeology and Archaeometry*, 13.1 (2013): 153–160.

Ames, Christine. *Medieval Heresies: Christianity, Judaism, and Islam*. Cambridge: Cambridge University Press, 2015.

Anderson, Benedict. *Imagined Communities Reflections on the Origin and Spread of Nationalism*. London: Verso, 1983.

Andrade, Nathaniel. *Syrian Identity in the Greco-Roman World*. Cambridge: Cambridge University Press, 2013.

_____. *Zenobia: Shooting Star of Palmyra*. Oxford; New York: Oxford University Press, 2018.

Andrae, Tor. *Der Ursprung der Islams und das Christentum*. Uppsala: Almqvist & Wiksells, 1926, trans. Jules Roche, *Les origines de l'Islam et le Christianisme*. Paris: Adrien-Maisonneuve, 1955.

Al-Ani, Ayad. *Araber als Teil der hellenistisch-römischen und christlichen Welt: Wurzeln orientalistischer Betrachtung und gegenwärtiger Konflikte: von Alexander dem Großen bis zur islamischen Eroberung*. Berlin: Duncker & Humblot, 2014.

al-Ansari (al-Ansary), 'Abd al-Rahman. "Adwa' jadidah 'ala dawlat kindah min khilal athar wa nuqush qaryat al-faw." *al-'Arab* 11–12 (1977): 864–875.

_____. "al-Qaba'il al-ba'idah kama arrakhaha al-qur'an al-karim." *Al-Manhal* 66 (2004): 64–69.

_____. *Qaryat al-faw: surah lil-hadarah al-'arabiyyah qabl al-islam fi-l-mamlakah al-'arabiyyah al-su'udiyyah / Qaryat al-Fau: A Portrait of Pre-Islamic Civilization in Saudi Arabia*. New York: St. Martin's Press, 1982.

_____ and F. Yusuf. *Ha'il: dayrat hatim*. Riyadh: Dar al-Qawafil, 2005.

_____. *Tayma' multaqa al-hadarat*. Riyadh: Dar al-Qawafil, 2002.

Ardener, Shirley. "Sexual Insult and Female Militancy." *Man* 8.3 (1973): 422–440.

Ariño-Durand, Miguel. "La Vie de la bienheureuse Vierge Marie dans les traditions apocryphes syro-orientales." PhD diss. Université Paris-Sorbonne/Institut Catholique de Paris, 2014.

Anthony, Sean. *Muhammad and the Empires of Faith: The Making of the Prophet of Islam*. Oakland: University of California Press, 2020.

_____. "Why Does the Qur'an Need the Meccan Sanctuary? Response to Professor Gerald Hawting's 2017 Presidential Address." *Journal of the International Qur'anic Studies Association* 3 (2018): 25–41.

Athanassiadi, Polymnia. *Mutations of Hellenism in Late Antiquity.* London; New York: Routledge, 2017.

Ayad, Mariam. *God's Wife, God's Servant: The God's Wife of Amun (ca. 740–525 BC).* London; New York: Routledge, 2009.

Ayubi, Zahra. *Gendered Morality: Classical Islamic Ethics of the Self, Family, and Society.* New York City: Columbia University Press, 2019.

Badareen, Nayel. "Shi'i marriage law in the pre-modern period: Who decides for women?" *Islamic Law and Society* 23.4 (2016): 368–391.

Bahay, Jihan Shah. *"al-Ihtilal al-rumani li-mamlakat al-anbat wal-wilayah al-'arabiyyah 106–305 miladiyah."* PhD diss. King Saud University, 2010.

al-Bajawi, 'Ali and Muhammad al-Mawla. *Ayyam al-'arab fi al-jahiliyyah.* Beirut; Sidon: al-Maktabah al-'Asriyyah, 1998.

Baldick, Julian. *Black God: Afroasiatic Roots of the Jewish, Christian and Muslim Religions.* London: Bloomsbury Academic, 1997.

Ball, Warwick. *Rome in the East.* London; New York: Routledge, 2002.

Baranov, Vladimir. "The iconophile fathers," *The Wiley Blackwell Companion to Patristics,* ed. Ken Parry. Chichester: John Wiley & Sons, 2015.

Bardy, Gustave. *Paul de Samosate: étude historique.* Louvain; Paris: Spicilegium Sacrum Lovaniense; Champion, 1923.

_____. *La question des langues dans l'église ancienne.* Paris: Beauchesne et ses fils, 1948.

Bauer, Walter. *Rechtgläubigkeit und Ketzerei im ältesten Christentum.* Tübingen: J. C. B. Mohr, 1964.

Bell, Richard. *The Origin of Islam in its Christian Environment: The Gunning Lectures 1925, Edinburgh University.* London: F. Cass, 1926.

Benko, Stephen. *The Virgin Goddess: Studies in the Pagan and Christian Roots of Mariology.* Leiden: Brill, 1993.

Berger, Philippe. "Les inscriptions hébraïques de la synagogue de Palmyre." *Mémoires de la Société de linguistique de Paris* 7 (1889): 65–72.

Bernal, Martin. *Black Athena: The Afroasiatic Roots of Classical Civilization.* New Brunswick: Rutgers University Press, 1987.

Betancourt, Roland. *Byzantine Intersectionality: Sexuality, Gender, and Race in the Middle Ages.* Princeton: Princeton University Press, 2020.

Block, Corrie. *The Qur'an in Christian–Muslim Dialogue: Historical and Modern Interpretations.* London; New York: Routledge, 2013.

Blue, Debbie. *Consider the Women: A Provocative Guide to Three Matriarchs of the Bible.* Grand Rapids: Eerdmans, 2019.

Le Bohec, Yann. *The Imperial Roman Army.* London; New York: Routledge, 1989.

Bowersock, Glenn. *The Crucible of Islam.* Cambridge: Harvard University Press, 2017.

_____. "Limes Arabicus." *Harvard Studies in Classical Philology* 80 (1976): 219–29.

_____. "Mavia, queen of the Saracens," *Studien zur antiken Sozialgeschichte: Festschrift F. Vittinghoff*, eds. Werner Eck, Hartmut Galsterer, and Hartmut Wolff. Köln; Vienna: Böhlau, 1980.

_____. *Roman Arabia*. Cambridge: Harvard University Press, 1983.

Bowles, David and José Meléndez. *Ghosts of the Rio Grande Valley*. Charleston, SC: Haunted America, 2016.

Brent, Allen. *Hippolytus and the Roman Church in the Third Century: Communities in Tension before the Emergence of a Monarch-Bishop*. Leiden; New York; Köln, Brill, 1995.

Brock, Sebastian. *An Introduction to Syriac Studies*. Piscataway: Gorgias Press, 2017.

_____. *Spirituality in the Syriac Tradition*. Kerala: St. Ephrem Ecumenical Research Institute, 2005.

Brock, Sebastian and Susan Harvey. *Holy Women of the Syrian Orient*. Berkeley: University of California Press, 1998.

Brown, Peter. *The Cult of the Saints: Its Rise and Function in Latin Christianity*. Chicago: University of Chicago Press, 2009.

_____. "The Rise and Function of the Holy Man in Late Antiquity." *The Journal of Roman Studies* 61 (1971): 80–101.

_____. *Society and the Holy in Late Antiquity*. Berkeley: University of California Press, 1989.

_____. *Power and Persuasion in Late Antiquity: Towards a Christian Empire*. Madison: University of Wisconsin Press, 1992.

Bucur, Bogdan. *Scripture Re-Envisioned: Christophanic Exegesis and the Making of a Christian Bible*. Leiden: Brill, 2018.

Burke, Peter. *Varieties of Cultural History*. Ithaca: Cornell University Press, 1997.

Burkitt, F. C. *Early Christianity Outside the Roman Empire: Two Lectures Delivered at Trinity College, Dublin*. Glasgow: Cambridge University Press, 1899.

Burris, Catherine and Lucas Van Rompay. "Thecla in Syriac Christianity: Preliminary Observations." *Hugoye: Journal of Syriac Studies* 5.2 (2002): 337–342.

al-Bustani, Butrus. *Muhit al-muhit: Qamus mutawwal lillugha al-ʿarabiyyah*. Beirut: Maktabat Lubnan, 1965.

Cameron, Averil. "The Cult of the Virgin in Late Antiquity: Religious Development and Myth-Making." *Studies in Church History* 39 (2004): 1–21.

Carroll, Michael. *The Cult of the Virgin Mary: Psychological Origins*. Princeton: Princeton University Press, 1986.

Chadwick, Henry. *The Church in Ancient Society: From Galilee to Gregory the Great*. Oxford; New York: Oxford University Press, 2001.

El Cheikh, Nadia. *Women, Islam, and Abbasid Identity*. Cambridge: Harvard University Press, 2015.

Cheikho, Louis. *Shuʿara' al-nasraniyyah qabl al-islam*. Beirut: Dar al-Mashriq, 1967.

Chelhod, Joseph. "Du nouveau à propos du 'matriarcat.'" *Arabica* 28.1 (1981): 76–106.

Cole, Juan. *Muhammad: Prophet of Peace Amid the Clash of Empires*. New York: Public Affairs, 2018.

_____. "*Paradosis* and monotheism: a late antique approach to the meaning of *islam* in the Quran." *Bulletin of the School of Oriental and African Studies* 82.3 (2019): 405–425.

Constantinou, Stavroula. "Thekla the Virgin: Women's Sacrifice and the Generic Martyr," *The 'Other' Martyrs: Women and the Poetics of Sexuality, Sacrifice, and Death in World Literatures*, eds. Alireza Korangy and Leyla Rouhi. Wiesbaden: Harrassowitz Verlag, 2019.

Croix, Geoffrey. *Christian Persecution, Martyrdom, and Orthodoxy*. Oxford: Oxford University Press, 2006.

Crone, Patricia. *The Nativist Prophets of Early Islamic Iran: Rural Revolt and Local Zoroastrianism*. Cambridge; New York: Cambridge University Press, 2012.

_____. *The Qur'anic Pagans and Related Matters: Collected Studies in Three Volumes, Volume 1*. Leiden: Brill, 2016.

Coulter-Harris, Deborah. *The Queen of Sheba: Legend, Literature and Lore*. Jefferson, NC: McFarland and Co., 2013.

The Darb al-Bakrah: A Caravan Route in North-West Arabia Discovered by Ali I. al-Ghabban, Catalogue of the Inscriptions, ed. Laïla Nehmé. Riyadh: Saudi Commission for Tourism and National Heritage, 2018.

Dawud, Ahmad (Daoud). *al-'Arab wa al-samiyyun wa al-'ibraniyyun wa banu isra'il wa al-yahud*. Damascus: Dar al-Mustaqbal, 1991.

de Boer, Theo. "Identité narrative et identité éthique," *Paul Ricoeur, L'hermeneutique a l'ecole de la phenomenology*, ed. Jean Greisch. Paris: Beauchesne, 1995.

De Fina, Anna. *Identity in Narrative: A Study of Immigrant Discourse*. Amsterdam; Philadelphia: John Benjamins Publishing Company, 2003.

Dennett, Daniel. *Consciousness Explained*. New York: Little, Brown & Co., 2017.

al-Dhib [al-Theeb], Sulayman. *al-Kitabat al-qadimah fil-mamlakah al-'arabiyyah al-su'udiyyah*. Riyadh: Kitab al-Majallah al-'Arabiyyah, 2018.

Dijkstra, Klaas. *Life and Loyalty: A Study in the Socio-Religious Culture of Syria and Mesopotamia in the Graeco-Roman Period Based on Epigraphic Evidence*. Leiden; New York; Köln: Brill, 1995.

Diwan, 'Abd al-Hamid. *Mawsu'at ashhar al-nisa' fi al-tarikh al-qadim: Mundhu fajr al-tarikh hatta al-'asr al-jahili*. Mansouria, Lebanon: Kitabuna li al-Nashr, 2009.

Donner, Fred. *Muhammad and the Believers: At the Origins of Islam*. Cambridge, MA: Harvard University Press, 2012.

_____. *Narratives of Islamic Origin: The Beginnings of Islamic Historical Writing*, Princeton: Darwin Press, 1998.

Dorra-Haddad, Joseph. *al-Qur'an da'wah nasraniyyah*. Beirut: Durus Qur'aniyyah, 1970.

Drake, Hal. *Constantine and the Bishops: The Politics of Intolerance*. Baltimore: Johns Hopkins University Press, 2002.

Drake, Susanna. *Slandering the Jew: Sexuality and Difference in Early Christian Texts*. Philadelphia: University of Pennsylvania Press, 2013.

Drijvers, H. J. W. *Bardaisan of Edessa*. Assen: Van Gorcum & Comp, 1966.

_____. *Cults and Beliefs at Edessa*, Leiden: Brill, 1980.

_____. "Die Dea Syria und andere Syriche Gottheiten im Imperium Romanum," *Die Orientalischen Religionen Im Römerreich*, ed. Maarten Vermaseren. Leiden: Brill, 1981.

_____. "East of Antioch: Forces and Structures in the Development of Early Syriac Theology," *East of Antioch*, ed. H. J. W. Drijvers. London: Variorum, 1984.

Drory, Rina. "The Abbasid construction of the Jahiliyya: Cultural authority in the making." *Studia Islamica* 83 (1996): 33–49.

Eadie, John and John Oleson. "The Water-Supply Systems of Nabataean and Roman Humayma." *Bulletin of the American Schools of Oriental Research* 262 (1986): 49–76.

Ehrman, Bart. *How Jesus Became God: The Exaltation of a Jewish preacher from Galilee.* San Francisco: Harper One, 2014.

_____. *Lost Christianities: The Battles for Scripture and the Faiths We Never Knew.* Oxford; New York: Oxford University Press, 2005.

El-Badawi, Emran. "From 'clergy' to 'celibacy': The development of *rahbaniyyah* between Qur'an, Hadith and Church Canon." *Al-Bayān: Journal of Qur'an and Hadith Studies* 11.1 (2013): 1–14.

_____. *The Qur'an and the Aramaic Gospel Traditions.* London: Routledge, 2013.

Elias, Jamal. "Prophecy, power and propriety: The encounter of Solomon and the queen of Sheba." *Journal of Qur'anic Studies* 11.1 (2009): 57–74.

Elliot, Dyan. *Spiritual Marriage: Sexual Abstinence in Medieval Wedlock.* Princeton: Princeton University Press, 1995.

al-Fassi, Hatoon. "*al-'Anasir al-sukkaniyyah al-wafidah 'ala shamal gharb al-Jazirah al-'arabiyyah fil-fatrah min muntasaf al-qarn al-sadis q.m. wa hatta al-qarn al-thani lil-milad.*" *Dirasat Tarikhiyyah* 2.56 (1995): 3–41.

_____. "*Aswaq al-'arab,*" *al-Kitab al-marja' fi tarikh al-ummah al-'arabiyyah*, vol. 1. Tunis: al-Munadhamah al-'Arabiyyah li-Ttarbiyah wa-Ththaqafah wal-'Ulum, 2005.

_____. "*al-Awda' al-siyasiyyah wal-ijtima'iyyah wal-iqtisadiyyah wa-ththaqafiyyah fi jazirat al-'arab,*" *al-Kitab al-marja' fi tarikh al-ummah al-'arabiyyah*, vol. 1. Tunis: al-Munadhamah al-'Arabiyyah li-Ttarbiyah wa-Ththaqafah wal-'Ulum, 2005.

_____. "*al-Jazirah al-'arabiyyah bayn istrabu wa blini: qira'ah fi al-masadir al-klasiki-yyah.*" *Majallat al-Khalij lil-Tarikh wa-l-Athar* 8 (2013): 55–91.

_____. "Kamkam the Nabataean priestess: Priesthood and society in ancient Arabia," *From Ugarit to Nabataea: Studies in Honor of John F. Healey*, eds. George Kiraz and Zeyad al-Salameen. Piscataway: Gorgias Press, 2012.

_____. "*Malikat al-'arab fil-alf al-awwal qabl al-fatrah al-mu'asirah.*" *Adumatu* 7 (2012): 13–50.

_____. "*Malikat al-anbat: dirasah tahliliyyah muqaranah.*" *Adumatu* 16 (2007): 11–39.

_____. "*Mintaqat al-ha'il qabl al-islam,*" *Mawsu'at al-mamlakat al-'arabiyyah al-su'udiyyah/Encyclopedia of Saudi Arabia.* Riyadh: Maktabat al-Malik 'Abda al-'Aziz al-'Ammah, 2007.

_____. "*al-Nizam al-umumi bayn al-nuqush al-hasa'iyyah (al-thajiyyah) wal-nuqush al-nabatiyyah.*" *Adumatu* 28 (2013): 35–50.

_____. "*Nuqtat al-bad' al-tarikhi, min ayn? ru'yah marja'iyyah jadidah.*" *GCC Society for History and Archeology* 9 (2008): 123–140.

_____. *Women in pre-Islamic Arabia: Nabataea*. Oxford: Archaeopress, 2007.

Fawwaz, Zaynab. *al-Durr al-manthur fi tabaqat rabbat al-khudur*. Kuwait: Maktabat Ibn Qutaybah, 1891, repr. Cairo: Hindawi, 2014.

Ferguson, R. B. "Masculinity and war." *Current Anthropology* 62.23 (2021): S112–124.

Fiema, Zbigniew, Ahmad al-Jallah, Michael Macdonald, and Laïla Nehmé. "*Provincia Arabia*: Nabataea, the emergence of Arabic as written language, and Graeco-Arabica," *Arabs and Empires before Islam*, ed. Greg Fisher. Oxford: Oxford University Press, 2015.

Finlayson, Cynthia. "The women of Palmyra: Textile workshops and the influence of the silk trade in Roman Syria." *Textile Society of America Symposium Proceedings* 385 (2002): 1–12.

Fisher, Greg. "From Mavia to al-Mundhir: Arab Christians and Arab tribes in the late antique Roman East," *Religious Culture in Late Antique Arabia: Selected Studies on the Late Antique Religious Mind*, eds. Kirill Dmitriev and Isabel Toral-Niehoff. Piscataway: Gorgias Press, 2017.

_____. "Reflections on Arab leadership in Late Antiquity," *To the Madbar and Back Again: Studies in the Languages, Archaeology, and Cultures of Arabia Dedicated to Michael C. A. Macdonald*, eds. Laïla Nehmé and Ahmad Al-Jallad. Leiden: Brill, 2018.

_____. *Rome, Persia, and Arabia: Shaping the Middle East from Pompey to Muhammad*. London: Routledge, 2019.

Fisher, Greg, Philip Wood, George Bevan, Geoffrey Greatrex, Basema Hamarneh, Peter Schadler, and Walter Ward. "Arabs and Christianity," *Arabs and Empires before Islam*, ed. Greg Fisher. Oxford: Oxford University Press, 2015.

Fowden, Garth. *Before and after Muhammad: The First Millennium Refocused*. Princeton; Oxford; Princeton University Press, 2014.

Fowlkes-Childs, Blair and Michael Seymour, *The World between Empires: A Picture Album*. New York: Metropolitan Museum of Art, 2019.

Frymer-Kensky, Tikva. *In the Wake of the Goddesses: Women, Culture, and the Biblical Transformation of Pagan Myth*. New York: Ballantine Books, 1992.

Ghaffar, Zishan. *Der Koran in seinem religions- und weltgeschichtlichen Kontext: Eschatologie und Apokalyptik in den mittelmekkanischen Suren*. Leiden: Brill, 2017.

Gibbon, Edward. *The Decline and Fall of the Roman Empire (Edited and Abridged)*. New York: Random House, 2009.

Gibbons, Ann. "Why 536 was 'the worst year to be alive.'" *Science*, 15 November 2018.

Giri, Jacques. *Les nouvelles hypothèses sur les origines du christianisme: Enquête sur les recherches récentes*. Paris: Karthala, 2010.

Graf, David. *Rome and the Arabian Frontier: From the Nabataeans to the Saracens*. London: Ashgate, 1997.

Grasso, Valentina. "The gods of the Qur'an: The rise of Hijazi henotheism during late antiquity," *The Study of Islamic Origins: New Perspectives and Contexts*, eds. Mette Mortensen, Guillaume Dye, Isaac Oliver, and Tommaso Tesei. Berlin: De Gruyter, 2021.

Gray, Patrick. "The Legacy of Chalcedon Christological Problems and Their Significance," *The Cambridge Companion to the Age of Justinian*, ed. Michael Maas. Cambridge, Cambridge University Press, 2006.

Griffith Sidney. *The Bible in Arabic: The Scriptures of the "People of the Book" in the Language of Islam*. Princeton: Princeton University Press, 2015.

_____. "Monks, 'Singles,' and the 'Sons of the Covenant,' Reflections on Syriac Ascetic Terminology," *Eulogema: Studies in Honor of R. Taft*, eds. E. Carr and Robert Taft. Rome: Pontificio Ateneo S. Anselmo, 1993.

Gruendler, Beatrice. *The Development of the Arabic Scripts: From the Nabataean Era to the First Islamic Century According to Dated Texts*. Atlanta: Scholars Press, 1993.

Grunebaum, G. E. Von. "The nature of Arab unity before Islam." *Arabica* 10.1 (1963): 5–23.

Guidère, Mathieu. "Les poètes et le prophète au debut de l'Islam." *Quaderni di Studi Arabi* 5.6 (2010–2011): 121–138.

Gzella, Holger. *A Cultural History of Aramaic: From the Beginnings to the Advent of Islam*. Leiden; Boston: Brill, 2015.

al-Hadrani, Balqis. *al-Malikah balqis: al-tarikh wal-usturah wa-rramz*. Cairo: Matba'at Wahdan, 1994.

Haeri, Shahla. *The Unforgettable Queens of Islam: Succession, Authority, Gender*. Cambridge: Cambridge University Press, 2020.

Hage, Wolfgang. *Das orientalische Christentum*. Stuttgart: Kohlhammer, 2007.

Halter, Marek. *La Trilogie: Les Femmes de l'Islam (Khadija, Fatima et Aisha)*. Paris: Groupe Robert Laffont, 2015.

Hamur, 'Irfan Muhammad. *al-Mar'ah wa al-jamal wa al-hubb fi lughat al-'arab*. Beirut: Dar al-Kutub al-'Ilmiyyah, 1971.

al-Hariri, Abu Musa. *Qiss wa nabi: bahth fi nash'at al-islam*. Beirut: s.n., 1979, trans. Joseph Azzi, *Le prêtre et le prophète: aux sources du coran*. Paris: Maisonneuve et Larose, 2001.

Harnack, Adolf von. *Die Mission und Ausbreitung des Christentums in den ersten drei Jahrhunderten*. Leipzig: J.C. Hinrichs, 1902.

Harvey, Susan. "Feminine imagery for the divine: The Holy Spirit, the Odes of Solomon, and early Syriac tradition." *St. Vladimir's Theological Quarterly* 37 (1993): 111–139.

_____. "Revisiting the Daughters of the Covenant: Women's choirs and sacred song in ancient Syriac Christianity." *Hugoye: Journal of Syriac Studies* 8.2 (2005): 125–149.

Hawting, Gerald. *The Idea of Idolatry and the Emergence of Islam: From Polemic to History*. Cambridge: Cambridge University Press, 1999.

Healey, John. *The Religion of the Nabataeans: A Conspectus*. Leiden: Brill, 2001.

_____. "Were the Nabataeans Arabs?" *Aram* 1 (1989): 38–44.

Heide, Gale. *Timeless Truth in the Hands of History: A Short History of System in Theology*. Eugene: Wipf and Stock Publishers, 2012.

El-Hibri, Tayeb. *Reinterpreting Islamic Historiography: Harun al-Rashid and the Narrative of the Abbasid Caliphate*. Cambridge: Cambridge University Press, 1999.

Hitti, Philip. *History of the Arabs: From the Earliest Times to the Present*. Basingstoke: Palgrave Macmillan, 2002.

Hodgson, Marshall. *The Venture of Islam*, vol. 1. Chicago: University of Chicago Press, 1977.

Holma, Harri. "Que signifie, chez Diodore de Sicile, le nom propre arabe Βανιζομεν(εῖς)?" *Orientalia* 13 (1944): 356–360.

Holt, Maria. *Violence against Women in Peace and War: Cases from the Middle East*. Lanham: Lexington Books, 2021.

Hoyland, Robert. *Arabia and the Arabs: From the Bronze Age to the Coming of Islam*. London; New York: Routledge, 2010.

_____. "The Jews of the Hijaz in the Qur'an," *New Perspectives on the Qur'an: The Qur'an in Its Historical Context 2*, ed. Gabriel Reynolds. London; New York: Routledge, 2011.

_____. "Late Roman provincial Arabia, Monophysite monks and Arab tribes: A problem of centre and periphery." *Semitica et Classica* 3 (2010): 117–139.

_____. *Seeing Islam as Others Saw it: A Survey and Evaluation of Christian, Jewish and Zoroastrian Writings on Early Islam*. Princeton: Darwin Press, 1997.

Hunt, Emily. *Christianity in the Second Century: The Case of Tatian*. London: Routledge, 2003.

Hurwitz, Siegmund. *Lilith: Die erste Eva Eine historische und psychologische Studie über dunkle Aspekte des Weiblichen*. Einsiedeln: Daimon verlag, 1980.

Identity and Story: Creating Self in Narrative, eds. D. P. McAdams, R. Josselson, and A. Lieblich. Washington: American Psychological Association, 2010.

Intagliata, Emanuele. *Palmyra after Zenobia, 273–750: An archaeological and historical reappraisal*. Havertown, PA: Oxbow Books, 2018.

'Iqab, Fathiyyah. "*al-'ilaqat al-siyasiyyah bayn al-anbat wa-l-yahud fi filastin wa mawqif al-dawlah al-rumaniyyah minha: min awakhir al-qarn al-thani qabl al-milad ila al-qarn al-awwal al-miladi*." PhD diss. Abd al-Aziz University, 2000.

Jayyusi, Lena. *The Adventures of Sayf Ben Dhi Yazan: An Arab Folk Epic*. Bloomington: Indiana University Press, 1996.

Jones, Stephanie. "Emboldening Dinarzad: The Thousand and One Nights in contemporary fiction," *New Perspectives on Arabian Nights*, ed. Geert Jan van Gelder. London: Routledge, 2014.

Kaelin, Oskar. "*Modell Ägypten*," *Adoption von Innovationen im Mesopotamien des 3. Jahrtausends v. Chr*. Fribourg: Academic Press Fribourg, 2006.

Kahalah, 'Umar. *A'lam al-nisa' fi 'alamay al-'arab wa-l-islam*. Beirut: Mu'assasat al-Risalah, 2008.

Kateusz, Ally. "Collyridian Déjà Vu: The Trajectory of Redaction of the Markers of Mary's Liturgical Leadership." *Journal of Feminist Studies in Religion* 29.2 (2013): 75–92.

Kazan, S. "Isaac of Antioch's Homily against the Jews." *Oriens Christianus* 45 (1961): 30–53.

Kemezis, Adam. *Greek Narratives of the Roman Empire under the Severans: Cassius Dio, Philostratus and Herodian*. Cambridge: Cambridge University Press, 2014.

King, David. "The Petra fallacy: Early mosques do face the sacred Kaaba in Mecca but Dan Gibson doesn't know how," 2018, 1–54, https://www.researchgate.net/publication/330221815_King_The_Petra_fallacy_The_Petra_fallacy_-_Early_mosques_do_face_the_Sacred_Kaaba_in_Mecca_but_Dan_Gibson_doesn%27t_ know_how_Comparing_historical_orientations_with_modern_directions_can_lead_to_false_re (accessed April 4, 2022).

Kinzig, Wolfram. *Christenverfolgung in der Antike*. Munich: Verlag C. H. Beck, 2019.

Kister, M. J. "A bag of meat: A study of an early Hadith." *Bulletin of the School of Oriental and African* 33.2 (1970): 267–275.

_____. "The sons of Khadija." *Jerusalem Studies in Arabic and Islam* 16 (1993): 59–95.

Klein, Wassilios. *Syrische Kirchenväter*. Stuttgart: Kohlhammer, 2004.

Kofsky, Arieh. "Mamre: A Case of Regional Cult?" *Sharing the Sacred: Religious Contacts and Conflicts in the Holy Land, First–Fifteenth Centuries CE*, ed. Guy Stroumsa. Jerusalem: Yad Izhak Ben Zvi, 1998.

Kosinski, Rafal. *Holiness and Power: Constantinopolitan Holy Men and Authority in the 5th Century*. Berlin: De Gruyter, 2016.

Krag, Signe. *Funerary Representations of Palmyrene Women: From the First Century BC to the Third Century AD*. Turnhout: Brepols, 2018.

Lammens, Henry. *L'Islam: Croyances et Institutions*. Beirut: Imp. Catholique, 1943.

Langford, Julie. *Maternal Megalomania: Julia Domna and the Imperial Politics of Motherhood*. Baltimore: Johns Hopkins University Press, 2013.

Lassner, Jacob. *Demonizing the Queen of Sheba: Boundaries of Gender and Culture in Postbiblical Judaism and Medieval Islam*. Chicago: University of Chicago Press, 1993.

Lenski, Noel. *Failure of Empire: Valens and the Roman State in the Fourth Century A.D.* Berkeley; Los Angeles; London: University of California Press, 2002.

Lieu, Samuel and Mary Boyce. *Manichaeism in the Later Roman Empire and Medieval China: A Historical Survey*. Manchester: Manchester University Press, 1985.

Limberis, Vasiliki. *Divine Heiress: The Virgin Mary and the Making of Christian Constantinople*. Routledge: New York; London, 1994.

Lowin, Shari. *The Making of a Forefather: Abraham in Islamic and Jewish Exegetical Narratives*. Leiden: Brill, 2006.

Maalouf, Amin. *Les jardins de lumière*. Paris: J. C. Lattès, 1991.

Mabra, Joshua. *Princely Authority in the Early Marwanid State: The Life of 'Abd al-'Aziz ibn Marwan (d. 86/705)*. Piscataway: Gorgias Press, 2017.

Macdonald, Michael. "Arabs, Arabias, and Arabic before Late Antiquity." *Topoi* 16.1 (2009): 277–332.

_____. "Goddesses, dancing girls or cheerleaders? Perceptions of the divine and the female form in the rock art of pre-Islamic North Arabia," *Dieux et déesses d'Arabie: Images et représentations*, eds. Isabelle Sachet and Christian Robin. Paris: De Boccard, 2012.

_____. "Three dimensions in two: Convention and experiment in the rock art of Ancient North Arabia," *The Archeology of North Arabia: Oases and Landscapes*, ed. Marta Luciani. Vienna: Austrian Academy of Sciences, 2016.

Macina, Menachem. "Les bnay et bnat qyama de l'Église syriaque: Une piste philologique sérieuse." *Patrimoine Syriaque* 6 (1999): 13–49.

MacMullen, Ramsay. "Roman imperial building in the provinces." *Harvard Studies in Classical Philology* 64 (1959): 207–235.

Maghen, Zeev. "Davidic Motifs in the Biography of Muhammad." *Jerusalem Studies in Arabic and Islam* 35 (2008): 91–139.

al-Mallah, Hashim. *al-Wasit fi tarikh al-'arab qabl al-islam*. Beirut: Dar al-Kutub al-'Ilmiyyah, 1971.

Maraqten, Mohammed. "Der Afkal/Apkallu im arabischen Bereich: eine epigraphische Untersuchung." *Alter Orient und Altes Testament* 252 (2000): 263–283.

Marzolph, Ulrich, Richard van Leeuwen, and Hassan Wassouf. *The Arabian Nights Encyclopedia*. Santa Barbara, CA: ABC-CLIO, 2004.

Masarwah, Nader. "Marriage in Pre-Islamic Arabia as Reflected in Poetry and Prose: The Social and Humane Relations between Husband and Wife." *Sociology Study* 3.11 (2013): 847–857.

McHugh, John. *Emperor Alexander Severus: Rome's Age of Insurrection, AD 222–235*. Barnsley, UK: Pen & Sword Military, 2017.

Mernissi, Fatima. *Sultanes oubliées: femmes chefs d'État en Islam*. Paris: Albin Michel; Éditions Le Fennec, 1990, trans. Mary Jo Lakeland, *The Forgotten Queens of Islam*. Minneapolis: University of Minnesota Press, 2003.

Meshorer, Ya'akov. *Nabataean Coins*. Jerusalem: Hebrew University of Jerusalem, 1975.

Millar, Fergus. "Ethnic identity in the Roman Near East, 325–450: Language, religion and culture." *Mediterranean Archaeology* 11 (1998): 159–176.

———. "Hagar, Ishmael, Josephus, and the origins of Islam." *Journal of Jewish Studies* 44 (1993): 23–45.

———. *The Roman Near East, 31 BC – AD 337*. Cambridge, MA: Harvard University Press, 1993.

———. "Paul of Samosata, Zenobia and Aurelian: The Church, Local Culture and Political Allegiance in Third-Century Syria." *The Journal of Roman Studies* 61 (1971): 1–17.

Miller, Patricia. *Women in Early Christianity: Translations from Greek Texts*. Washington, D.C.: The Catholic University of America Press, 2005.

Morris, Ian. "Mecca and Macoraba." *Al-'Usur al-Wusta* 26 (2018): 1–60.

Moussalli, Ahmed. "An Islamic model for political conflict resolution: *Tahkim* (Arbitration)," *Peace and Conflict Resolution in Islam: Precept and Practice*, eds. Abdul Aziz Said, Nathan Funk, and Ayse S. Kadayifci. Washington, D.C.: University Press of America, 2009.

Muhanna, 'Abd. *Mu'jam al-nisa' al-sha'irat fi al-jahiliyyah wa al-islam*. Beirut: Dar al-Kutub al-'Ilmiyah, 1990.

Murray, Robert. *Symbols of Church and Kingdom: A Study in Early Syriac Tradition*. London: Cambridge University Press, 1975.

Nashif, Halah. *Urid huwiyyah: qisas qasirah*. Beirut: al-Mu'assasah al-'Arabiyyah lil-Dirasat wal-Nashr, 1993.

Nehmé, Laïla. "A glimpse of the development of the Nabataean script into Arabic based on old and new epigraphic material," *The Development of Arabic as a Written Language*, ed. Michael Macdonald. Oxford: Archaeopress, 2010.

_____. "Aramaic or Arabic? The Nabataeo-Arabic Script and the Language of the Inscriptions Written in This Script," *Arabic in Context: Celebrating 400 years of Arabic at Leiden University*, ed. Ahmad Al-Jallad. Leiden: Brill, 2017.

Nielsen, Ditlef. "Die altsemitische Muttergöttin." *Zeitschrift der Deutschen Morgenländischen Gesellschaft* 92.17 (1938): 504–551.

Ni'mah, Nihad. *al-Jinn fil-adab al-'arabi*. Beirut: American University in Beirut Press, 1961.

Norris, Jerome. "Peuples et groupes sociaux en Arabie du nord-ouest aux époques nabatéenne et romaine." PhD diss. Université de Lorraine, 2014.

Ohlig, Karl-Heinz. "Vom muhammad Jesus zum Propheten der Araber: Die Historisierung eines christologischen Prädikats," *Der frühe Islam eine historisch-kritische Rekonstruktion anhand zeitgenössischer Quellen*, ed. Karl-Heinz Ohlig. Berlin: Verlag Hans Schiller, 2007.

Olinder, Gunnar. *The Kings of Kinda of the Family of Akil al-Murar*. Lund: C. W. K. Gleerup, 1927.

Ong, Walter. *Orality and Literacy*. New York: Methuen & Co., 1982.

Osman, Ghada. "Pre-Islamic Arab converts to Christianity in Mecca and Medina: An investigation into the Arabic sources." *The Muslim World* 95 (2005): 67–80.

Ouardi, Hela. *Les Derniers Jours de Muhammad*. Paris: Albin Michel, 2016.

Papakonstantinou, Zinon. "Wine and wine drinking in the Homeric world." *L'Antiquité Classique* 78 (2009): 1–24.

Parker, Samuel and John Betlyon. *The Roman Frontier in Central Jordan: Final Report on the Limes Arabicus Project, 1980–1989*. Washington, D.C.: Dumbarton Oaks Research Library and Collection, 2006.

Payne-Smith, J. *A Compendious Syriac Dictionary*. Oxford: Clarendon Press, 1979.

Pennacchietti, Fabrizio. *Three Mirrors for Two Biblical Ladies: Susanna and the Queen of Sheba in the Eyes of Jews, Christians, and Muslims*. Piscataway: Gorgias Press, 2006.

The Petra Papyri, eds. Antti Arjava, Matias Buchholz, and Traianos Gagos. Amman: American Center of Oriental Research, 2002–2018.

Photo 3946, *Corpus Inscriptionum Semiticarum* 2.3 (1953): 12.

Potter, David. *The Roman Empire at Bay, AD 180–395*. London: Routledge, 2004.

Powers, David. "Demonizing Zenobia: The Legend of al-Zabba' in Islamic Sources," *Histories of the Middle East*, eds. Roxani Margariti, Adam Sabra, and Petra Sijpesteijn. Leiden: Brill, 2010.

_____. *Muhammad Is Not the Father of Any of Your Men: The Making of the Last Prophet*. Philadelphia: University of Pennsylvania Press, 2009.

_____. "Sinless, sonless and seal of prophets: Muhammad and Kor 33, 36–40, revisited." *Arabica* 67 (2020): 333–408.

_____. *Zayd*. Philadelphia: University of Pennsylvania Press, 2014.

al-Qimani, Sayyid. *al-Hizb al-hashimi wa ta'sis al-dawlah al-islamiyyah*. Cairo: Maktabat Madbuli al-Saghir, 2008.

_____. *al-Usturah wal-turath*. Cairo: Maktabat Ibn Sina, 1999, repr. Cairo: Hindawi, 2017.

Rapp, Claudia. *Holy Bishops in Late Antiquity: The Nature of Christian Leadership in an Age of Transition.* Berkeley: University of California Press, 2013.

Rathjens, Carl. "Die alten Welthandelsstrassen und die Offenbarungsreligionen." *Oriens* 15 (1962): 115–129.

Retso, Jan. *The Arabs in Antiquity: Their History from the Assyrians to the Umayyads.* London; New York: Routledge, 2014.

Reynolds, Gabriel. "On the Qur'an and Christian heresies," *The Qur'an's Reform of Judaism and Christianity: Return to the Origins,* ed. Holger Zellentin. London: Routledge, 2019.

———. *The Qur'an and Its Biblical Subtext.* London; New York: Routledge, 2010.

Robin, Christian. "À propos des 'filles de dieu." *Semitica* 52–53 (2002–2007): 139–148.

———. "Arabia and Ethiopia," *The Oxford Handbook of Late Antiquity,* ed. Scott Johnson. Oxford: Oxford University Press, 2012.

———. "'Athtar au féminin en Arabie méridionale," *New Research in Archaeology and Epigraphy of South Arabia and its Neighbors,* ed. A. V. Sedov. Moscow: State Museum of Oriental Art and Institute of Oriental Studies, 2012.

———. "Chrétiens de l'Arabie heureuse et de l'Arabie déserte: de la victoire à l'échec." *Dossiers Archéologie et sciences des origines* 309 (2005–2006): 24–35.

———. "Faut-il réinventer la Jahiliyya?" *Orient et Méditerranée* 3 (2009): 5–14.

———. "Himyar et Israël." *Comptes rendus des séances de l'Académie des Inscriptions et Belles-Lettres* 148 (2004): 831–908.

———. "'La caravane yéménite et syrienne' dans une inscription de l'Arabie méridionale antique," *L'Orient au cœur: en l'honneur d'André Miquel,* eds. André Miquel and Floréal Sanagustin. Paris: Maisonneuve et Larose, 2001.

———. "L'attribution d'un bassin à une divinité en Arabie du Sud antique." *Raydan* 1 (1978): 39–64.

———. "L'évêché nestorien de Mashmahig dans l'archipel d'al-Bahrayn (Ve–IXe siècle)." *Berliner Beiträge zum Vorderen Orient* 2 (1983): 171–196.

———. "Les Arabes de Himyar, des Romains et des Perses (iiie–vie siècles de l'ère chrétienne)." *Semitica et Classica* 1 (2008): 167–202.

———. "Les 'Filles de Dieu' de Saba' à La Mecque: réflexions sur l'agencement des panthéons dans l'Arabie ancienne." *Semitica* 50 (2001): 113–192.

———. "Les religions pratiquées par les membres de la tribu de Kinda (Arabie) à la veille de l'Islam." *Judaïsme ancien/Ancient Judaism* 1 (2013): 203–261.

———. "Les rois de Kinda," *Arabia, Greece and Byzantium. Cultural Contacts in Ancient and Medieval Times,* eds. Abdulaziz al-Helabi, Dimitrios Letsios, Moshalleh al-Moraekhi, and Abdullah al-Abduljabbar. Riyadh: King Saud University, 2012.

———. "Quel judaïsme en Arabie?" *Le judaïsme de l'Arabie antique: Actes du colloque de Jérusalem,* ed. Christian Julien Robin. Turnhout: Brepols, 2015.

———. "Soixante-dix ans avant l'Islam: l'Arabie toute entière dominée par un roi chrétien." *Comptes rendus des séances de l'Académie des Inscriptions et Belles-Lettres* 156.1 (2012): 525–553.

Rodinson, Maxime. *Les Arabes.* Paris: Presses Universitaires de France, 2002.

Romney, B. T. H. *Religious Origins of Nations? The Christian Communities of the Middle East*. Leiden: Brill, 2010.

Röttgers, Kurt. *Identität als Ereignis: Zur Neufindung eines Begriffs*. Bielefeld: Transcript Verlag, 2016.

Rowan, Clare. *Under Divine Auspices: Divine Ideology and the Visualisation of Imperial Power in the Severan Period*. Cambridge: Cambridge University Press, 2012.

Ruffini, Giovanni. *Medieval Nubia: A Social and Economic History*. Oxford: Oxford University Press, 2012.

Ryan, M. K., Alexander Haslam, Mette Hersby, and Renata Bongiorno. "Think crisis—think female: The glass cliff and contextual variation in the think manager—think male stereotype." *Journal of Applied Psychology* 96.3 (2011): 470–484.

El-Saadawi, Nawal. *al-Untha hi al-asl*. Cairo: Hindawi Foundation, 2017.

Sabbagh, Layla. *al-Mar'ah fi al-tarikh al-'arabi: fi tarikh al-'arab qabl al-islam*. Damascus: Wizarat al-Thaqafah wa al-Irshad al-Qawmi, 1975.

Sahner, Christian. *Christian Martyrs Under Islam: Religious Violence and the Making of the Muslim World*. Princeton: Princeton University Press, 2018.

Said, Salah. "Two New Greek Inscriptions with the Name YTWR from Umm al-Jimal." *Palestine Exploration Quarterly* 138.2 (2006): 125–132.

Saint-Laurent, Jeanne-Nicole Mellon. *Missionary Stories and the Formation of the Syriac Churches*. Berkeley: University of California Press, 2015.

Sánchez, Francisco. *Nabatu: The Nabataeans through Their Inscriptions*. Barcelona: University of Barcelona, 2015.

al-Sawwah, Firas. *Lughz 'ishtar: al-uluhah al-mu'annathah wa asl al-din wal-usturah*. Damascus: Dar 'Ala' al-Din, 1996.

Scully, Jason. *Isaac of Nineveh's Ascetical Eschatology*. Oxford: Oxford University Press, 2017.

Segovia, Carlos. "Messalianism, Binitarianism, and the East Syrian Background of the Qur'an," *Remapping Emergent Islam: Texts, Social Settings, and Ideological Trajectories*, ed. Carlos Segovia. Amsterdam: University of Amsterdam Press, 2020.

Shaddel, Mehdy. "Studio onomastica coranica: *al-Raqim*, caput nabataeae." *Journal of Semitic Studies* 62.2 (2017): 303–318.

Shahid, Irfan. *Byzantium and the Arabs in the Fourth Century*. Washington, D.C.: Dumbarton Oaks, 1984.

_____. *Byzantium and the Arabs in the Fifth Century*. Washington, D.C.: Dumbarton Oaks, 1989.

_____. *Byzantium and the Arabs in the Sixth Century*. Washington, D.C.: Dumbarton Oaks, 2002.

_____. *Byzantium and the Arabs in the Seventh Century*. Washington, D.C.: Dumbarton Oaks, 2010.

_____. "Byzantino-Arabica: The Conference of Ramla, A.D. 524." *Journal of Near Eastern Studies* 23 (1964): 115–131.

_____. *Rome and the Arabs: A Prolegomenon to the Study of Byzantium and the Arabs*. Washington, D.C.: Dumbarton Oaks, 1984.

Shahin, Aram. "Struggling for communitas: Arabian political thought in the great century of change (*ca.* 560–*ca.* 660 AD)." PhD diss. University of Chicago, 2009.

Shariati, Ali. *Fatemeh fatemeh ast*. Tehran: Nashr-i-Ayat, 1978, trans. Laleh Bakhtiar, *Ali Shariati's Fatima is Fatima*. Tehran: Shariati Foundation, 1981.

Shoemaker, Stephen. *Ancient Traditions of the Virgin Mary's Dormition and Assumption*. Oxford: Oxford University Press, 2002.

_____. "Epiphanius of Salamis, the Kollyridians, and the Early Dormition Narratives: The Cult of the Virgin in the Later Fourth Century." *Journal of Early Christian Studies* 16 (2008): 369–99.

_____. *Mary in Early Christian Faith and Devotion*. Newhaven; London: Yale University Press, 2016.

Slade, Darren. "*Arabia Haeresium Ferax* (Arabia Bearer of Heresies): Schismatic Christianity's Potential Influence on Muhammad and the Qur'an." *American Theological Inquiry* 7.1 (2014): 43–53.

Soroush, Abdolkarim. *Bast-i tajrubay-i nabavi*. Tehran: Moasese Farhangi Serat, 1999, trans. Nilou Mobasser, *The Expansion of Prophetic Experience*. Leiden: Brill, 2008.

Smith, Robertson. *Religion of the Semites*. London: Adam and Charles Black, 1894.

Smith, T. M. *Arabs: A 3,000–Year History of Peoples, Tribes and Empires*. New Haven: Yale University Press, 2019.

Southern, Pat. *Empress Zenobia: Palmyra's Rebel Queen*. London: Bloomsbury, 2008.

Spencer, Robert. "Arabian matriarchate: An old controversy." *Southwestern Journal of Anthropology* 8.4 (1952): 478–502.

Stinchcomb, Jillian. "The Queen of Sheba in the Qur'an and late antique Midrash," *The Study of Islamic Origins: New Perspectives and Contexts*, eds. Mette Mortensen, Guillaume Dye, Isaac Oliver, and Tommaso Tesei. Berlin: De Gruyter, 2021.

Stoneman, Richard. *Palmyra and Its Empire: Zenobia's Revolt against Rome*. Ann Arbor, MI: University of Michigan Press, 1992.

Streete, Gail. *The Strange Woman: Power and Sex in the Bible*. Louisville, KY: Westminster John Knox Press, 1997.

Stroumsa, Guy. *Self and Self-Transformation in the History of Religions*. Oxford: Oxford University Press, 2002.

The Syriac World, ed. Daniel King. London: Routledge, 2018.

Szilágyi, Krisztina. "Muhammad and the monk: the making of the Christian Bahira legend." *Jerusalem Studies in Arabic and Islam* 34 (2008): 169–214.

Tamcke, Martin. "The relationship between theological teaching and religious practice by the East Syrian Christians in Qatar (sixth–seventh centuries)," *Religious Culture in Late Antique Arabia: Selected Studies on the Late Antique Religious Mind*. Piscataway: Gorgias Press, 2017.

Tannous, Jack. *The Making of the Medieval Middle East: Religion, Society, and Simple Believers*. Princeton: Princeton University Press, 2020.

Teixidor, Xavier. *The Pagan God: Popular Religion in the Greco-Roman Near East*. Princeton: Princeton University Press, 1977.

_____. "Palmyra in the third century," *A Journey to Palmyra: Collected Essays to Remember Dilbert R. Hillers*, ed. Eleonora Cussini. Leiden; Boston: Brill, 2005.

_____. *The Pantheon of Palmyra*. Leiden; Boston: Brill, 1979.

Teubal, Savina. *Sarah the Priestess: The First Matriarch of Genesis*. Columbus, OH: Swallow Press, 1984.

al-Tizini, Tayyib. *Muqaddimat awwaliyyah fi al-islam al-muhammadi al-bakir nash'atan wa ta'sisan*. Damascus: Dar Dimashq li al-Tiba'ah wa al-Sahafah wa al-Nashr, 1994.

Toral-Niehoff, Isabel. *al-Hira: Eine arabische Kulturmetropole im spätantiken Kontext*. Leiden; Boston: Brill, 2013.

Tougher, Shaun. "In praise of an empress: Julian's speech of thanks to Eusebia," *The Propaganda of Power: The Role of Panegyric in Late Antiquity*, ed. Mary Whitby. Leiden; Boston; Köln: Brill, 1998.

Trimingham, John. *Christianity among the Arabs in Pre-Islamic Times*. London; New York: Longman, 1979.

al-Turki, Hind. *al-Malikat al-'arabiyyat qabl al-islam: dirasat al-tarikh al-siyasi*. al-Jouf: Mu'assasat 'Abd al-Rahman al-Sudayri al-Khayriyyah, 2008.

Urbainczyk, Theresa. *Slave Revolts in Antiquity*. London: Routledge, 2016.

Vergote, J. "L'Expansion du Manichéisme en Égypte," *After Chalcedon: Studies in Theology and Church History Offered to Professor Albert Van Roey for His Seventieth Birthday*, ed. Carl Laga, Joseph A. Munitiz, and Lucas Van Rompay. Ann Arbor: University of Michigan Press, 1985.

Vööbus, Arthur. *History of Asceticism in the Syrian Orient: A Contribution to the History of Culture in the Near East*. Louvain: Secrétariat du Corpus SCO, 1958.

Warner, Marina. *Alone of All Her Sex: The Myth and the Cult of the Virgin Mary*. New York: Vintage Books, 1986.

Warren, Larissa. "The women of Etruria," *Women in the Ancient World: The Arethusa Papers*, eds. John Peradotto and John Sullivan. Albany: SUNY Press, 1984.

Watts, Edward. *The Final Pagan Generation*. Berkeley: University of California Press, 2015.

_____. *Hypatia: The Life and Legend of an Ancient Philosopher*. Oxford: Oxford University Press, 2017.

Webb, Peter. *Imagining the Arabs: Arab Identity and the Rise of Islam*. Edinburgh, Edinburgh University Press, 2017.

_____. "al-Jahiliyya: Uncertain times of uncertain meanings." *Der Islam* 91.1 (2014): 69–94.

Weitz, Lev. *Between Christ and Caliph: Law, Marriage, and Christian Community in Early Islam*. Philadelphia: University of Pennsylvania Press, 2018.

Westfall, Cynthia. *Paul and Gender: Reclaiming the Apostle's Vision for Men and Women in Christ*. Ada, MI: Baker Publishing, 2016.

Wilson, Stephen. "Annotated bibliography," *Saints and Their Cults: Studies in Religious Sociology, Folklore and History*, ed. Stephen Wilson. Cambridge: Cambridge University Press, 1985.

Winnett, F. V. *Ancient Records from North Arabia.* Toronto: University of Toronto Press, 1970.

Wolkstein, Diane and Samuel Kramer. *Inanna: Queen of Heaven and Earth: Her Stories and Hymns from Sumer.* New York: Harper & Row, 1983.

Wood, Philip. *The Chronicle of Seert: Christian Historical Imagination in Late Antique Iraq.* Oxford: Oxford University Press, 2013.

_____. "Peter Webb, Imagining the Arabs: Arab Identity and the Rise of Islam." *Al-ʿUsur al-Wusta* 25 (2017): 178–183.

_____. *"We Have No King but Christ": Christian Political Thought in Greater Syria on the Eve of the Arab Conquest (c. 400–585).* Oxford: Oxford University Press, 2010.

Yamut, Bashir. *Shaʿirat al-ʿarab fi al-jahiliyyah wa al-islam.* Kuwait: al-Maktabah al-Ahliyyah, 1934.

Yaʿqub, Ighnatyus. *al-Kanisah al-suryaniyyah al-antakiyyah al-urthuduksiyyah.* Damascus: Alif Baʾ al-Adib Press, 1974.

Zafer, Hamza. *Ecumenical Community Language and Politics of the Ummah in the Qurʾan.* Leiden: Brill, 2020.

Zahran, Yasmine. *Zenobia between Reality and Legend.* Oxford: Archaeopress, 2008.

Zargar, Cyrus. "Virtue and manliness in Islamic ethics." *Journal of Islamic Ethics* 1.1–2 (2020): 1–7.

Zaydan, Jirji. *Tarikh al-ʿarab qabl al-islam.* Cairo: Matbaʿat al-Hilal, 1922.

al-Zayyat, Habib. *al-Marʾah fi al-jahiliyyah.* Cairo: Wikalat al-Sahafah al-ʿArabiyyah, 2018.

Zellentin, Holger. "Ahbar and Ruhban: Religious leaders in the Qurʾan in dialogue with Christian and Rabbinic literature," *Qurʾanic Studies Today,* eds. Michael Sells and Angelika Neuwirth. London; New York: Routledge, 2016.

_____. *The Qurʾans Legal Culture.* Tübingen: Mohr Siebeck, 2013.

Index